Coloring
Outside
the
Lines

Mentoring Women into School Leadership

Mary E. Gardiner
Ernestine Enomoto,
and
Margaret Grogan

State University of New York Press

Published by
State University of New York Press, Albany

© 2000 State University of New York

For information, address State University of New York Press,
State University Plaza, Albany, N.Y., 12246

Production by Michael Haggett
Marketing by Fran Keneston

Library of Congress Cataloging-in-Publication Data

Gardiner, Mary E., 1953–
    Coloring outside the lines : mentoring women into school leadership /
  Mary E. Gardiner, Ernestine Enomoto, and Margaret Grogan.
        p. cm. — (SUNY series in women in education)
    Includes bibliographical references (p.) and index.
    ISBN 0-7914-4581-X (HX : acid free)—ISBN 0-7914-4582-8 (PB : acid free)
        1. Women school administrators—United States—Interviews.
    2. Feminism and education—United States—Case studies.
    3. Mentoring in education—United States—Case studies.
    I. Enomoto, Ernestine, 1949–   II. Grogan, Margaret, 1952–
    III. Title.   IV. Series.

    LB2831.82 .G37 2000
    371.2´011´82—dc21

                                                        99-049936

10 9 8 7 6 5 4 3 2 1

Coloring
Outside
the
Lines

SUNY series in Women in Education
Margaret Grogan, editor

To David, Ryan, and Kyle—Mary

To Misao Fujio Enomoto,
my first mentor and mom—Ernestine

To Michael and Klara—Margaret

Contents

Acknowledgments

We have been friends and colleagues for many years, but this was our first major collaborative research venture. It was a challenging and exhilarating experience. We faced the difficulties of different viewpoints, different schedules and priorities, and the problem of carrying out the study across long distances. Technology was our friend in enabling this study to come together.

As most researchers, we had to fit this project in amongst many other competing demands. Work of this nature requires much support, patience, and general goodwill to be accomplished. Our gratitude and thanks goes to each other, and to our numerous colleagues, friends, and family, without whom this study would never have been completed.

In Mary's words:

> The completion of this book is due to the generous support that I have received from family and friends. Thank you, Mum and Dad, for loving me unconditionally, and forgiving me for living so far away. I want to name all the Gardiners in my immediate family: Walter, Kath, David, Robyn Jeanette, Kurt, Mark, Tara, Tim, Anne, Thomas, Jonathon, Ben, Robyn Jane, Erin, Miriam, and Jacob Gardiner. I love you all. Special thanks also to JoAnn and Greg Fenton, who have provided essential care for Ryan and Kyle during work hours. They have thrived in their home day-

care, thanks to their creation of an environment where children and their parents are part of an extended family who help each other. The close friendship of Gisela Ernst-Slavit, David Slavit and baby Max, Pam and Wayne Peterson and son Sean, Eileen Oliver, Bronwyn Davies, Gail Furman, Pat Krysinski, Darcy Miller, Patti Komp, Don and Helen Reed, Mimi and Marv Wolverton, and Sherry Vaughan has also been very important to me. In addition to friendship, many of these women are mentors to me. In particular I want to thank Sherry Vaughan, who is a goddess of education, and a mentor like no other. Numerous graduate students have also had a tremendous impact on my life and thinking; I am privileged for having worked with all of them. Above all, my husband David, and our sons Ryan and Kyle, have made this book possible. Their presence, joy, and laughter gave me the emotional energy to write this book and enjoy the process.

In Ernestine's words:

I wish to thank my colleagues and staff in the Department of Education Policy, Planning and Administration at the University of Maryland, College Park for their collaborative spirit and ongoing support throughout the data collection phase of this project. I am deeply grateful to Dr. Robert Dubel, who as a former school superintendent and professor of education, offered me direction in making contacts throughout the state. Special thanks to program area colleagues, Drs. Betty Malen and J. Edward Andrews. I would like to thank former students like Dr. Clarissa B. Evans, Mrs. Pamela Akers, Mr. Heath Morrison, Dr. Brenda P. Shockey, and Dr. Carey Wright, whose work in school leadership has been inspiring to me as a teacher of educational administration. I feel honored to work with them in school improvement and educational reform efforts. I am indebted to faculty mentors like Drs. Louise Berman, Sharon Conley, Jessie Roderick, and Linda Valli for their constant encouragement throughout my work and studies at Maryland. Many friends provided support by reading drafts, providing encouraging words, and offering counsel in difficult times. My heartfelt thanks go to Mary Antony Bair, Cassandra Constantino, Bob Croninger, Clare Ginger, Julie Matthaei,

Jamie Metsala, Victor Nolet, Margaret Rogers, Eileen Tamura, Marguerite and Allan Wigfield.

In Margaret's words:

This has been a very rewarding professional experience. I could not have put my heart and soul into it as I have done without the wonderful support I received from my colleagues and graduate assistants here at the Curry School of Education. I am very grateful to Hal Burbach, Chair of the Department of Leadership, Foundations and Policy for supporting me in the study leave I took during the write-up of the project. During that time, colleagues Pam Tucker and Al Butler graciously helped out with teaching my classes and Chuck Jones and Ana Curado expertly kept the administrative machinery moving for my various other responsibilities. I could not have managed without the help and encouragement I received from graduate assistant, Sheryl Cohen, and student / colleague Monica Gillespie who expressed their faith in me and kept me sane. Many thanks must also go to Phyllis Palmore and Peggy Marshall for the many hours of painstaking transcription. My calm, competent, good-humored administrative assistant, Betty Brown, always made sure everything proceeded smoothly.

I would particularly like to thank my good friends and colleagues in the field who helped shape my concept of the study early on and offered ideas for contacts: Deanna Gordon, Margaret Blackmon, Eleanor Flora-Smalley, Sue Burgess, Linda Weber, Diane Bostain, Harriet Morrison, Sandra Mitchell, Becky Sutherland, and Juliet Jennings.

My deep thanks go also to the colleagues who read drafts of my work, commented on presentations of it and offered encouragement throughout: Dan Duke, Eric Bredo, Herb Richards, Walt Heinecke, and Gabriel Lakomski.

I would also like to recognize and thank my own early mentors: my parents, Thérése D'Arcy, Ruth Sheehy and Mary Gardiner for being instrumental in my career development. If it were not for these caring family and friends who encouraged me in my aspirations, I would not have made it to a place where I could write about mentoring. Most important in this regard are my husband, Michael Wahlster and daughter Klara. They deserve special thanks for loving me and giving me the freedom and the energy to do my writing.

We also thank the many people at State University of New York Press who helped with this project. In particular we want to thank Jennie Doling, Priscilla Ross, Acquisitions Editor, and Michael Haggett, Production Editor.

And most importantly, we owe a debt of gratitude to the courageous and pioneering women and men whose voices are heard in this book.

1　Introduction to the Study

Coloring Outside the Lines, the title of this book, represents two current aspects of educational administration, that we, the women authors of this study, hope to change. First we wish to alter the image of administration. Educational administration is a predominantly white male occupation, with 93 percent men (Schmuck 1999, ix), and 96.6 percent whites, in superintendencies nationwide (Chase 1995, 36). We would like to see many more women, white and of color, in leadership positions in our public schools. Second, coloring "outside the lines" refers to changing the lines that have been drawn, the unwritten rules, the culture or "medium within which we exist" (Cole 1996, 8) that defines educational administration. We argue that the dominant culture of educational administration is androcentric, meaning informed by white, male norms. Mentoring has been a part of this androcentric culture of educational administration. Women have been, and still are in many respects, on the borders, with "outsider" status in educational leadership (Tallerico, Poole and Burstyn 1994, 439). They may have gained entry into educational administration, but they are still seen as new and different. However, women are in a position as newcomers, to transform leadership through mentoring. It is from the borders and margins that we are best positioned to open up new forms of understanding.

Much has been written about mentoring in the literature of education, business, and the professions. (See for example, the extensive references on mentoring women in education in Hall and Sandler 1983; Johnsrud 1990, 1991; Stalker 1994). Yet many of the studies are limited in that they either advocate uncritically for mentoring as a necessary key to women's and men's career success (*e.g.*, Roche 1979; Schmidt and Wolfe 1980, 45; Lively et. al. 1992; Bizzari 1995; Didion 1995; Stevens 1995); assume traditional models of mentoring (Bova and Phillips 1982; Daloz 1991); or are practical, commonsense directives to women (*e.g.*, Sandler's 1995 "Ten Commandments of Mentoring"). A more promising line of research critiques the dominant framework of the mentoring literature (*e.g.*, Swoboda and Millar 1986; Haring-Hidore and Brooks 1987), suggesting that traditional mentoring relationships are hierarchical, with an inherent possibility to be dependent and exploitative, given the power differentiation inherent in the relationships. The work of L. K. Johnsrud (1990) and J. Stalker (1994), in this critical vein is cogent and well researched. However, they are conceptual pieces based solely on the literature, while calling for further research informed by the lived lives and actual experiences of women.

As a study of mentoring this book makes three main contributions. First, it is an empirical study, including fifty-one in-depth interviews with women administrators in mentoring relationships, either mentors or protégés, across three states in the United States: Maryland, Virginia, and Washington state. Four men administrators are also included in this study as mentors, with a total of fifty-five participants. When women today hold administrative positions, such as superintendent, the most prestigious and powerful position in the public schools, or school principal, we wondered what are their mentoring experiences. The literature on mentoring makes the point that for women, mentoring is rare, and that when they do receive mentoring, for women their experience too often is "debilitating rather than empowering" (Johnsrud 1991, 7). We wanted to know much more about the experiences of women being mentored into educational leadership in public school systems. We were interested in finding out who were the people doing the mentoring, and how they were accomplishing this work. What do these special relationships entail? Is mentoring a gendered and racialized practice? This book offers readers insights into the changing face of mentoring and educational leadership in public schools, and is intended to show some of the unspoken assumptions, the unwritten rules that those aspiring to administrative positions in the public school systems often do not know. We show how women respond to those tacit rules, and how they are changing the rules.

Second, we use a feminist poststructuralist framework (Capper 1993; Davies 1994; Weedon 1997) to deconstruct the mentoring of women within the cultures of K-12 public school administration in which they work. The study examines mentorship from the perspective of women in professional relationships with a mentor in the field of education. We question the very assumptions of mentoring which has tended to be grounded in traditional leadership notions of power and authority. Rather than abandon mentoring, though, we explore possibilities for transformation and change towards new kinds of mentoring. We consider both the problems of mentoring for mentors and protégés as well as the benefits. We also take into account that schools are located in a broader context of a gendered and racist society. Following S. Chase (1995), we offer women's accounts of power and subjection / oppression in their professional lives as educational administrators, with a focus specifically on mentoring for educational leadership. We show that women are not reproducing the patriarchy. Instead, we show women leaders who are on one level, "same" with their male colleagues, conforming to the expectations and essentially presenting no problems, and simultaneously they are "other" (different / marginalized) and engaging in subversive and overt practices to change the system (Stalker 1994). Third, it is a collaborative, qualitative study by three women professors of educational leadership, who have their own mentoring experiences, knowledge of K-12 public schools, and the process of this research to share with the reader.

The book is not only for women who aspire to school leadership positions and those who will mentor them, but also for both women and men who have a critical role to play, and a responsibility to redefine mentoring in order to bring forth the best new leaders for our schools. Some mentors, for example, white males, may represent different styles, interests, and voices to those represented here, but they also have an interest in learning from, understanding, and accessing the talents and abilities of all potential leaders, not just those who are similar to them. And as Kristeva argues men can exist in so-called feminine mode and women can exist in so-called masculine mode; to think otherwise is to force men and women into patriarchy's straitjacket (Tong 1993, 230). Thus, women and men may find the issues and directions discussed in this book part of their ongoing struggle in working towards pluralistic leadership. A brief description of the structure of the book follows.

In this chapter, we examine: (a) the context of women in educational leadership; (b) the concept of mentoring—what is mentoring / how is mentoring; and (c) briefly introduce the reader to our field study. Later chapters give details on the mentoring of women, white and of color, why it affects one's life and career, and how mentoring can be informed by feminist theory. In addition, three state chapters develop key ideas found in the complete dataset: on women's conflicts as they are mentored into educational leadership (Washington state); mentoring as caring and caregiving (Virginia); and cultivating feminist educational leadership through mentoring (Maryland). The concluding chapter pulls the threads together and critically discusses issues and concerns with mentoring, as well as outlining the potential for mentoring to transform educational leadership.

WOMEN IN EDUCATIONAL LEADERSHIP

Nationwide in K-12 education, women, white and minority, do not have adequate entry into the most prestigious leadership positions. K-12 public education has traditionally been and is still characterized by a feminized profession with a predominance of women in the teaching ranks and fewer women in leadership, especially at the superintendent level. As J. Blount (1998, 3) explains, educational administration is a "traditionally male-identified educational domain." Low numbers of women are in "executive positions in education [K-12 school administration] as well as even fewer numbers of female professors in educational administration (fewer than 2 percent)" (Gupton and Slick 1996, 90). Among practicing superintendents nationwide, only 7.1 percent (Montenegro 1993) / 7.5 percent are women (Pence 1995), and only 7.6 percent of high school principals are women (Pence 1995, 136). The male dominance of leadership is "striking because superintendents rise from the ranks of teachers, 70 percent of whom are women" (Chase 1995, 36). Likewise, a color gap exists. Only 4 percent of superintendents nationwide are minorities (Glass 1992, 55). Almost all minority superintendents are black or Hispanic, with most minority superintendents in school districts with enrollments of more than three thousand students (Glass 1992, 55). The "glass ceiling" is a term that has been applied to explain the underrepresentation of women and minorities in leadership as a result of the presence of informal barriers that impose a ceiling on achievement. The number of women in educational administration has increased, "yet the glass ceiling has not been broken, especially in the high school principalship and the superintendency," which are the most prestigious positions in public education (Schmuck (1995, 213). Women who are school superintendents are, as S. Chase (1995, 12) argues, "at once powerful individuals and members of groups that have been subject to racism and sexism throughout American history."

So how do aspiring administrators gain entry to the profession? Educational administrators are encouraged to enter this professional realm through mentoring and role modeling. Mentoring, in addition to personal aspirations and talents, would seem to be critical for those aspiring to administrative positions (see Covel 1978; Daresh 1987; Daresh and Playko 1992; Klauss 1981; Pence 1995; Poll 1978; Price 1981; Shakeshaft 1989, 115–116; Stevenson 1974; Vertz 1985). D. J. Levinson and his colleagues, as early as 1978, reported that mentorship was critical for men's advancement in educational administration. Typically, mentorship is the special and favored relationship that is cultivated whereby the mentor counsels, guides, and helps the protégé to develop both personally and professionally. In educational administration, mentorship has traditionally been cast as an "old boy network." S. Gupton and G. Slick (1996, 91) put it this way, "older male executives and male professors typically prefer protégés who are junior versions of themselves." An invisible network of older professionals have groomed their protégés, younger versions of themselves, for top-level positions. They have largely been white men, who promoted younger white men, who have been expected to maintain their leadership styles, standards and cultural mores.

As R. Hall and B. Sandler (1983, 1) suggest for women seeking leadership positions, "success often depends not only on what you know but whom you know—not only on hard work, but also on encouragement, guidance, support and advocacy from those who are already established in the system." J. Alston (1999, 86) identifies one of the facilitators for black female superintendents' entry into the superintendency is the provision of a mentor or sponsor. M. Rowe (1981, 102) notes the lack of mentoring of women and advises women strongly to "go find yourself a mentor." Johnsrud (1990, 59) also affirms the importance of mentoring: "there is probably no other single relationship that can be instrumental in enhancing an administrative career in higher education than a quality mentoring relationship" (1990, 59). This comment applies equally well to K-12 public school administration.

The underrepresentation of women in high-level leadership positions is thought to be connected to mentoring. Mentoring and role modeling are essential for success in educational administration, and women have had limited access to both. As Nicolson argues:

> This informal model [of mentoring] is more effective in terms of career advancement and motivation than any formal system could be. The system cannot work for women in the same way because there is not the long term continuity or the number of women to make this possible, and neither is there a tradition of such practice. (1996, 106)

While most women have not had mentors, many of those who have been successful in acquiring administrative titles currently have or have had mentors in the past. In a study of aspiring school administrators by S. Edson (1995, 43) of those women "who identified mentors in 1979–80, 42 percent (or fifty-nine women) became principals or beyond by the end of ten years, whereas only 17 percent (or twenty-four women) who did not have mentors were able to advance." Similarly, Gupton and Slick's (1996, 92) survey of 151 women superintendents, assistant superintendents, and high school principals revealed that the majority of those women leaders had "significant numbers" of positive role models and supportive mentors in their lives. Mentoring, or the lack of it, has been a means of excluding other potential leaders from the system. In turn, with transformation, mentoring could become a means of opening up opportunities for those traditionally denied access, such as women and minorities. If the top management is held primarily by men and a few women who may have been enculturated into white, male-administrative norms, women, white and of color, may be at a disadvantage in not only finding a mentor, but in also identifying with and internalizing any mentoring that is given. Thus, M. Lang and C. A. Ford (1988) point out the need for building community and mentoring, particularly amongst women of color, if women of color are to succeed. C. Hetherington and R. Barcelo (1985, 14) call for cross-cultural mentoring or "womentoring," arguing that women, white and of color, need to work together if women are to be successful.

Furthermore, while it is agreed that mentors are almost essential for those aspiring to educational leadership (*e.g.*, Aisenberg and Harrington 1988, 47; Edson 1995, 43), insufficient details are given on just what it takes to establish, maintain, and benefit from mentoring relationships. Researchers (Merriam 1983, 171; Moore and Salimbene 1981, 64; Stalker 1994) conclude that more research is needed to clarify the actual workings of mentoring. At the same time, mentoring has been uncritically accepted by many educators as desirable, almost a panacea for women, and in need of formal implementation.

In many school districts and in professional educational organizations, such as state associations of school administrators, mentoring has become a formalized process. Since the 1970s, when mentoring became recognized as important to success in educational administration, efforts were made to actively recruit and promote women and minorities into administrative positions. Organizations began using formal mentorship to help guide the way of underrepresented groups to executive ranks. Formal mentorship programs of school districts and educational organizations range from being voluntary to being mandated at the state level (Pence 1995, 126–127). For example, in 1986 the U. S. Department of Education allocated seven million dollars for a project named LEAD which was to encourage the mentorship of underrepresented groups in administration. In a number of states participating in Project LEAD (Leadership for Educational Administration Development), centers were formed whereby administrators and university people came together to formally pair up mentors and protégés / mentees and provide a structured environment for them to network:

> The program designated mentors and protégés from different school districts. A steering committee matched mentors and protégés and developed plans for four statewide dinner presentation meetings. During the school year, mentors and protégés discussed important educational issues and shared their plans with other participants. These four dinner meetings served as the major activity to help mentors and aspirants clarify their work together and learn new ways to work together. (Pence 1995, 128) (Also see U. S. Department of Education 1992)

Likewise, the president of the Confederation of Oregon School Administrators developed a mentorship program including twenty selected administrative protégés (women and minorities) matched with twenty practicing administrators in districts other than their own. In this program, the mentor pairs meet and devise a plan for developing leadership skills, with meetings bringing together all participants to share their experiences (Schmuck 1995, 213). However, such formalized programs, which rely on an organization matching mentor and protégé, overlook the fact that "mentoring relationships demand a personal connection that cannot be mandated" (Johnsrud 1990, 62).

Women and minorities may also have special needs in mentoring and their voices need to be heard because the dominant culture of educational administration is androcentric, or that of white male-identified norms:

> Women administrators have additional difficulty learning their administrative role because there are conflicting attitudes about the stereotypes of what it means to be female and what it means to be an administrator. Developing relationships with veteran practicing administrators provides a link for neophytes and protégés that are important for learning the tasks and challenges of a new position. These relationships can especially be important to a woman or minority who is "different" from the stereotyped image of an administrator who is white and male. (Pence 1995, 125)

Perceptions of difference, different experiences or styles of leadership is not the problem; it is prevailing attitudes and assumptions concerning women in leadership:

> It is not viewing women as different from men that harms women, but rather identifying women and women's styles of leadership as inferior to men and men's styles of leadership. (Shakeshaft 1989, 115)

When mentoring does occur, in whose interest is mentoring? Women and minorities tend to feel that the powerful men who mentor them may be doing this as much to enhance their own careers as to help their protégés (also see Kanter 1977). Women may feel used in these relationships. As Johnsrud (1991, 8) argues, academic women are now being warned against engaging in traditional mentoring relationships, and to seek alternatives such as "peer pals, collegial networks and other developmental relationships" (Hall and Sandler, 1983; Kram, 1983; Nichols, Carter and Golden, 1985; Pancrazio and Gray, 1982; Shapiro, Haseltine, and Rowe, 1978; Swoboda and Millar, 1986). In the traditional mentoring relationship, the imbalance of power and the hierarchical nature of the relationship puts one person, the mentor, in a superior role, with the protégé dependent on the mentor's largesse. In alternative mentoring, women are encouraged to engage in more participatory and equal relationships of affiliation, collaboration, and sharing.

Finally, in using labels, such as "men," "white male," "women," and "women of color," this is not to imply common issues or conflicts. There may be as much variation within as between gender and ethnic groups, which are the two subjectivities / identities that are the focus of this book. For instance, placing personal and family relationships as more important than career success / goals / ambitions can also be a source of conflict for some men as well as for those particular women discussed in this book. And for many women such concerns may not exist. Some men also may be in need of some of the kinds of mentoring outlined in this book. While our focus here is on the intersection of race and gender, we also have to take into account the multiple identities of people, for example, Democrat, Catholic, gay parent, single mother, and so on, and how this plays into their perspectives on mentoring and leadership. Our goal is to work towards pluralistic schools and society unconstructed by gender and race. We believe that as a result of a policy of exclusion in educational leadership the leadership potential for our schools has been impoverished, and that attention needs to be given to the voices and experiences of those who might bring new awarenesses and insights to our schools.

THE CONCEPT OF MENTORING

Definitions of mentorship in the literature are varied, as evidenced in the following long list of synonyms:

> Words such as teaching, coaching, advising, training, directing, protecting, sponsoring, guiding and leading are among the terms used [for mentoring]. Similarly, words such as mentee, protégé, apprentice, learner and novice, used to describe the person being mentored, hint at the diverse nature of the mentoring activity. (Stalker 1994, 362)

In studying this topic, we found ourselves faced with word choices: mentoring or womentoring; protégé, protégée or mentee as the most common. Although our interviewees used the word mentee at times, as well as the word protégé, we as researchers decided to standardize our own usage. Mentee has yet to be used officially in standard English dictionaries, and protégée as the feminine form of protégé seemed outdated, therefore we decided to use the term protégé. We acknowledge that the words have slightly different connotations. Protégé is reminiscent of earlier times when men chose other men to sponsor and groom them for a particular role. Interestingly, in the end, this study confirms that this connotation is still relevant, which is perhaps our best reason for using the word protégé, since we hope to help change traditional mentoring practices.

The traditional mentoring model is that of the *mentoring dyad*, an "intense, lasting, and professionally centered relationship between two individuals" (Moore and Salimbene 1981). However, not everyone experiences this "strong, intense relationship." According to B. Sandler (1995, 105) "25 percent of professionals, or fewer, have had the strong, intense relationships that we traditionally call mentoring." People may have supportive relationships that they use for their professional or personal gain, but they may not identify these relationships as mentoring. In contrast to the dyad, more recent mentoring models emphasize peer relationships, and multiple ways of mentoring across large social networks (*e.g.*, Stalker 1994).

In what follows, we review some of the most commonly used metaphors for mentoring to illustrate the different forms that mentoring may take between these two extremes of the dyad and the large social networks of peers. It should be noted that many of the writings combine elements from various metaphors. Thus, the teacher metaphor may be dominant, but the mentor may also be likened to a parent or guide.

WHAT IS MENTORING?

What are the interactions like in mentoring relationships is a question we sought to clarify. Two types of interactions were identified by K. Moore and A. Salimbene (1981, 56): the superior / subordinate (what we call "mentor as boss" interactions); and the relationship between faculty members and students (what we call "mentor as adviser"). We suggest some additional types of interactions found in mentoring relationships: mentor as teacher, mentor as guide, mentor as parent, mentor as spiritual or philosophical guru, mentor as gatekeeper, mentor as public role model, and mentor as friend or peer.

Mentor as boss or superior. In the boss or superior model, mentoring is premised on one person having greater power and responsibility than the other. The superordinate who is also a mentor (for not all bosses are mentors) has the best interests of the subordinate in mind. But there is clearly a differentiation between the ability of one of the people in the relationship to garner resources than the other. The subordinate is dependent on the superordinate for his / her professional success. In this hierarchical, power relationship, the positive aspect is that a powerful mentor can open doors much more readily than a peer. The disadvantages are the potential for abuse, exploitation, and dependence (Gupton and Slick 1996, 93; Johnsrud 1990, 64). In addition, amongst other difficulties, when the supervisor is the mentor, there is a danger of other staff members under the same supervisor perceiving favoritism (Hennecke 1983; Johnsrud 1990, 63).

Mentor as adviser. This view is one typically associated with the graduate student in the university and the professor who serves as major professor or mentor. The professor is seen as a wise adviser in formal and informal settings initiating the protégé into the academy, and socializing her / him into scientific research norms, ethics, and a professional orientation (e.g., see Schmidt and Wolfe 1980). May (1990, 285) argues that the mentor teaches the student a "wide range of subjects ranging from specific techniques and experimental procedures to ways of thinking about research, science, and life in general. Much of what a student learns in a graduate program is obtained by modeling ideas and behavior on those of someone who has mastered the field." It is also argued that the once intimate and one-to-one relationship between mentor and protégé in the university has been replaced in many cases with "large research laboratories, employing dozens of technicians and professional staff as well as many graduate students and postdoctoral associates . . . large teams perform research under the direction of a busy, harried, and often remote supervisor" (May 1990, 287). Guidelines are sometimes developed by universities to outline the mentoring responsibilities of graduate faculty to their students. For instance, at Stanford

University the Graduate Student Academic Advising Guidelines for departments states that mentoring: "requires role modeling, intensive constructive dialogue, and especially a willingness to be hard-nosed. Most crucially it involves avoiding the two opposite dangers of nonconstructive hand holding and too much nurturing on the one hand and on the other zealous efforts to train students to deal with the challenge of working independently without guidance" (LaPidus and Mishkin 1990, 285).

Mentor as teacher.   Another frequent metaphor is that mentoring is a form of teaching. For instance, F. Parkay (1988, 195–196) writes that mentoring is an adult teacher-learner connection between two people whereby the teacher provides the student with a customized and individualized curriculum that is maximally growth promoting in all ways, for example, Socrates and Plato, Aristotle and Alexander the Great, Anne Sullivan and Helen Keller, and Freud and Jung. Mentoring is seen to go beyond formalized teaching in the following ways:

> First, the mentor-protégé relationship matures and develops over time, usually several years. Second, the degree and quality of caring a mentor extends to the protégé is similar to the intimacy that exists among family members. The relationship is deeper and more holistic than the teacher-student relationship; likewise, the psychological bond between mentor and protégé is more potent, more emotional. Third, the protégé learns from the mentor not only the objective, manifest content of professional knowledge and skills but also a subjective, nondiscursive appreciation for how and when to employ these learnings in the arena of professional practice. In short, the mentor helps the protégé to "learn the ropes," to become socialized into the profession. Finally, the essence of mentoring is to be found in the way the mentor inexplicably "teaches" him or herself to the protégé who, over time, internalizes much of this ego ideal—i.e., the set of "ideal" goals one has for oneself. (Erikson 1978; Parkay 1988, 195–196)

In the example just given, the view of mentoring that emerges can best be described as a combination of teacher-student, adviser and a parent-child relationship. Speaking of his own mentor, Dr. Herbert

Thelen, a professor at the University of Chicago, Parkay writes: "Not only was he more intelligent, experienced and well-known than I, the child, could ever hope to be, but he might (or so my unconscious imagined) turn against me, his 'son.' . . . The parent-child dynamics I have described are to be found, I feel, in all mentor-protégé relationships" (Parkay 1988, 199).

Mentor as guide. Another view of mentoring in the literature is that of the professional guide who socializes others into their professions in a nurturing, nonthreatening manner (*e.g.*, see Nichols, Carter and Golden 1985). For instance, mentoring is used as a concept to explain teachers socializing new teachers into the profession (*e.g.*, Gehrke and Kay 1984). On mentoring guidance for faculty, and specifically the professional challenge of gaining tenure in higher education, N. Aisenberg and M. Harrington write:

> Another woman tells of critical help [mentoring] she received during a recent, and positive, process of tenure decision. "I was very lucky to have a female chairperson who took me through tenure the way you would want a mother to stand by you as a guide, who really cared about you but wanted you to have your own independence. And tenure is normally for people here a pretty horrible process." (1988, 47)

In this case, the mentor is assisting the protégé to be guided and socialized into the profession, with its productivity demands of teaching, research, and service. We see some overlap with the parent metaphor, for the mentor acted "the way you would want a mother to stand by you."

Mentor as parent. Mentors are frequently seen as like loving and wise parents, nurturing their young, and promoting their professional growth and development. Children use the advice, guidance, resources, and protection of their parents as long as they are needed, and then they move on with their lives. The goal of the parent-mentor is for the protégé, seen initially as child-like, to be brought fully to adult status through the equivalent of the novice stages of infancy, childhood, and the teen years through to mature, equal, and responsible adult status. E. Bolton (1980) suggests that "the primary function of a mentor is to provide a transition from the child-parent relationship to the adult-peer relationship in the course of development. The mentor must then be a combination of these figures in order to guide this transition successfully" (Bolton 1980, 199). Obviously, care, concern and love are elements of the parent-child type relationship, and also greater power on the part of the "parent" figure, and dependence on the part of the protégé.

Mentor as spiritual or philosophical guru.   When mentorship is seen in terms of spiritual guidance, emphasis is placed on conceptual development according to some philosophy. A mentoring relationship with a guru is similar to that of rabbis or priests with their followers, and is based on the spiritual authority they are given. As an example, the mentor may be an ardent feminist or human rights activist and the protégé has never thought of him / herself in those terms and has never explored the particular literature or principles. The mentor may be the one responsible for awakening certain possibilities, ideas or consciousness within the protégé (see Kanter 1977; Carter 1982).

Mentor as gatekeeper.   When one is defined by oneself and others as a member of a certain group, certain rights, responsibilities, and privileges are granted. Elders of the group may look out for and promote the well-being of younger members, and those who do not belong may be ostracized or treated less well than insiders. This type of gatekeeping mentoring is embodied in the practice of the "old boy network" that has traditionally operated in educational administration whereby male-to-male relationships of men with like values and norms were established, and women and men of color received little or no opportunity to participate in educational administration. The gatekeeper invites the upwardly mobile into the select circle of the power elite (Moore and Salimbene 1981, 58). Mentors operating in this way have a strong influence on the careers of their protégés' (Roche 1979a). The negative aspect of this type of mentoring is the reproduction, carbon copy, mirror image outcome of the relationships and leadership that may ensue.

Mentor as public role model.   Here established professionals are highly visible in a public role and serve to inspire and give guidance and direction to younger professionals, in a similar way that basketball heroes serve as role models to thousands of young aspiring basketball players. For example, a woman professor may be a mentor to many young women who look up to her and try to follow her example and advice, even though they may never have the opportunity to meet her and know her personally (see Aisenberg and Harrington 1988, 47). This is a type of mentoring that does not apply to the women in this study, all of whom are in specific, cultivated mentoring relationships with one or more mentors.

Mentor as friend or peer.   The friendship approach to mentoring is similar to the peer relationship. Friend-as-mentor is an egalitarian relationship, one where the needs of both parties are negotiated and reciprocated. The personal and the professional are closely intertwined and connected. The mentor attends to the protégé as a whole person, rather than strictly differentiating between appropriate work needs. In our study, we found some apprehension and consciousness of the dangers of an intensely personal mentoring relationship turning into an accusation of sexual involvement. Most mentors and protégés are conscious of the need to not put themselves in a position of compromise, and to always act with integrity and professionalism. But many felt this kind of talk and innuendo occurs anyway, regardless of the professional nature of the relationship, because many people cannot believe that two individuals are capable of an intense Platonic and professional relationship. From a critical standpoint, however, there should be awareness of the sexualized environment of educational administration and the inherent power relations (Shakeshaft 1995). Thus, there may sometimes be problems when mentoring is intensely personalized. But we need to remember that claims such as that "men fear mentoring women" because of the possiblity of a sexual harrassment lawsuit (see Scott 1996, 35) is really part of an ongoing power struggle between men and women, and part of the sexualized environment of educational administration (Shakeshaft 1993, 101).

Recent literature advocates strongly for mentoring with peers, usually as part of large social networks and multiple relationships. In this model, women are encouraged to form networks with multiple mentors across different age and ethnic groups. Mentoring is a more egalitarian and reciprocal relationship. Professional peers have many different things to offer women, whereas the traditional mentoring dyad can be too isolating or create a false sense of security when the protégé overrelies on the mentor and places too much trust and responsibility in one person: "putting all one's eggs in one basket" (Gupton and Slick 1996, 93; Sandler 1995). These types of equal, helpful peer relationships "are seen as having a positive impact on people's professional success" (Johnsrud 1990, 58) (Also see Sandler and Hall 1983; Hill et. al. 1989). The advantages of peer relationships are the mutual sharing, emotional and career support that can occur. A disadvantage is that sometimes peers compete with one another, and the sharing in relationships can become compromised. We found many women who either practice or believe strongly in the idea of forming these connections and sharing power with others. Unlike the "old boy's network" which only transferred power to select, favored individuals, the networking that women say they seek and want would be a positive force for all women in educational leadership. Network in this sense is a verb, an active, informal helping process of empowerment for many, not a noun connoting a club with select membership.

Such mentoring networks have not yet been fully realized. S. Gupton and G. Slick's (1996, 96) survey of 151 women public school leaders found that 20 percent "have never mentored anyone—male or female." In the present study, women had one or more mentors, and had experienced mentoring from many people, women and men. But the women complained that women did not yet have in place the networks that they desired. They envisage a network of women and men helping women and men. J. Stalker paints this picture of women as transformers of society: "women as groups of active agents; actors who are able to take and shape space to their own ends" (Stalker 1994, 370). Women leaders are transforming schools and society by their leadership, as we show in this book. However, the process is by necessity incremental and less revolutionary than one might want, for women are both accommodating of / "same," and separated from the dominant patriarchal structures / "other" (Stalker 1994, 370). However, the results of women's influence on mentoring practices and educational leadership are profound, and are likely to continue for many years.

HOW IS MENTORING?

Favoritism, jealousy and competition in mentoring. Women sometimes complain that women are not mentoring women. They say it is the powerful, established men who are doing the mentoring. Is this the case? If so, why? Are women, white and of color, truly supportive of one another? Or do the white men who hold the bulk of the power and positions make it difficult for women to secure power? Do women end up in a colonized position, vying with each other for the seemingly limited patronage of their male mentor, and fighting with one another for recognition? S. Chase (1995, 5) points out that "even the most privileged women in the American work force [*e.g.*, superintendents] are subject to institutionalized male and white dominance." Why do some people seem to be favorites in the workplace, gaining the mentoring attention of superiors, and the advantages that ensue? Why are some women pushed to the margins despite their awesome talents and abilities, while others succeed? Why is the competition associated with advancement often a source of conflict for women, who may view the world differerently, in more collaborative terms, and be uncomfortable with winning at the expense of others? As one woman put it:

> In administration you need to get recognized to move ahead and to get recognized you have to do something that's particularly outstanding that is going to call attention to yourself and some people seem to go about that in a very personal way, trying to call attention to themselves perhaps even at the expense of the other people. I've always found that that was impossible for me to do. That what I enjoy doing is cooperating with other people and facilitating the sort of getting ahead for a group of people as opposed to me as a single individual getting ahead . . . I think it is a real problem, it has been a real problem for me. (Aisenberg and Harrington 1988, 60)

A further consideration is what happens in a mentoring relationship when the protégé becomes equal to or surpasses the mentor (Gupton and Slick 1996, 93). Jealousy has the potential to disrupt relationships and to poison efforts and motives. A common motif in the literature is that of the jealous powerful woman, the "Queen Bee" who guards and protects her exclusive status (see Benton 1980; Ginn 1989; Gupton and Slick 1996, 91–92). In this study, we include many counter examples to this motif, women who gladly and freely share power, knowledge, and their lives with each other, while acknowledging the existence of tensions and conflicts in these close relationships.

Stages in establishing mentoring relationships.   S. Acker (1995, 61) suggests that protégés will not gain mentoring unless they give evidence to the mentor that they are willing to stand apart from their peers and gain from the mentorship. Gaining the attention of a superior and cultivating a mentor is described in the following way:

> Some teachers seemed able to display some special qualities that triggered Liz's [principal Liz Clarke] strongest sponsor-ship efforts. A subtle labelling process seemed to be at work. In the schools I studied or visited, heads, including Liz, rarely did any systematic observation of teachers actually teaching classes, although they would pass by or through the classrooms frequently. Judgments about teaching compe-tence were not necessarily arrived at by direct empirical ev-idence derived from the classroom. . . . Mrs. Clarke had clear ideas about who was "like a rock" or a "good, average teacher" or "a brilliant teacher." In other words, mentorship is seen as a process of "labelling," encouraged by "triggering" mentorship efforts through appropriate behavior (such as agreeing to suggestions put forward by the mentor) and in-dications that the mentee is worthy of special efforts on the mentor's part. (Evetts 1989)

In this case, the protégé is seen as instrumental in helping set the conditions for the establishment of a mentoring relationship. Mentoring is thus often seen as occurring in stages, with an evolv-ing relationship that begins with the establishment of a connection between people, through mentoring which leads to greater inde-pendence on the part of the protégé. For instance, mentoring has been described as progressing from: (*a*) peer pals, (*b*) guide, (*c*) sponsor, and finally, (*d*) mentor, which is the highest level of inten-sity and commitment (Shapiro et. al. 1978, 57). In contrast, for K. Moore (1982, 24), the stages are seen to involve first the mentor, who is typically in a higher level position, recognizing the talents of a protégé (she may have distinguished herself as a teacher-leader for instance, and may be invited to consider joining the ad-ministrative ranks). Second, the mentor poses a series of tests and challenges to the protégé, although this stage is said to be usually brief. Third, the mentor consciously chooses to work closely with the protégé and begins intentional mentoring. Fourth, the protégé is put to work purposively with personal growth and career devel-opment goals.

Still other researchers focus on the work that the mentors do to encourage protégés through the various stages:

> There was a stage of getting her convinced that she can do it. And then there's the always inevitable stage of vice principalship and convincing them they don't know everything and they quit trying to act like they do. Then there's the period of frustrations—am I ever going to get one of those jobs? And you have to sort of take them through that. And that's a real tough one. You really have to hold some hands during that time because by that time they have got a vision and a dream and it doesn't look like it's going to happen. You have to counsel some patience and wait till the right thing comes along. Don't get too excited about this—your time will come. It will happen to you. So you go through that with them. Then, of course, there's the euphoria of when they get the job. Then there's the tears, or anger, or scared, actually it's fear after they have gotten it and they are faced with their first two or three big ones. I've really got to make this decision. Is it going to turn out all right? Is everyone going to hate me when I do it? Am I capable of doing a job this difficult? There's lots of stages through the whole thing. (Pence 1989, 130)

These references to stages of mentoring suggest the need to examine more systematically and in close detail the process of mentoring and the shift in relationship between mentor and protégé. In the example above, the mentoring that is occurring is primarily that of a junior novice being encouraged and counseled by a senior expert. Is that the only form of mentoring? Might there be other types of mentoring that women, white and of color, find more appealing and effective? In our study, some women did talk of stages in mentoring, and in some cases of being able to bypass stages, because the trust had already been laid down by many years of acquaintance and professional relationship. In later chapters, we conceptualize these stages, as well as detailing the types of relationships, and the outcomes that women anticipated and realized in their mentoring relationships.

Women's mentoring and an ethic of care.   Conventional wisdom also holds that women leaders are perhaps moral leaders, with a strong emphasis on what has become known as an ethic of care (Noddings 1984, 1992; Beck 1994). Sometimes this is mistakenly assumed to be oversentimental and emotional. C. Shakeshaft (1995) claims that women are uncomfortable using power—we care for others, we placate, we please, yet we have to learn how to use power, she argues. Is this the case? Do women, white and minority, have to learn to do things the white, male way, or are they able to do things differently and develop their own styles that may or may not use power, or power may be interpreted in another way? For instance, Mary Catherine Bateson, in her extraordinary biography, *Composing a Life* (1990) reveals the strength in leadership of five accomplished professional women. Each of the women in this book, Johnnetta Cole, president of Spelman College, Joan Erikson, dancer, writer, and jewelry designer, Alice d'Entremont, electrical engineer and entrepreneur, Ellen Bassuk, psychiatrist and researcher on homelessness, and Professor Mary Catherine Bateson herself, an anthropologist and professor, has enjoyed rich personal relationships, and mentoring from significant others. Further, each of the women display an incredible flexibility, an ability to adapt and adjust to whatever circumstances they find themselves in. Rather than a linear path to success in their professional lives, the women adapt and change in response to the unpredictable and sometimes fortuitous events and opportunities that occur in their lives. Bateson suggests that from their position on the margins of public life, women have been able to improvise and use the space and freedom that marginality provides. She argues that these women combine professional fulfillment with personal ideals of interdependence, an ethic of care grounded in reality, and imaginative creativity. What might also be seen as discontinuity, lost opportunities and marginal positioning for women, for example, following one's partner to new cities and countries and putting one's own career on a lower priority, Bateson turns into an affirmation of women's strength and ability to keep personal relationships intact while searching out new professional opportunities in the work world. On mentoring faculty as a dean, a position Bateson held for a number of years, she explains

> The appropriate degree of caretaking in such roles as dean can only be accessible to professional and conscientious men and women if it is freed from cliches and practiced with judgment: the best caretaker offers a combination of challenge and support, yet adults dealing with women administrators are sometimes as fretful as infants denied the breast. To be nurturant is not always to concur and comfort, to stroke and

flatter and appease; often, it requires offering a caring version of the truth, grounded in reality. Self-care should include the cold shower as well as the scented tub. Real caring requires setting priorities and limits. Even the hard choices of triage have their own tenderness. Again and again in myths and folklore, kindness to strangers or animals is enjoined and heroes are rewarded for pausing on their journeys to care for those in need. But psychologist Jean Houston points out an episode in the myth of Psyche and Eros that provides a useful balance. When Psyche is in search of Eros, she is enjoined to resist the cries and pleas of others. If she is to find her beloved, she must harden herself against inappropriate impulses to help and nurture. (Bateson 1990, 155)

From this we see that an ethic of care does not mean smothering dependency, but rather interdependency and connection that also contributes to growth and possibility.

In our study, it is interesting to examine the life choices of women, white and of color, traditionally marginalized in leadership, to see how they perceive mentoring and how they are experiencing their own mentorship by others. We show many cases of women leaders engaging in leadership informed by an ethic of care, and as in Bateson's account, this does not mean caring in the sense of loving unconditionally, but rather a full range of responses. The women each have their own approaches to mentoring and leadership, undergirded by a belief that they are doing this in the interests of children and improved teaching and learning. We might question whether this represents part of women's location in a sexist society, where it is acceptable for men to be career-oriented and focus on their own career advancement, but women feel compelled to claim higher moral causes and altruism, that they are working for instructional improvement, or for children, not themselves. Of course it may be both, but it is interesting that some women are not yet out-of-the-box that locates them as the selfless giver (see Seelinger 1998, for interesting insights into the way that women leaders see themselves as "fixing the system"). Women viewed as "fix-it women," selfless givers, or rescuers, can be both transformative and powerful, a representation of women's efficacy and power, or alternatively a traditional problem of women as self-deprecatory and accepting of themselves as leaders only if it is a service / serving role.

Politics underpins leadership.   Politics is so important in professional advancement, a notion that may be eschewed by some women, who may believe that simply doing good work is enough to be professionally rewarded. Politics means that one lives in a world inhabited by others and that one relates to them and forms alliances with others. In order to be more successful in leadership, one must collaborate and be a team player rather than doing one's work in isolation. This requires a rethinking of one's work to include relating to others as an integral part of it—along with other professional activities. N. Aisenberg and M. Harrington (1988) give the example of a woman medievalist scholar at a university who was very productive in tangible ways (articles published, a fellowship secured), but who shunned politics, refusing to engage in the work of relating to colleagues. She was ultimately denied tenure because she was removed from all channels of communication (she didn't even know her contract was up); she had no advocate in the department:

> "I do think tactically I was very foolish. I didn't make an effort to get close to anybody. I didn't . . . in the parlance of the business school, I did not seek a mentor and I should have done it. . . . I never even knew a decision was imminent. I assumed that there would be an automatic renewal, that I didn't have to get busy lining up the troops for another three years. . . . I should have been more present, I think now, looking back. I don't think I looked serious. I should have talked about my work all the time. . . . I should have been more conscious of the need to make that effort." But, she concluded, "I didn't even think of it. . . . I can't even say I made the wrong decision. I didn't make any decision, except, sort of, unconsciously. I never even said if I don't hang around, if I don't talk to this person and that person. . . . I'm running this risk. It never dawned on me." (Aisenberg and Harrington 1988, 52)

In academe and in the public schools there are clearly consequences to nonpolitical behavior. Merit alone is not enough. Building relationships and being a colleague are political acts in themselves. Dedication and practical accomplishments are insufficient in the world of educational leadership: one must also be prepared to engage in conversations, and to do the necessary interpersonal work of relating to others (also see Beekley 1999, 168). Of course, the opposite is also true, in that one cannot merely shake hands and be collegial toward others every day and expect to be rewarded if one has not also contributed substantively to the production of the workplace, for example, improving student learning, building relationships with parents and community, curriculum improvement. We were interested in the women in leadership positions in the public schools and how they manage the politics. Have they simply embraced the male model of politics, or are they relating and engaging in politics and leadership in their own styles? Thoughout this book you will find interesting portraits of women and their approach to being both a leader and a woman, and in some cases a woman of color, amongst other identities.

OUR FIELD STUDY

We purposively selected our participants according to certain criteria. We were looking for school leaders, such as union presidents, central office specialists, assistant principals, principals, assistant superintendents, and superintendents. We also chose women who are white and of color. Someone, typically a principal, assistant / deputy superintendent, or superintendent has taken on the role of mentor and has a special interest in these women, with a view to helping prepare them for higher level educational leadership positions. The women have been brought up through the ranks, and are now being actively mentored by a person in a higher leadership position. While we began the study with the notion of mentoring pairs, and this continued to be important, we also found mentoring triplets, or three women connected as mentors and protégés, and some mentoring networks.

Interviews addressed first information about participants in order to gain a sense of the mentor's or protégé's background, and experiences that may have contributed to their philosophy and leadership. Second, their professional beliefs about mentoring were examined. Participants were asked to define mentoring for school leadership and their own practice of school leadership. They were also asked to tell stories and recount critical incidents in their mentoring relationships that helped shape their knowledge and practice of leadership. We agree with S. Chase (1995, 7) that "contrary to commonsense which assumes that our lives determine our stories, narrative scholars argue that our stories shape our lives and that narration makes self understanding possible." Finally, issues that have posed difficulty for the women, the conflicts involved in mentoring, and tensions between the personal and the professional were addressed (see chapter two for methodology).

CONCEPTUAL FRAMEWORK FOR MENTORING

For each of the particular life stories, we have tried to examine them reflexively—looking inward and outward. We cannot claim to speak for each of the people in the study. Instead we seek to provide some new viewpoints on everyday experiences. Through the process of gathering data and simultaneously trying on new ways of looking at the data—or theorizing—we seek to challenge conventional wisdom and accepted mundane views of reality. For example, we found that notions of relationships, outcomes, power, subjection, conflicts, and marginality, helped explain the data, even though our participants did not use these theoretical frameworks to make sense of their world. While protégés were concerned with their mentors opening doors and new possibilities for them, it was also clear that contextual norms of educational administration were helping define the ways that their mentors related to them. Theorizing does not invalidate the mundane realities of everyday lives. Rather, the theoretical perspectives are different ways of making sense. They are reflexive accounts of participant and social science explanations. As P. Alasuutari (1996, 383) notes "when the routines and self-evident notions of everyday life are shattered, we always take reflexive distance from them and consider an event or encounter from other perspectives to figure it out."

We try to conceptualize mentoring and how it occurs, and find that there is a broad range of definitions of what are mentoring relationships (also see Romero and Storrs 1995, 79). As Johnsrud (1990, 59) notes, the difficulty in conceptualizing mentoring results from the ambiguity that surrounds the functions of mentoring:

> According to Kram (1985), the functions of the mentoring relationship are developmental and can be divided into *career* functions and *psychosocial* functions. The career functions she describes include sponsorship, coaching, provision of exposure and visibility, and challenging work assignments. These specific career-enhancing efforts are differentiated from [psychosocial] functions that attend to the development

of the whole person, such as acceptance and confirmation, counseling, role modelling, and friendship. Essentially, mentors enhance the position of the protégés by enabling the development of their skill and competence in a supportive environment.

Thus, to mentor may mean many different things to many people when mentors respond to the unique and specific needs of protégés. In this study, our work was informed by the work of J. Stalker (1994) who differentiates between relationships (which encompasses the psychosocial) and outcomes (which includes career advancement). *Relationships* includes both structural relationships, for example, hierarchical or lateral connections between people, and personal relationships, for example, how people relate as friends / intimates and / or with impersonal challenges and support. *Outcomes* refers to the benefits that may accrue from the mentoring relationships. The literature acknowledges that ideal mentoring relationships are reciprocal, with benefits coming to both mentors and protégés. Outcomes thus includes: (*a*) career advancement, for example, acquisition by protégés of practical, technical skills, and formal knowledge, and raised visibility for the mentor as a result of being a mentor to a "rising star," resulting in career advancement for both mentors and protégés; (*b*) personal development, for example, increased emotional growth, self-understanding and self-confidence for mentors and protégés, and; (*c*) professional identification, for example, socialization into the profession. Stalker (1994, 369) argues that research designs for mentoring studies have frequently been androcentric, that gender issues have not been given enough attention, and that too often the literature portrays women as victims of the patriarchy, an unacceptable view of "paralysis." We use a feminist poststructuralist conceptual framework to examine numerous cases of mentoring women, white and of color, into leadership in public schools. We give details of how and why mentoring occurs, and the particular circumstances that arise around mentoring women.

CONCLUSIONS

A key issue is what it means to be an administrator as we approach the twenty-first century, with changing administrative norms such as the empowerment of teachers, parents, and community members, site-based management, and decentralization of authority. The theory, practice and culture of administration is changing. Administrators who are women, white and of color, are struggling to find their own voices as they bring their unique heritages to the bureaucracy of schools. In this study of mentoring, what leadership means to women is drawn out, and more important, the strategies employed to facilitate quality mentoring relationships are discussed. We show how women are establishing their own styles of leadership and their own voices, even where the mentor's approach may be quite different.

The study contributes theoretically by adding to our understanding and knowledge about mentorship, how it occurs, and the problems that arise. For the next generation of women and minority leaders in K-12 public education such understandings are critical. The study also contributes practically, as an expected outcome is the development of educational materials on mentorship that can be used to improve educational administration preparation programs across the country, and for leadership academies designed to increase women's success in educational leadership positions. Questions often asked about women's success in educational leadership include:

> Have successful women worked at changing the structures and practices of the white and male dominated institutions in which they work, or have they been coopted by those institutions? . . . Why are there still so few women? Is it because women do not want the responsibility that comes with power? Because women are not as good as men at exercising power? Or because women face glass ceilings, persistent discrimination, and other insurmountable obstacles along the way. (Chase 1995, 12)

We show that women leaders *are* transforming schools and changing images of administration by their mentoring and leadership. Mentoring is lending personal and career support, and not just giving the rules that are available about how to be successful. It is sharing inside information that allows one to have an edge in making sound decisions, adding value to the organization, and leading others. Many women, white and of color, who are as groups relative "newcomers" to visible leadership positions, find themselves in a largely traditional and conservative profession. While this has changed somewhat with the influx of some women and minorities into high-level positions, the general conservatism of the culture of educational administration remains. Mentors have the special capacity to help women to garner the political support that they need from others, by sharing the inside information about the organization. They can help protégés to keep their own identities and selves, not to prostitute themselves to organizational cultures, nevertheless to position themselves in a positive light, so that they are not only doing good things for the organization, but also are seen to be doing good things for the organization. These shared insights may be more general norms, such as appropriate relationships with parents, and school policies on student enrollment. Or they may be more specific norms, such as sharing the list of names of influential Hispanic leaders in the community, and giving ideas on how to involve them in the public schools. Mentors assist protégés in working smarter, with more return for time and effort invested in a particular initiative, not necessarily harder.

Furthermore, these accounts of women's mentoring and leadership do not show only status quo reproduction of existing social mores and norms, but of women's resistance and proactive shaping of new agendas for our nation's schools. Women can be transformers; many women are resisters. Women are located in a position to know and understand the system, and to defy and change it. Mentoring is a mechanism for these changes. Women mentors work in the interstices (both "same" and "other") to change the system. As Stalker notes, "women mentors act out complex and often contradictory roles of resistance, contestation, mediation and reproduction of patriarchal, institutional and societal structures" (Stalker 1994, 366). Women are sharing inside information and teaching other women how to work within the power structures, and also to change the dominant system, to go with their strengths and bring women's voices to bear on leadership. The women's voices that you are about to hear are brilliantly diverse, sometimes discordant, and a cacaphony of hopes, disappointments and triumphs.

2

Feminist Research

For this study of mentoring women, we interviewed fifty-five purposively selected mentors and protégés (fifty-one women and four men) in leadership positions in public schools or central office positions in the states of Washington, Virginia, and Maryland in the United States. Our intent was both to further academic theory on mentoring, and to bring about change in educational leadership by enhancing leadership opportunities for women. We include some compelling stories that illustrate how traditional mentoring can fail women and how mentoring can be used to transform the face of educational leadership. Details are provided of the mentoring relationships and the people involved.

Feminist research was our chosen methodology for several reasons. First, we wanted to represent women's thinking, to show the mentoring experiences of women administrators from their own experiences and perspectives. Feminist research validates multiple and diverse perspectives, in particular the value of examining these perspectives to clarify one's own beliefs and values, and for the pedagogical opportunities to help one to consider the viewpoints of other individuals. Women learn from other women's voices and experiences. Second, we deconstruct the whole notion of mentoring. Traditionally, leadership has meant having power, influence, and control over one's subordinates. Thus, mentoring for educational administration has included the use of power and authority to frame leadership. We wanted to look under the assumptions, to question and explore the very notion of mentoring.

Mentoring has been part of a hierarchical educational environment, whereby the experienced and powerful elders controlled access and mobility into educational administration. Knowledge and authority have been the possession of those in power as superintendents and principals, while younger and inexperienced novices (teachers or beginning administrators) benefited from the counsel, advice, and mentoring of their superiors. The idea is that novices become experts, eventually reproducing the leadership, so that mentors retire and their protégés succeed them in the hierarchy. Thus, mentoring can be interpreted as socialization into current school practices (Lees 1998, 6). This reproduction model is similar to Paulo Freire's (1970) well-known "banking" model of education, essentially a knowledge-dispensing model, whereby experts convey what they know to novices. There is no sense of reciprocity, of wisdom shared or equal participation, or of the novice simultaneously teaching the mentor to see in new ways. We wanted to challenge the traditional notion of mentoring, to find some ways that it might be working by and for women, and to use this study to help further women's leadership in the public schools.

Feminist Poststructuralist Approach

Using a critical approach of feminist poststructuralist theories (Capper 1993; Davies 1994; Weedon, 1997), the study examines mentoring from the perspective of women in professional relationships with a mentor in the field of public school K-12 education. The study aims to clarify the ways in which women are located in a struggle to construct their own lives and meanings against the structural constraints (*i.e.*, patriarchy, racism, Eurocentrism). We contend that the dominant perspective in educational administration has been androcentric or male-biased, and that the contradictions arising from this bias are best exposed by utilizing feminist poststructuralism. Drawing from the work of Jacques Derrida, J. Lacan, Julia Kristeva, Louis Althusser, and Michel Foucault, this body of theories reveals socially constructed meanings through language, suggesting ways in which competing language patterns might produce current notions of gender. Scrutinizing these established meanings is key to the transformative process as it interrogates the familiar, and questions the premises upon which the meanings are based.

As our field of investigation consists of women and men mentoring women, we propose that a feminist orientation best addresses the issues of this domain. We refer to M. K. Tetreault's (1976) phase theory which identifies the common ways of thinking about women as reflected in the academy. She argues that when characterizing women's experiences, scholars tend to do the following: (a) assume the male experience is universal; (b) identify only outstanding women as worthy of attention; (c) provide a census of the number of women in a given field or discipline for purposes of affirmative action; and (d) view men and women as "separate, equal and complementary sexes." Less likely is a feminist orientation, which values women's experiences as the focus of attention, that is, "women studied on their own terms" (Tetreault, 1976, 51). We chose to take this feminist orientation, asking such questions as: What were women's mentoring experiences? What are the historical and cultural contexts of these experiences? How might these experiences and contexts relate to a diversity of perspectives?

Feminist poststructuralist theory rests on assumptions of the social creation of realities and the nexus between oppression and personal and collective actions. The oppression of women, white and of color, historically and in contemporary society and organizations, is recognized and named. Day-to-day interactions, intentions, and actions are also seen as part of the creation of multiple identities, gendered, social class, religious and race relationships. People are recognized as active agents participating in their own realities, and not simply powerless participants in social reproduction. Deconstruction and analysis of our own socially constructed realities and multiple identities can help us understand our struggles and location in society, and empower us to reposition and rename our contributions to personal and public worlds, and to understand their intersection. Subjectivity is seen as socially constructed, and the nature of the self is considered unstable and changeable. The self is constantly being created and recreated through new forms of discourse and new forms of social relationships.

Even though we use the terms "woman" or "woman of color" in this book, we acknowledge the variety of experiences of women, and the constantly changing form of these identities which are "precarious, contradictory, and in process, constantly being reconstituted in discourse each time we speak" (Weedon 1997, 33). In other words, though our focus here is on integrating the issues of gender and race, there is no universal experience of "being a woman" or a "woman of color": "female experience is never as unified, as knowable, as universal, and as stable as we presume it to be" (Fuss 1989, 114). For feminists of many different orientations, those with different religious beliefs, gays, parents, and those who are not parents, and so on, there are as many different voices and experiences as there are people and lives. Any search for universal truths is useless (Tong 1993, 219). Feminist research allows for a multiplicity of truths, none of them complete, and values those studies that begin with the lives and voices of women's experiences. Different perspectives help illuminate the kalidescope of women's lives.

A feminist approach thus validates personal experience, and is theoretically informed by an understanding of marginality, given women's history of social and cultural subordination in the public world. Feminist social science also rests on the assumption that all knowledge forms must be locatable. We must be able to see in whose interests and puposes particular knowledge claims are made and from whose experience such findings are generated. In other words, it is not enough to simply claim to view the world from the position of those marginalized, although this may be useful and new knowledge, we must also contextualize our accounts, "an argument for situated and embodied knowledges and an argument against various forms of unlocatable, and so irresponsible, knowledge claims" (Haraway 1988, 583–584). B. Davies and R. Hunt (1994, 391) put it this way:

> Dona Haraway suggests there is much to be learned from studies of the world from the perspective of the marked or subjugated, and that any claims to truth are best drawn from such studies of partial and situated experiences. One reason for this claim is that the positions from which seeing and knowing are done are more readily visible for marked category positions, whereas those who are habitually positioned in unmarked categories, such as male, white, heterosexual, and the ruling class, often manage to generate an illusion of positionless speaking.

Feminist poststructuralism cautions that one should make careful note of all actions taken, all data generated, all interpretations made. The approach served to guide our analytic processes, forcing our own reflection on ourselves as researchers and as data collectors. In short, feminist theories were drawn on which validated and contextualized the personal experiences of our respondents; highlighted gender differences if possible; identified and exposed power relationships and authority conflicts; and purposefully included multiple and diverse perspectives for consideration. Our rationale for utilizing feminist poststructuralism is to correct an imbalanced male-biased perspective held about educational administration by offering a feminist orientation and scrutinizing the alternative premises suggested about mentoring and leadership.

OVERVIEW OF THE STUDY

An Inital Design

Mary initiated our mentoring study by developing a research proposal and building the collaborative research team. She shaped its original design as an in-depth ethnographic study of selected mentoring pairs from the three states in which we lived and worked: Ernestine in Maryland, Margaret in Virginia, and Mary in Washington state. The focus would be on women and minorities in K-12 public school administration who were participating actively in informal mentoring relationships. It was anticipated that there would be nine mentoring pairs in each of the three sites, totally fifty-four participants, who would be studied for three academic years or until data saturation had occurred and no new knowledge was forthcoming.

The criteria for selecting these mentoring pairs were the following: (a) that the protégé had a working relationship with the mentor for at least one year or more; (b) that the protégé identified the mentor as someone who had been instrumental in her career development; (c) that the protégé was at the level of assistant principal or higher; and (d) that the protégé was a woman or minority aspiring to positions in educational administration. Among the other concerns and possible selection criteria discussed were: (1) site and regional specificity, such as sampling across urban, suburban, and rural areas; (2) various levels of administration beyond schools as, for example, in central office administration or in school district positions; (3) insuring minority representation with an over sampling of minorities within the different regions, as is often done in quantitative sampling; and (4) selecting to interview an equal number of minority male respondents.

Data collection would consist of a series of intensive interviews with mentors and protégés, and observations of mentoring behaviors. The interview questions for primary informants were semi-structured, aimed at describing the nature of the relationships, obtaining general descriptions and comments about good mentorship, and soliciting strategies that might encourage success for women and minorities particularly. For example, questions included the following: Who is mentoring the next generation of women and minority public school leaders? How did your mentoring relationship begin? Who initiated the relationship? How did it develop? How was rapport established? What were the conflicts that arose, if any? How were these conflicts and difficulties resolved? What strategies did the mentor use to encourage women and minorities to be successful in educational leadership?

It was anticipated that data analysis would follow the qualitative research methods outlined by the study's ethnographic approach. Solicited from people in professional relationships in education, data would be coded according to concepts and ideas from the literature, but advanced and developed by subjecting findings to closer scrutiny in field study. As researchers, we would attempt to make visible what people were doing, thinking and desiring in their day-to-day mentoring relationships through our prolonged engagement and persistent observation.

We chose a feminist social science approach to provide theoretical grounding for the study. Given women's history of social and cultural subordination in the public arena, we felt that this approach would force an interrogation of the values and viewpoints being legitimated in a traditionally white male-dominated educational administration. This approach allowed us to deconstruct mentoring in practice, to examine closely accepted assumptions about mentoring and leadership, to use the theoretical ideas in relationship to practice, and to generate new insights for practice. We, as researchers, would question whose interests were being advanced and whose viewpoints were being legitimated. We would begin with the personal experiences and lives of the respondents, placing women's views at the center of the discourse. Further, we would contextualize our own accounts and interrogate our own subjectivities and biases. Self-analysis as well as critical analysis is part of the process of examination, interpretation, and understanding. Unlike the interpretivist or constructivist tradition in qualitative research, which seeks to provide one account, the feminist social science approach validates the multiplicity of perspectives and experiences. Thus, while we, as researchers, would integrate and interpret the data, we would be inclusive of the participants' voices, even if they might differ from or contradict our interpretations.

Building a Collaborative Research Team

To build a research team, Mary invited two of her colleagues to join her efforts. We three researchers were similar in interest, philosophy, and choice of methodologies. All three of us were women in higher education with backgrounds in K-12 public education. We were currently faculty members teaching in educational administration and leadership programs in state universities. We had participated in educational environments where as women in educational administration, we were in the minority. Our work as faculty members was to encourage and mentor students in their career development in the field. This study would contribute to our own understandings, and help in our mentorship of our graduate students. We were aligned in our feminist approaches as well as our qualitative research orientations. Mary had used a feminist social science approach in her book *Parent-School Collaboration: Feminist Organizational Structures and School Leadership* (Henry, 1996). Margaret had also recently written a book on women aspiring toward the superintendency, entitled *Voices of Women Aspiring to the Superintendency* (1996). Ernestine was engaged in studies of minorities in different school contexts (1997). Among us, we felt that we could both engage in a study that would be richer for our varied contributions, and that we would be fulfilled through the exciting opportunity to work together on a project of mutual interest.

We three researchers are also different. While we were all interested in K-12 public school administration and educational leadership, Margaret was particularly interested in central office leadership and the superintendency. She desired to focus on women aspirants who sought the superintendency, because she had written on that topic previously. Mary was interested in mentoring as a social relationship and the process of how women were mentored into school administration in general, while Ernestine favored a broader look at the trajectory of women in leadership throughout school systems in the state. These individual differences shaped what we thought we were studying. We questioned whether we were looking at the phenomenon of "mentoring" or of "mentoring women" more specifically. We discussed whether minority referred to "women as minority" or whether we could distinguish race and gender issues separately in considering "women and minorities." We challenged the notion of mentoring pairs, asking whether these relationships were groups or networks or generations rather than exclusively pairings. We also realized we could not adequately study both women and minorities, so the focus of the study was changed to mentoring women only.

In terms of research methodology, we three considered ourselves qualitative researchers, but brought our own specific approaches and methods to doing research in qualitative ways. For example, Mary emphasized an ethnographic study approach, while Ernestine preferred utilizing oral history to direct the interviewing process. We attempted to put forth our own viewpoints and relied upon the support of our colleagues to negotiate our differences. Data were collected in the 1996–97 and 1997–98 school years, and were coded according to concepts and ideas from the literature on leadership, administration, and mentorship. Those concepts were further refined in light of data generated in the field study. The study evolved as we implemented the initial design and negotiated our different perspectives on the subject of mentoring relationships.

Selection and Sampling

As noted by M. LeCompte and J. Preissle (1993), qualitative researchers employ a selection process which attempts to specify the kinds of individuals involved in the investigation as well as the circumstance under which they are studied. Sampling involves creating a more restricted set from the original population, directed by the purpose of the investigation.

While quantitative research methodologies define quite specifically how selection and sampling techniques are to be undertaken and executed, qualitative research methodologies offer greater flexibility and adaptability. With several researchers working collaboratively, the process of determining who will be studied is an interactive and often dynamic one. A research study might be initiated by identifying a particular group—individuals in a school, bilingual teachers in a particular region, building administrators in an urban setting, members of a specific cultural minority in a particular region. Once access is obtained, selection of informants and sampling might occur in numerous ways. Researchers must confront problems and issues related to selection and sampling in the process of conducting their study.

In this mentoring study, our aim was to focus on mentoring practices of women, both white and of color, in educational leadership. We were interested in the relationships between the mentor and the protégé whom they mentored. We developed specific criteria for considering who would constitute a mentoring pair or twosome. Protégés would be women, white and of color, aspiring to hold educational leadership positions, most likely as administrators at various levels. We anticipated the person who was mentored would be at the level of assistant principal, assuming that such an individual had expressed interest in educational administration. There could be other kinds of mentoring, such as mentoring of teachers in instructional leadership, but we were directing our efforts toward prospective administrators. The protégé might have identified the mentor as someone who was instrumental in their career development in a variety of ways. And the mentoring pair would have developed a long-term working relationship, perhaps a year or more. The assumption was that mentoring occurred over a sustained period of time, rather than a single occurrence.

But as noted by M. Zelditch (1962), qualitative research selection is not static; rather it is "dynamic, phasic and sequential." While we began with selection and sampling to define an initial group, we attempted to use our informants to expand the scope of the study, refine our questions, and generate new lines of inquiry as we proceeded in our investigation. Because of the iterative nature of the process, we felt that it was important to detail our selection and sampling as it occurred.

Selection of Mentoring Pairs

Overall, we were consistent in applying the selection criteria, identifying participants through our personal and professional contacts. There were, however, individual variations in how we defined the participants in our respective samples and how we sought representation among women, white and minority.

Washington state.   To identify possible mentoring pairs, Mary utilized her own knowledge of people in administrative positions, as well as solicited the knowledge of others who were connected to

Washington public schools. She consulted with administrators in the schools and some professors of educational administration, and compiled lists of possible mentoring pairs, noting who had recommended those individuals as possible study participants. She called the mentors and told them about the study. When someone had referred them, she mentioned the referral. In two cases she was turned down, the individuals citing that they did not feel comfortable having their perspectives and activities as mentors examined, since they did not believe they were exemplary as mentors. In other cases, the person suggested as a mentor felt more comfortable being identifed as a protégé. Mary allowed for this alteration because the respondents were usually interested in participating, and seemed to have much to share. In some cases, she was able to contact that respondent's mentor as well. Furthermore, although none of us used pairings based upon a formal university mentoring program or a school district internship, one pair (Pat Sorensen and Eileen Hales) is included where they are engaged in an internship. This is because the mentor relationship has spanned some fifteen years, and is the kind of naturally occurring phenomenon we sought to study, rather than a short-term arranged mentorship. The notion was that the mentoring phenomenon would be best examined as informally occurring in the school or school district setting.

When completed, Mary interviewed sixteen participants (ten protégés and six mentors), of which there were fourteen women and two men. One of the men was white and the other Hispanic. The latter served as mentor to two of the women. Of the women, nine were white, four were Hispanic, and one was African-American (see table 2.1). To ensure the confidentiality of our interviewees, all proper names used for individuals, schools, schools districts, and cities in this study are pseudonyms (for more details on participants in the study see appendix A).

Virginia. For the Virginia sample, Margaret's selection of her mentoring pairs originated with women who were already administrators and mentors. She initially approached three women superintendents, told them about the mentoring study, and asked if they had ever mentored women into educational administration. Explaining that our interest was in mentoring pairs, she asked them to have a particular woman in mind in answering interview questions. Following the interviews, she was put in touch with the respective protégés.

TABLE 2.1   Washington State Mentoring Participants

Mentor	Protégé
Dr. Jeff Stewart (white male) Assistant Superintendent	Dr. Susan Rembert (white female) Assistant Principal
Dr. Pat Sorensen (white female) Principal Elementary School	Eileen Hales (white female) Central Office Specialist
Dr. Les Johnson (Hispanic male) Superintendent	Dr. Meredith Koval (white female) Assistant Superintendent
Dr. Les Johnson (Hispanic male) Superintendent	Diane Lynch (white female) Principal Elementary School
Marcia Francis (white female) Principal Elementary School	Reneé Miles (Hispanic female) Assistant Principal
Gabriela Ramirez (Hispanic female) Community College Professor	Leticia Martinez (Hispanic female) Assistant Principal
Joyce Stearns (white female) President of Education Association	Lesley Kinnard (white female) Union leader / Teacher
Othene Kirkland (African-American female) Retired Principal	Doreen Ballard (African-American female) Principal Elementary School
Dr. Barbara Hansen (white female) Currently Law School Student	Maria Valdez (Hispanic female) Director of Special Programs, Elementary
Dr. Carlos Domingos (Hispanic male) Dean of Community College	Ramona Gonzales (Hispanic female) Director of Special Programs, Secondary
Dr. Sherrill Williams (white female) Assistant Superintendent	Peggy Hoffman (white female) Central Office Specialist
Dr. Barbara Hansen (white female) Currently Law School Student	Emilia Head (white female) Assistant Director, Special Progams, Elementary

In a second stage of selecting interviewees, Margaret approached three or four women administrators who were not yet superintendents, but whom she knew either from class or from other professional connections. She asked them whether they had ever been mentored or whether they had ever mentored a woman into educational administration. At this stage she also consciously sought minorities and approached three male superintendents. Two of the male superintendents said they had not mentored any women into educational administration. The third man said he could probably think of someone, but he would have been a reluctant participant. Consequently, he was not interviewed.

Margaret discussed the study with colleagues in different parts of the state to secure a geographical mix of respondents. From these discussions, she was referred to several potential participants by some of these colleagues and by participants who had already been interviewed. She chose to follow up on such referrals based on ethnicity, location, and lack of personal connection to her. She considered such things as size of district, kind of administrative position. Her purposive sampling in this stage was to obtain a rich variety of relationships. She also chose to avoid students who were in her classes, although she did select two. When contacting those who had been referred, Margaret explained the need for mentoring pairs and subsequently eliminated some potential participants whose pair was out of state. She did ask that her interviewees identify either the protégé or mentor who had been most instrumental or meaningful in their lives.

All together she interviewed eighteen participants, of which there were seventeen women and one man. Of the women, there were five who were African-American, the rest were white. Although some of the participants in the study knew other interviewees, Margaret chose not to discuss who the other participants were. Only one cross connection came up, in which one participant mentioned getting help from one other person in the study different from the person who was identified as her pair.

Maryland.   In her selection process for Maryland, Ernestine spoke first with a faculty colleague who had been a former superintendent with close ties to the current state and city superintendents, as well as numerous others in educational leadership throughout the state. She met with this individual on three occasions to record his administrative background and note his mentoring experiences. In the course of these conversations, she identified his mentors as well as

TABLE 2.1   Virginia Mentoring Participants

Mentor	Protégé
Dr. Mary Ellen Remington (white female) Superintendent	Dr. Julia Dawson (white female) Associate Director of Instruction
Dr. Patty Burns (white female) Superintendent	Beverly Thompson (African-American fem.) President of Education Association Teacher
Dr. Sarah Anderson (white female) Superintendent	Bobbi Reeves (white female) Elementary School Principal
Dr. Pam Egan (white female) Middle School Principal	Dr. Brenda Monroe (African-American fem) Director of Human Resources/ Staff Development
Dr. Mary Ann Chase (white female) Middle School Principal	Carol Pierce (African-American female) Principal of Alternative High School
Dr. Marsha Poole (white female) Superintendent	Sara Murphy (white female) Elementary School Principal
Dr. George Street (white male) Superintendent	Dr. Janet Cochran (white female) Dir. Staff Development and Program Evaluation
Joan Lewis (white female) Retired Assistant Superintendent	Dorothy Hunnicutt (African-American fem.) Curriculum Coordinator
Dr. Eve Farley (white female) Superintendent	Vicky Fletcher (African-American female) Director of Instruction

his protégés. While there were some defined pairs of mentor and protégé, the emerging pattern seemed more of a web of relationships. There was also the possibility of tracing leadership development in the state as her colleague provided names of top women leaders identified as potential interviewees. Ernestine used this list as the start of her interview prospects.

Letters were sent to these individuals. The first respondent was an assistant superintendent who was in charge of the professional development unit of an urban school district. During this interview, the assistant superintendent gave her several other possible interviewees. Ernestine asked that the assistant superintendent contact these individuals and if they were willing, then they would call the researcher. By the next day, additional interviews were set up with two others, one protégé, who was an assistant principal in an alternative school, and the other, a director working under the assistant superintendent. A similar protocol was followed with the individuals contacted via letter.

In addition, Ernestine pursued her own leads derived from personal contacts. For example, there were interviewees of students who had completed the university program in educational administration. One graduate was an assistant principal with a mentor who was her principal. Another former student was a newly appointed high school principal who had been Ernestine's dissertation advisee. A third graduate was an assistant superintendent who had recently completed her doctorate in the educational administration program. Ernestine selected to ask individuals not currently in the program, but rather those who had completed the program, and were no longer advisees or students.

Perhaps the most interesting story was how Constance, a school district superintendent, became a participant. She had been identified on the initial contact list of top women leaders. Ernestine sent her a letter but did not hear back from her. Months later, at a party, Ernestine happened to be speaking with a former graduate of the university's doctoral program about the mentoring study. The graduate mentioned Constance by name as she had been in the same school district serving as an administrator. Recounting how Constance had mentored many women in the district, she emphatically said, "Oh, you have to talk with her!" This prompted a follow-up call and an interview with Constance.

For the most part, Ernestine followed the criteria for selecting individuals. However, it is noteworthy that the initial informants came from those individuals at high ranks, that is at the level of deputy superintendent or higher. Thus, her interviewees were mostly mentors who identified protégés, rather than the other way around. In only two cases, were there protégés who in turn identified mentors that were subsequently interviewed. At the same time, mentors frequently spoke about their own experiences, mentioning former mentors and their influences.

Ernestine sought individuals beyond the usual pairing of mentor and protégé, usually in clusters of three. Her sets were of a mentor and usually two protégés, or of one mentor, a protégé, and that protégé's protégé. She intended to explore the proposition that one individual was linked with a multiplicity of relationships, not strictly a one-on-one relationship. Also she was interested in how individuals were mentored by previous generations in educational leadership, and further, how these individuals established the leadership within the school districts they served.

In the Maryland sampling, there were twenty-one interviewees in total, fifteen discrete pairs of mentor and protégé. Interviewees consisted of twenty female respondents; one male; eight who identified themselves as African-Americans, thirteen who were white; ten mentors, and eleven protégés, among whom there were some who identified themselves as both mentor and protégé at different times in response to the questions.

Interviewing

The interviewing at all three sites followed the same procedure. Prior to the data collection, Mary completed the necessary paperwork for human subjects review and received approval from the Office for Grants and Research Development at Washington State University in Spring 1996. Each subsequent year, she updated the request and was granted continuing approval. We used standard forms granting informed consent as stipulated by the university (see appendix B).

Interviewees were contacted either by phone or by letter and told about the study, its protocol, and the questions to be asked. In most cases, individuals readily consented to be interviewed and a convenient date and time were established for a meeting. The location was usually at the school or district site, in part for the interviewee's convenience, but also to gather additional contextual data about the educational organization or system. Mary noted that because she lived on the eastern side of the state of Washington, she often drove considerable distances to these sites, often as much as three to four hours one way. She opted for this situation, rather than selecting participants closer to home, because the larger districts at a distance offered more diversity in school populations and participants. Margaret

TABLE 2.3   Maryland Mentoring Participants

Mentor	Protégé
Dr. Winoa Chambers (white female) Elementary School Principal	Angela Patterson (white female) Elementary Assistant Principal
Clara Barnes (African-American female) Associate Superintendent/ staff development	Lauren Kente (African-American female) Alternative High School Assistant Principal
Clara Barnes (African-American female) Associate Superintendent/ staff development	Jennifer Davies (white female) Director of School Improvement
Dr. Roberta Paulie (white female) Superintendent	Elaine Bennett (white female) Elementary School Principal
Dr. Martha Ellison (African-American female) Deputy Superintendent	Dr. Denise Oscar (African-American female) Supervisor of Parent/ comm. relations
Dr. Martha Ellison (African-American female) Deputy Superintendent	Marion Bateson (African-American female) Magnet School Principal
Dr. Glenda Alcott (white female) Superintendent	Cassie McHenry (white female) Alternative High School Principal
Dr. Glenda Alcott (white female) Superintendent	Dr. Denise Oscar (African-Amer. female) Supervisor of Parent/ community relations
Dr. Glenda Alcott (white female) Superintendent	Marion Bateson (African-American female) Magnet School Principal
Chuck Donnelly (white male) Associate Superintendent	Dr. Sharon Perta (white female) High School Principal
Dr. Sharon Perta (white female) High School Principal	Frances Dawton (white female) Middle School Principal

(Continued)

TABLE 2.3   *(Continued)*

Mentor	Protégé
Dr. Constance Lee (white female) Superintendent	Grace Holly (white female) Elementary Principal
Dr. Paula Jenkins (white female) Retired Deputy Superintendent	Dr. Constance Lee (white female) Superintendent
Dr. Nanette Morrison (African-American female) Private School Principal	Dr. Ellie Carlye (African-American female) Assistant superintendent C & I
Dr. Monique Avery (African-American female) High School Principal	Dr. Ellie Carlye (African-American female) Assistant Superintendent C & I

also drove between two and three hours each way to conduct all but four interviews, which were local or within half an hour's drive. The interviews in Ernestine's sample were conducted at the respondent's site, except for two out of the twenty-one interviews. One exception was a curriculum director who had concluded a meeting at a professional development site and arranged for her interview to be conducted there on a Saturday afternoon. A second exception was a retired educator who lived out of state and had been invited to the college for a presentation. Her interview was conducted in Ernestine's office. In all cases, we sought to make interview times and locations comfortable and convenient for our respondents.

The interview protocol was to introduce ourselves and ask for their consent in tape recording. Consent forms were then signed. The interviews were conducted face-to-face in the person's office and tape recorded and later transcribed (see appendix C for the interview questions). We generally would begin with the first question, asking the interviewee to describe themselves, their career in education, and their work. For instance, Margaret asked for background information telling how the respondent obtained her or his current position in order to develop an idea of that individual's career in education. That would be followed by more free-flowing questions and answers as the conversation developed. To insure that all questions of importance to the respondent were covered, respondents were asked that they review the questions and highlight any that they particularly wanted to address. The interviews generally lasted 60–75 minutes, keeping to our agreement of time.

In addition to tape recording, we took extensive notes during the sessions. Following the interview and on the long drive home, Mary thought through the interview and made verbal and sometimes written notes of significant points. She also wrote descriptive narratives on each participant based on the interactions with them, and analytic notes following the interviews. These narratives covered not only the interviews, but often the lunch, coffee, or dinner conversations following the scheduled appointments. Similarly, Ernestine wrote field notes following each interview, noting when, where, key points, any impressions. She found these "snapshots" to be quick refreshers and helpful in conceptualizing what each respondent had to say. These field notes also served as backups, until the actual interview tapes were transcribed.

At the schools and offices of our respondents, we also often requested and collected information sheets, pamphets on display for parents and citizens, school newsletters, and any other documents that would provide some insight into the participants in the study, their school organizations, leadership styles, current issues of the school system, and so on. In one case, an interviewee brought in her resume for reference. However, this was not systematically collected from all respondents. This would have been useful for documentation and validation purposes in confirming the career histories of our mentors and protégés.

Additional input was solicited in this study after the preliminary analysis and writing had been completed. Preliminary writings were shared with some but not all interviewees, who were asked to comment on what had been said and how they were represented. All respondents were positive and supportive of the discussions.

Data Analysis and Writing

Our strategies in conducting data analysis and writing were based upon qualitative research methodologies. In general, we engaged in the analytic process by immersing ourselves in the data of our respective samples. Mary read and reread her interview transcripts, making notes in the margins, looking for patterns, anomalies, and points of interest. To further the inquiry, she clustered her examination around questions from the data and the literature such as what is mentoring, what characterizes mentoring, how are women doing leadership in their own styles, what are the problems, and how they are benefiting from mentoring. Margaret's initial inquiry was directed by the interview questions as well as by asking what could be understood about the mentoring relationship as seen through pairings. In a second iteration, she looked more broadly at the themes and ideas emerging that might not specifically relate to the questions asked in the interview. Ernestine's strategy was to base her initial inquiry upon a particularly rich interview data set, generated by a mentor who was a principal and her protégé, the assistant principal. She proceeded first to examine those transcripts, drawing from the analysis of that base and identifying other threads that would be pursued in subsequent transcripts. This strategy enabled a validation of what might be overall themes, occurring through the data set in contrast with anomalies more specific to individual interviewees.

In attempting to compare the three states, we formulated general questions that became the organizing rubric for our collective data. We also utilized the feminist social science approach as a means of interrogating our data and thus, challenging the male hegemony predominant in educational administration, management, and leadership. Two of us used qualitative software package for organizing the data but we employed different packages. Mary used HyperQual2; Ernestine employed Nudist. All three of us also employed traditional qualitative analysis techniques.

Our Personal Subjectivities

Recognizing that no research is value free and that our viewpoints as researchers hold biases, we examined our own personal subjectivities and biases in doing this study. As mentioned earlier, we shared similar philosophical orientations, but we acknowledged our contrasting ways of thinking about the subject of mentoring. Our individualized viewpoints both personalized our representations of our mentoring data sets, while emphasizing different aspects of the phenomenon in our analysis and writing.

Mary spoke of her specific interest in a feminist perspective in conducting this study. "I think our location in a sexist society means that our experiences are still of a professional and social context where women are less financially and socially rewarded professionally than men."

Margaret identified herself as a university professor whose work on women in leadership was recognized by some women she interviewed:

> Two or three of them have read my book and know that I use feminist theory in my research and in some of my teaching. Some of these women also know that I teach a superintendent's preparation course and that I am actively encouraging women to consider the superintendency as a career possibility in the future. I do seminars and participate in workshops on women's leadership approaches.

For Ernestine, while gender was an important factor to be considered in a study of mentoring minorities, she identified as much with the confounding nature of racial, ethnic, and other diverse differences that impact our identities as professionals and our career advancement in systems that are traditionally sexist, racist, and hegemonic.

> I think of myself as an Asian-American minority first, before I think of my sexuality as a woman in American society. I believe I am viewed in this light. This colors my thinking about how professionals would succeed as minorities. This is essentially what we are examining as we consider the successful mentoring of women, both white and nonwhite, in our American society.

Both Mary and Margaret are originally from Australia and have immigrated to the United States. Margaret has also experienced living in Japan for some seventeen years, with numerous nationality, race, and cultural experiences there. Concerning race and ethnicity issues, in Mary's words, "For me sexism is just one small piece of the problem of oppression. My sensitivity to the larger race issues has also been heightened by the experiences of my son Ryan, who is African-American, and those of my friends of color."

Ernestine brought to our discussions a fragmented or differentiated sense of culture, where in any one group there might be less convergence of values and more ambiguity over what was shared and common. She advocated for an orientation to larger contextual, organizational issues related to how individuals advance and are mentored, proposing that we would examine relationships within the context of the school and school district, not in isolation. Moreover, she adhered to a notion of webbings or interconnectedness in which the roles of mentor / protégé are muted, multiplied, confounded in various ways. Constant use of conference calls, e-mail discussions and continual writing and rewriting on shared documents became necessary tools to bridge these distances and differences, and to allow for collaboration which also preserved our distinct voices.

Conclusion

While we found the process of doing collaborative research over long distances extremely challenging, we also found it to be one of our most rewarding research experiences. The experience tested our friendships, made us question ourselves at every turn, and created additional work since we were forced to collaborate, to explain our positions and processes, and take the time to reach agreement on matters of critical importance. However, we felt the additional difficulties made for a stronger study, and enhanced our individual understandings of feminist research and qualitative inquiry.

Across the states, our data show women mentors and protégés who are making a difference in public schools. We see women caught in conflicts, dilemmas, choices, and possibilities, as they struggle to redefine themselves on their own terms, not as others see them, as leaders in their own right. We also see evidence of multiple selves, such as women leaders who are aware of their leadership possibilities, but who are presently choosing to move at a slower pace for personal fulfillment, rather than career enhancement. Other women are enthusiastically moving ahead as fast as the opportunities present themselves—excited by their dreams to improve education. We applaud all the women in this book, who, whether they acknowledge it or not, by their very location on the periphery of the patriarchal system of educational administration, are making changes to the very heart of educational leadership. The next two chapters report our findings on what quality mentoring means in general terms to the participants in the study (chapter 3) and what specific mentoring experiences women perceive are needed in order for them to be successful in K-12 public school administration (chapter 4). We later critique current mentoring practices, show some of the contradictions and double-binds in which women find themselves, and suggest some new possibilities for mentoring and leadership.

3

Quality Mentoring
Relationships for Women

Not all so-called mentoring relationships are helpful. To our way of thinking, all relationships that are truly mentoring relationships are by definition helpful, because mentoring implies furthering the professional development of the protégé in a way that is personally rewarding. Oftentimes people can be caught in relationships that are not helpful, when they have a mentor who is experienced or powerfully connected but not providing mentoring. Connections with powerful people are not always worthwhile to cultivate, for it is the quality of the relationship that characterizes mentoring. Johnsrud (1990, p. 61), for example, describes a mentoring relationship in which the protégé was unable to discuss his concerns about his future with his mentor. Lack of communication between mentor and protégé is a serious flaw in a mentoring relationship. The protégé may feel an intense loyalty to the mentor, but the mentor is not responsive to the protégé's desires and ambitions. Perhaps those ambitions are considered excessive, or perhaps the mentor does not value the protégé as much as she should, or she may not want to lose the protégé as an immediate employee, in a situation where the mentor is also a boss. Thus, a lack of trust may exist between mentor and protégé, and possibly the relationship may be exploitative. In a worst case scenario, "protégés are exploited: emotionally, sexually, and professionally.

Inappropriate emotional ties have been forged, sexual harassment is all too common, and original work has been stolen" (Johnsrud 1990, 61). We agree that some mentoring relationships do indeed hinder, and others can be exceptionally helpful. The aim of the chapter is to clarify what the participants saw as helpful or quality mentoring by reporting on the analysis which draws upon data collected in the three states. We explain in chapters 3 and 4 what good mentoring means for the participants in this study, and distinguish it from what might be characterized as mentoring that is poor or insufficient. This definition of mentoring is a beginning framework for the kinds of mentoring based on care and collaboration that we propose in later chapters. We begin by presenting our findings, the perspectives of the women in our study, on quality mentoring as it presently occurs. It is our belief that in understanding how women view the mentoring process and the assumptions of mentoring, together with an analysis of the conflicts and contradictions in their lives (in later chapters), we are better positioned to empower women and men to redefine mentoring and leadership.

DEFINITION OF QUALITY MENTORING

Mentoring is characterized as an active, engaged and intentional relationship between two individuals (mentor and protégé) based upon mutual understanding to serve primarily the professional needs of the protégé. Quality mentoring relationships can be distinguished by certain ways of relating, by expectations and parameters placed on the relationships that serve to promote the protégés' professional success and well being. These relationships are also valued by mentors. Our participants defined mentoring as an dynamic process clearly focused on the needs of the protégé:

> [Mentoring is] actively helping that person, training, advising, talking with her, picking her up when she is low, and laughing with her when she has been successful. (Mentor, Pam Egan)

> Number one, one of the biggest jobs that I feel that I have [as mentor] is to provide the leadership and the guidance and the experiences with Angela that are going to make her a stronger assistant principal. To develop her so that by the

time she assumes a principalship, she's had a variety of experiences. She's not feeling that there's gaps in her education or there's holes out there somewhere. She's feeling secure, confident in her abilities. She knows what she knows and she knows what she doesn't know. (Mentor, Winoa Chambers)

Mentors in this study spent a great deal of time with their protégés, listening to them, talking with them, and creating opportunities for them. Generally speaking, good mentors engage in the following behaviors that are inextricably interwoven, but will be discussed separately to clarify the nature of mentoring relationships.

Open communication and personal connection. Good mentors connect well on an emotional and personal level with their protégés, inviting them to work together and "ride the train" with them. They have a desire to take the time to care for and encourage their protégés, and get to know them really well. Understanding the needs and concerns of their protégés, good mentors are able to advocate for them on a variety of levels.

The mentor-protégé pair of Glenda Alcott and Cassie McHenry exemplify an active, intentional, and mutually supportive relationship with connectedness. According to Cassie, both sides actively sought each other out. You want to spend time so you make time to be together even with busy schedules. "You seek that person and their company." This mentoring relationship began when she and her mentor were in the same building but on two different floors. They sought each other out for conversation and idea sharing. Later, the protégé worked for the mentor as her administrative assistant. Now over sixteen years later, they are in different school systems but still have a strong relationship.

Another example is principal Dorren Ballard, an African-American woman with an African-American woman mentor who has invested enormous amounts of time and energy to help her gain the principalship and then be successful in her position. Note the imagery of the parent-child relationship with all the love and connectedness and time spent that it conveys: "She adopted me as her child, another child. But I think she sees the growth in me, the progression from a very neophyte, naive principal to someone who's stronger every year because of the challenges" (Protégé, Doreen Ballard). Part of being empathetic is listening really well, and having a sensitivity to gender and race concerns. Good mentors are perceptive, able to read people and see others' potential that they may not see in themselves. They have a perception and awareness of people's conditions, and they listen very carefully to what they're saying, and may use a story to illustrate what they did in a similar situation.

> I think it helps [a woman protégé] if they come to me and say, "I'm not sure what's going on here. Do you think it has to do with my gender? Or do you think it has to do with my skills?" I can talk to them from my experience, which is everything. . . . It's not a white male saying to them, here's what I can tell you." Maybe the white male wouldn't know. (Mentor, Marsha Poole)

The emotional commitment and connection in quality mentoring might be called "chemistry." Chemistry allows for the pair to spend a great deal of time together, and also to deal with any conflicts and tensions that arise: "I don't see how you can have a really strong mentorship without chemistry because you'd be driving each other nuts all the time I think. The chemistry is whatever allows you to want to spend great deals of time together and be friends and be happy" (Mentor, Joyce Stearns).

> When you're mentoring someone, sometimes, you find that you've got an awful lot in common and that your personalities click. Brenda and I have a particular sense of humor; we find certain things funny. No one else can even think of them as funny, but she and I will be in a meeting or someone says something that everyone else is just sitting there and we're looking at each other, and we both want to laugh. (Mentor, Pam Egan)

Good communication between mentor and protégé is evident when both can freely speak their minds and express differences of opinion. Speaking as a protégé, this respondent remarked:

> Communication is critical. I wouldn't want to embarrass the superintendent [her mentor], but we were at a meeting and I just took the completely opposite perspective to him and I asked him "Was that okay?" And he said, "If I wanted someone who would say exactly what I would say to them I wouldn't need that person here. What I need is a person here

who would say something different or look at it a different way." So I thought it was kind of neat. The mentor needs to never be threatened by another's thought or another's position. (Mentor, Marcia Francis)

Often good communication can be facilitated by good humor between mentor and protégé. Protégés sometimes acknowledged the sense of humor that their mentors displayed consistently in dealing with others:

> Glenda [mentor] has a consistent good humor. She is a good humored person. I don't think I've ever seen her honestly in a bad mood, really. She's always focused on something or pumping [excited] about something, or concerned but not worried. I'm the same way. So that is the chemistry that we had. I think the good humor was an underpinning of the relationship. That's what allowed us to enter into a mentoring relationship professionally. (Protégé, Cassie McHenry)

Also critical to good communication is the trust that is a necessary foundation to good communication. Good mentors build trust with their protégés, and encourage them to have faith in their abilities and to "trust the process" (Protégé Diane Lynch); "trust is critical" (Protégé Reneé Miles). "Good mentors let their protégés try something new or something their own way, even if it doesn't turn out the way they would like. There's no undermining of the protégé's efforts, and the protégé knows they have the unequivocal support of the mentor. Such mentors build a whole person relationship, a trusting relationship, providing support and encouragement.

> I feel very comfortable on a one-on-one basis letting [my mentor Clara] know, "I'm not real sure how I should approach this particular situation." And then sharing with her what I think that I would do and listening to see if she has any other recommendations. But I think that's critical for a mentor when you talk about "trust" and "rapport," because maybe it's some people's human nature—it's mine—to not have any problem opening up to those folks that I feel want to make it a win-win. I always feel that is Clara's goal as well, what can she do to support me as her subordinate. (Protégé, Jennifer Davies)

> In a mentoring situation you need to build respect otherwise it's going to be a drag. You must be able to trust each other and also find the time to spend with the person. . . . There needs to be a great deal of trust built up between you, and not only trust but a respect for each other's competencies. . . . The protégé can contribute to the mentor's growth as well. Neither person can be threatened in this situation. There has to be a sense of openness and trust. (Mentor, Pat Sorensen)

Reflection on leadership thinking and actions.   Good mentors also have an ability to offer to the protégé access to their reflection on their leadership, thinking and actions. They freely offer their thoughts on their plans and actions to their protégés, encouraging them to talk through situations and problem solve together. They model reflection, and thereby encourage their protégés to also be reflective, as well as providing information and answering questions in difficult situations. As an example, mentor Barbara Hansen explained to her protégé throughout the entire last year that they were working together as boss and subordinate, all the details of her job as Director of Special Programs, as she was working on them on a month by month basis. Similarly, George Street trained protégé Janet Cochran in every facet of finance and budget during his tenure as Assistant Superintendent for Finance. This shows a genuine desire to pass on everything that the mentors have learned and gained through experience, even while recognizing that the protégé will do things her own way. In addition, even now that the pairs no longer work in close proximity, these protégés still consult with their former mentors on professional matters. When Emilia Head (protégé) needed help with assessment, she called her mentor, who gladly assumed the role of guiding her protégé through "the assessment piece." Many protégés have similar accounts of reflection-on-action and directed guidance:

> The very last year she [mentor] ran me through what she would do each month. She was preparing me for her role, although she really couldn't [assume that I was going to get this position]. I mean she said, "These are the things you need to know if I'm here or not here." And so we went through every piece of what is required of all the programs that we supervise. (Protégé, Maria Valdez)

> Joan, my mentor, required that we watch her . . . when she had a dilemma as an administrator, she walked it through with us as to what was going on in her head. . . . She required that we have daily logs . . . it was very laborious and I hated doing it . . . but we were new, we had to prove ourselves to these other people out there. (Protégé, Dorothy Hunnicutt)

Good mentors take time to consult with their protégés throughout the process in which they are involved. They understand the value of this reflection on what the problem was, what occurred, what worked and what might be done differently next time. As part of a caring relationship they engage in continual debriefing with their protégés:

> One of the main things is that she's [protégé] able to gain access to all kinds of information, for example, what I'm doing, what I'm thinking, how I'm doing things. She knows what she wants to look for, the things she needs to build on in herself, and she is looking for different approaches and what works. There's the modeling aspect. She gets to see how I do things and how they turn out—and some things work better than others. We also talk about what I'm doing or what she's doing and try to analyze the situation. How could we do something better. (Mentor, Pat Sorensen)

> You're guiding them through the experience. They're getting the advantage of the wisdom that you have, having to learn trial by fire, and you're able to pass some of these things along, like, "Hey don't go there, that's going to blow up in your face." And they can really learn a lot and not have to make the same mistakes. . . . I try to feed her information that she wouldn't normally get, so that she has the information with which to build. (Mentor, Joyce Stearns)

Acting as a sounding board.   Mentors in quality relationships give feedback and serve as sounding boards for their protégés (also see Pavan 1999, 107). The sounding board function is critical as the protégé struggles with issues and tries to figure out her own leadership skills, abilities, and aspirations. The protégé knows that she has the mentor's unequivocal support. Furthermore, good mentors, when acting as a sounding board, do not simply provide the answers. They help their protégés develop their own style of leadership and their own philosophy of education that they can communicate with others, rather than trying to make the protégé into a carbon copy of themselves. By not giving the answers to particular problems, the mentor empowers the protégé to figure out her own responses and her own rationale for decision-making, and the protégé is thus able to refine her own strengths.

> Having someone to discuss things with and be a sounding board with . . . I see this person as being there to say, "What do you think of this? Give me your opinion on this. What do you think I should do? This is what I think I've done. What do you think I should do?" And just having a sounding board. (Protégé, Ramona Gonzales)

> You also have to be willing to give honest feedback to a person. I don't think a mentor relationship is one where you tell people just what they want to hear . . . and they have to be willing to accept it . . . that the mentor is always going to give them the best advice they have. Whether it's what they really want to hear or not. . . . But, if you don't have the kind of relationship between you and the mentee that will allow you to do those things, then I don't know that you can really help them. (Mentor, Clara Barnes)

Good mentors also evaluate protégés and encourage ongoing self-evaluation. Feedback on performance and growth is done directly and in person to the protégé herself, not to other people. The mentor may say privately to the protégé that wasn't a good plan, or that didn't work well, but the mentor would never say that in public or to anyone else. The mentor is candid, open, and honest about the protégé's shortcomings, while protecting the public image of the protégé. The underlying quality is the mentors' care and commitment to promoting the person they are mentoring, and they know that evaluation, particularly self-evaluation, is a key component to growth.

In other words, good mentors will not shy away from letting protégés know when they make a mistake, and they will encourage mistakes, for there can be no growth without risk taking and mistakes. However, the protégé does not want to feel that they are merely being critiqued or observed by the mentor. As protégé Susan Rembert explains, what she values in her mentor is that he will attend her functions, and following them he will discuss with her what happened and help formulate the next plan. "It wasn't that he was watching my performance. He didn't come in and say, "'Oh you did a good job at that."' Rather than an observer, he is more of a colleague who wants her to succeed, and uses his experience to help set the conditions for her success.

Protégés appreciate it when mentors give feedback on their performance on specific tasks. They see their role as not only that of learner, but also questioner; they have a responsibility to get information from the mentor on their growth and development in the particular position. The mentor's professional judgment is highly valued by the protégé, for she may not have many other sources that she can call upon for trusted evaluation. The mentor thus becomes a yardstick for the protégé to get feedback on how she is doing and the different plans that she has and to encourage self-evaluation and self-improvement.

> I think a lot of people in our profession are really good self-evaluators, and so I think that giving people challenges that they might take on and then helping them evaluate how well it went and what they might do differently next time. And encouragement is needed too for a person's not going to do everything that's correct everyday. There's just no way a person can do that. No one is perfect. So sometimes making sure that she doesn't get discouraged in the process is important. (Mentor, Marcia Francis)

A telling example of the feedback function of a mentor is the candid comments of mentor Othene Kirkland to her protégé Doreen Ballard, an African-American woman. Kirkland recognized Ballard's leadership potential, but warned her that her sensitivity to criticism could be a barrier to her success, and that she would have to work on this skill: "She said that I would make a good principal," but then she said, "I don't know about your sensitivity, because you're so sensitive" (Protégé, Doreen Ballard). Criticism or advice about one's personal qualities from a mentor is more likely to be accepted when the trust and connections are strong. The two women in the example above belong to the same church, are the same race, and attend the same sorority organization. Their relationship has also spanned some sixteen years, with a great deal of trust shared.

Opening doors and creating critical opportunities.   Opening doors or creating opportunities for leadership and visibility is another important function of good mentors. Today as in the past, opening doors continues to be important. If an aspirant does not have a mentor, it is difficult to get the necessary exposure, backing, and opportunities to work on critical projects.

> Mentoring is critical in terms of being allowed the opportunity to work on the projects and that can be cut off if you're not mentored. The opportunities just don't open up for you. (Protégé, Meredith Koval)

> I'm really looking at trying to create situations for them, where they will have the opportunity to be a leader; organize people, tasks to be done. And so, for example, one of the women at [the middle school] that I mentored in central administration, I made sure she had experience as department chair. I made sure she was on the school improvement team and had experience there. And now is the chair. (Mentor, Sharon Perta)

Examples of opening doors are when the mentor nominates the protégé for awards, or gives them opportunities to serve on high-level committees and projects that will bring visibility and credit to the protégé. At times mentors insisted that protégés do something that the protégé felt she was neither ready for nor capable of doing. Protégés recalled feeling anger and even frustration with the mentor at these times, but all claimed that the experience "by fire" was worth it. Mentor, Pam Egan described an incident this way:

> When [Brenda] first came on board, I said, "One of the first things you have to do is get out there and meet those principals." . . . I remember her coming in one day and just crying in my office and saying this one particular principal, she must have left five or six different messages, refused to return her call. I said, "You need to get in the car and go out there and just show up at his school." She was horrified that I would make her do that. (Mentor, Pam Egan)

Unprompted, protégé Brenda Monroe also remembered this incident where she was encouraged to take on a challenge that she didn't want to accept initially:

[Pam] made me get in the county vehicle and drive out there to this principal's school and confront him. I said, "You have got to be kidding!" But she wasn't. She didn't do it in a mean way or anything. She said, "You need to do this, you will appreciate it later, you will grow from this." . . . I still haven't to this day told [Pam] I appreciate it, but I do. And she knows that I do. (Protégé, Brenda Monroe)

Vicky Fletcher characterized a similar incident of being pushed beyond her comfort level to engage in public speaking that resulted in national recognition as a very significant experience in her development as an administrator. It becomes clear that whatever opportunity the protégé takes advantage of or task the protégé undertakes, she does so supported by her mentor's confidence in her. While the assignments are important as part of the learning process, they are also valuable in helping to cement the relationship. As one protégé puts it, "[The mentor] has faith and trust and they are going out on a limb. So I need to go out on that limb as well. . . . you want that person to know that they invested well" (Protégé Beverly Thompson).

Some mentors open doors in a very direct and forceful way, and they are highly visible in a school or school district. Other mentors take a more indirect, caregiving role, yet their function in opening doors may still be considerable. They may be behind-the-scenes mentors that some women talked about, and to whom they attribute much of their success, for example, Diane Lynch, Emilia Head, Maria Valdez, Ramona Gonzales. What matters is the purposeful acts and intentions of the mentor to create and sustain meaningful leadership opportunities for their protégés.

Advocacy for change.   Specifically for women, good mentors have a change agenda, and an activist view of administration. They empathize with women, white and of color, and others excluded from opportunity. They believe strongly in women's leadership capabilities and encourage them to aspire higher than they might have otherwise. As mentor Eve Farley puts it:

The key needs to be [has the protégé] thought about what she would want to do in the future. . . . As the conversation evolves, particularly what I find with women is it's always something lower and I'd say, "Whoa, I mean I know you are saying you want to be assistant principal, but you could be principal. Now, of course, you need to be assistant principal in the system first, but see [the principalship] is where you're headed." (Mentor, Eve Farley)

I can remember my thinking, "Why would you want me to do that?" [Women] don't see themselves in that [leadership] role. So until you ask them to go there, they won't, because they won't seek it out themselves. (Protégé, Maria Valdez)

Good mentors deliberately mentor women into leadership positions, and are passionately committed to equity and social justice. They recognize that conscious intervention is needed to ensure that equality of opportunity and outcomes is available for all. For instance, the white woman mentor described below by her Hispanic woman protégé, believes passionately in increasing the representation of women, particularly women of color, in educational leadership positions. Her agenda has became well-known throughout the district, and her positive stance has helped inspire confidence amongst women considering educational leadership positions.

Barbara is just awesome. She deliberately mentors women. She's made it a point to do this, and I think she gives me a lot of confidence working within the school district structure to know protocol and what's right and wrong and so forth. She is a very strong mentor. Very sensitive woman. (Protégé, Ramona Gonzales)

For women of color, a mentor also needs to share certain cultural understandings about oppression, and be able to support the protégé through instances of racism and challenges to their leadership. It may help for women of color to have a mentor who shares their history of oppression and courage, and possibly religion as well, so that the connections are deep, and the trust indisputable. African-American protégé Carol Pierce talks of a special bond between her mentor and herself that she believes grew out of shared experiences of different kinds of discrimination.

[Mary Ann] is Jewish though, and you know it's funny. . . . The two big pushes I have had in administration, both of the principals have been Jewish, . . . when you look at discrimi-

nation, or oppression and minorities, you know, so quickly
when we say minority, we think of the Black in this country.
But, everybody doesn't see it that way, because Jews were
oppressed and they were the minority. I mean six million
Jews were killed, not six million Blacks in Germany. . . . I
say it's just ironic that the two principals that really helped
me were Jewish. (Protégé, Carol Pierce)

When a mentor is able to connect with the protégé on a psychological level, the practical assistance and guidance that is necessary is
facilitated. Listen to this African-American principal describe her relationship with her mentor, another African-American woman who
was a principal for many years and now retired. The two women
share understandings about racism.

She [mentor] always related to Black history, slavery times
or after slavery times. This is what happened when the
Blacks were released, you know, they were free and they
were oppressed and we are still, because they are still trying
to make us feel inferior. So you read your history. And then
she said, "Hold onto your religion. It's no different." You've
got to be strong. You've got to believe in yourself. You know
that you're just as intelligent, you're just as capable and as
long as you know it, you can survive. (Protégé, Doreen
Ballard)

As women move into educational leadership, the support of others
who share similar principles or experiences can be invaluable in
helping women to be supported and believe in themselves.

Encouragement of risk taking.   Good mentors ask questions, always
pushing their protégés to think beyond the previous level, to always
question and explore new possibilities and new ideas and directions:
"Mentoring is letting people go to take a risk" (Mentor, Maria
Francis). Such caregiving mentors gradually increase expectations
and responsibility for their protégés: "It's the one plus one, where
you are, and moving on to the next step" (Protégé, Maria Valdez);
"Always expecting more from me than I thought I had to give"
(Protégé, Diane Lynch). These mentors never let their protégés
reach a *status quo* situation, but rather are always refining and
reevaluating where to go from here. Very high expectations are set.

Good mentors also have the courage to give up some of their own power and responsibility. They move protégés beyond their comfort zone, explaining and modeling and bringing in other people to assist them as necessary. Mentors have to be realistic in what they expect, and make every new experience challenging. It is not enough for the mentor to be a cheerleader alone, without providing the experiences and the guidance for the protégé to take on something more difficult than they had previously been able to do. It isn't enough to get the "pat on the back," without the challenge and the knowledge that they have grown and improved, both for themselves and for the organization. The challenges begin with relatively small things that the protégé can do; then the mentor helps build the protégé's professional repertoire and confidence in order to engage in risk taking. There are also some risks for the mentor in doing this, because the mentor must accept the potential political fallout of a possible failure on the part of the protégé.

> Stretch them, stretch them. Put them in situations that take them beyond their comfort zone. Put them in situations that won't damage them very much even if it screws them up a little bit; it won't hurt them terribly. It's important to have them move beyond the comfort zone where everything's just wonderful and sweetness and life and you sit around and talk, have a cup of coffee, and you don't get down to the serious work. Instead you have to take them in a direction that will give them confidence, and yet make them a little nervous about what they're trying to do. (Mentor, Les Johnson)

> [Mentoring] means giving up control of some things, so women leaders can try their own way of managing things and doing projects, and it's trust that they can try their own way to get there and you let them try that. (Protégé, Meredith Koval)

Buffering from criticism and providing advocacy.   Good mentors give the challenge, which can sometimes involve stress for the protégé as they take on a new responsibility, either level or project. The difference, however, between good and poor mentoring is that in quality mentoring the mentor is there as a buffer to protect, assist and guide the protégé.

I remember very clearly the superintendent . . . he was getting ready to go on . . . I think it was like two-and-a-half weeks vacation. . . . And he had his executive team together; he was giving us the days that we would be in charge; it was important because it was summer. A lot of people were going on leave and there were I guess four or five of us. I had the whole week. I had the last week before he was coming back that I was to be in charge. And I thought to myself, well, if there's a problem, I can just say, "Oh we'll wait for Dr. F to come back." And no sooner had I said that, then out of his mouth was, "And I don't want anyone to say we're going to wait for (Dr. F) to come back. We hired you. You're competent. If you make a mistake, we'll fix it when I get back." And I thought, "Oh that's a good way of looking at it." (Mentor, Constance Lee)

Good mentors are advocates for their protégés' position; they back their actions in public one hundred percent of the time, even if they disagree privately. They advocate strongly for the person—giving visibility, "painting a picture of her as a leader" (Mentor, Marcia Francis). They showcase their protégé's talents in the school or school district, allowing them to show their expertise in the public forum, with many opportunities to display their knowledge and skills in particular areas. The difference between a boss and a mentor is that the boss wants him / herself to succeed, and if the protégé assists in that then it is valued. In contrast, the mentor really wants the protégé to succeed, irrespective of the mentor's career outcomes. It helps when the protégé's success also means success for the mentor, but this is not a prerequisite. Instead, unequivocal, caring support is given: "He would back up what I did so I never waffled in terms of should I ask him first, or should I wait and see what he wants me to do" (Protégé, Meredith Koval). The words and actions of the mentor constantly conveys to others that she believes in her protégé, and that they also ought to be putting their trust in her. The protégé typically hears back from others in the community that their mentor thinks they are outstanding, or that they are being referred to her as the expert in a particular field. In this way, the mentor helps build public credibility, goodwill, and trust in the public arena for the protégé.

That's really important to anybody to know that there's someone out there that as you step out on the edge, they'll be there with a little tether. Even if you fall over and you make a really big mistake, they are going to reel you back in. They're just not going to watch you fall to the bottom of the canyon. (Protégé, Diane Lynch)

I don't like using the word protect, but buffer is maybe the best word. He would help buffer situations for me in order for me to take risks. (Protégé, Susan Rembert)

An everyday example of the "covering" that a mentor might engage in for a protégé, would be the following, described by Doreen Ballard: "If I missed a meeting she would always get a packet and send it to me. I didn't even have to ask her. I think a mentor wants you to succeed so they take every measure possible to help you succeed." Of course, the mentor can't cover to the extent that the protégé continually misses meetings that are her responsibility, or she fails to keep herself informed or learn some important lessons, but every administrator at some point is unable to do everything by themselves. The mentor is there to give that extra helping hand, to ensure that the protégé is informed, and that her reputation and credibility is enhanced at every opportunity. They must also provide the necessary teaching and give the public and private support (to be a caring "buffer" for harmful criticism or attacks) that is needed for the protégé to be successful in their work.

DISTINCTIONS BETWEEN POOR AND QUALITY MENTORING

Contrastingly, our notion of poor mentoring relationships are those where the mentor is considered competent, but is not necessarily providing the information, training and opportunity for her or his protégés. For example, a supervisor is viewed as qualified and competent, but does not necessarily facilitate opportunities and experiences that could broaden the protégé. There is an opportunity for mentoring in these relationships, but there is no active and committed response on the part of the mentor.

Even in the long lasting and helpful mentoring relationships seen in this study (some of these spanned twenty years), difficulties and problems can arise, for no mentoring relationship is free of the tensions and difficulties that typically exist in relationships. How these difficulties are handled makes the difference between good and poor mentoring. In what follows we discuss some of these difficulties that can lead to poor mentoring, from the points of view of women in mentoring relationships.

Conflicts over gender differences.   Those women in this study who have or have had male mentors value and appreciate them, but some argued that there are things that a male mentor may handle differently than a woman, and that this can create mentoring difficulties.

> I learned [things] from the superintendent, that I've copied and am using now, but he didn't really include me. It wasn't a situation where he said, for example, "Now this is the way to do the finance part. In fact he never pulled me into that procedure and I thought that would be a problem for me. . . . But he was just an older white male looking at another white person, a woman and just thinking why would she like, want [a superintendency]? . . . he told me more than once that the board was very angry with me for applying for a superintendency. (Mentor, Eve Farley)

Some women argued that a woman is more sensitive, and a woman mentor will handle things more thoughtfully than a man. Ramona Gonzales, for instance, thinks her male mentors are "harder" on her than her female mentors. She compares his style with that of her white female mentor, whom she describes as "awesome," "a friend," a person who does possess the leadership qualities of sensitivity to people and situations.

> With my [Hispanic male] mentor . . . we have a lot of differences. I think some of that may be male / female differences. . . . He doesn't understand the female portion of administration and how difficult it might be. It's always, "Oh brush yourself off and keep going." It's not that easy sometimes I think males—it doesn't matter what culture they're from— tend to feel that way. The two male [Hispanic] mentors that I have right now, both can be kind of hard on me sometimes when they're trying to make me understand. Whereas a woman would have a softer touch, listen, and lead me through a decision. (Protégé, Ramona Gonzales)

Some men and some women may have different interactional styles, and the protégé has the challenge of communicating with the mentor about the desired manner of response and interactions. For example, one male mentor only wanted to deal with facts and ideas, not emotions, and so the protégé had to always couch things in an objective, factual manner, rather than conveying the personal or emotional context of a particular issue. The protégé faced the difficulty of reframing issues in a nonemotional way, which was the language of administration that her mentor knew and understood.

> The challenge to me was to keep things on a logical, factual basis because that was his style of communication and to approach things in that way. He didn't want to hear, "They'll feel bad if they have to do that" or "They'll be upset if they find out." He wanted to hear that if they run out of paper they're not going to be able to give the final, not that if they run out of paper they're going to be upset. So the challenge to me was how to put things in logical, action terms so that we could communicate well. (Protégé, Meredith Koval)

Dr. Koval's mentor made it clear that he was not interested in serving as an emotional support, and that he expected his protégé to deal with those kinds of issues and get the support she needed at home or elsewhere. At the same time, he valued these qualities of emotional sensitivity in her as a leader. In this case, the protégé accommodated and worked with the conditions of her male mentor. She believed that if she had been unwilling to work with him in this way, it is unlikely that he would have maintained the support level that she received.

Most of the women wanted a woman mentor, and most of them were either currently in mentoring relationships with women, or had received critical mentoring from women during their careers. But matching gender alone is not enough to guarantee a good mentoring experience. Sometimes women are not supportive of other women, for example when the protégé has a different belief system than the mentor. In this study, for instance, mentor Marcia Francis had an assistant principal once who was very focused on her own career development, instead of on children's learning, which was Marcia's emphasis. Marcia found she could not be a mentor to her assistant principal because she saw her as self-serving. While pointing out how liking each other ("chemistry") and philosophical similarities are often the basis for establishing mentoring relationships, we also need to question here what is wrong with women being focused on career. Men have been doing this for years, and very successfully elevating themselves to positions of power and responsibility. If women are good at their jobs, and in the case of education that means bringing about successful learning for children and all around healthy development, why is there a double standard when it comes to benefiting from career successes?

Irreconcilable differences of opinion and leadership styles.   It is vital that protégés and mentors feel free to express different viewpoints, or even to disagree vehemently or express disappointment with each other. For instance, Ramona Gonzales, a female Hispanic Director of Special Programs, Secondary Education, felt that her male Hispanic mentor handled a situation very badly, and that he had behaved unprofessionally. To their credit, she was able to confront him on this situation, and he apologized to her.

> Basically I was raking him over the coals about it. I didn't appreciate how he went about the situation. And he apologized and said, "You're right. You're absolutely right. I apologize to you about it. I feel bad that I did that." So that was the confrontation that was most difficult for me, to tell him, "You were wrong. Totally wrong." Because I had never seen that unprofessional side of him, and he appreciated that, or so he said. (Protégé, Ramona Gonzales)

If Romana's mentor had not been open to her feedback and criticism, this conflict could possibly have resulted in a decrease in mentoring or the termination of the mentoring. In this case, however, the mentor handled the criticism from his protégé with courtesy, and an appreciation for the ways that her insights could help him improve his leadership. Thus, at times, the protégé becomes the "mentor" for the mentor.

Conflicts, arguments and tensions occur occasionally with many of the mentoring pairs, because very rarely do two leaders see exactly eye to eye on every issue. It is valuable to have differing opinions, the only real difficulty arises when one party is overly sensitive to the disagreements of the other party, or when one party tries to coerce or manipulate the other into adopting her viewpoint. When both parties hold a respectful acceptance of different points of view, such conflicts simply serve to give each party an alternative viewpoint, even though it may not alter the outcome of the decision being made.

When the mentor has a different style than the protégé and they are learning to work together, such differences need to be worked out. For instance, Assistant Principal Reneé Miles, an Hispanic woman, was being mentored by Marcia Francis, a white woman principal, and the two women had very different patterns of interaction. It took Reneé quite some time to feel comfortable with her mentor and develop the rapport that was necessary. Marcia's more distant "professional" style made it more difficult for Reneé to get to know her and to trust her, but the relationship proved to be invaluable. Admiring her mentor's leadership, Reneé is now using some of her principles, such as taking the personal element out of interactions and decision making.

> It took a while [to develop rapport] because she's so professional and not at a personal level. It took almost two years to get to a level where we felt really comfortable with each other and we'd go to lunch and be able to talk about anything. I think rapport came with success, being able to count on me, being assured that I will deal with kids and parents in an appropriate way. (Protégé, Reneé Miles)

Poor mentoring can also occur when the protégé feels compelled to be like the mentor and always agree with her / him, rather than being themselves and using their own strengths.

> I've worked with people where you have to try to figure out what they expect so they stay on your good side. I imagine a bad marriage is that way. You just keep thinking that if you try harder you can work with them and so I'll try harder to capture their key phrases or their key values so there isn't a conflict. (Protégé, Meredith Koval)

Poor mentoring also occurs when some of the tenets or principles on which the mentoring relationship have been established, such as trust, are seen to be broken or betrayed. Relationships are built and rebuilt with every encounter and endeavor, and when some of the foundation of the trust relationship is eroded, it is easy to lose faith in the other person. For instance, one day in a public setting, Dr. Domingos [mentor] criticized the words and actions of one of his protégé's Hispanic male friends. She was dismayed and offended: "I felt like he was airing dirty laundry in public and I don't think he ought

to be doing that. . . . I felt like he was breaking that trust factor"
(Protégé, Ramona Gonzales). Ramona's mentor had breeched her
trust. She believed that if he had a problem or issue with her friend,
he should have mentioned that to her privately or taken it up with
her friend himself. She felt that one of her close Hispanic friends had
been ridiculed publicly, and that instead, as a fellow Hispanic educational leader he should have had the support of Dr. Domingos. Her
view was that her mentor had acted inappropriately. In this instance, the relationship was strong, and she was able to convey her
feelings and to later reestablish that trust.

Communication difficulties.   Poor mentoring can occur if the protégé is not open to hearing any criticisms, or if the mentor is not prepared to give honest feedback when it is needed. In the example that
follows, the woman protégé appreciated the open communication
that she was able to establish with her two mentors, whereby she
was given an honest rebuke when appropriate, without taking of-
fense. If this were not possible, the mentor might begin to resent the
undermining of her efforts by the protégé, and the protégé might resent not being given the direction and guidance that she needs.

> They've [mentors] just come out and told me, "This didn't
> work." Instead of not trying to deal with the situation. He's
> told me, "I don't appreciate it when I've been telling a parent
> one thing and you tell her another." I said, "Oh, you know, I
> think it was a miscommunication. Let's get together and find
> out what we were both doing." We just weren't communicat-
> ing. And I think that's happened with her [other mentor] too,
> where she was just really open about conflict. You need that
> because if he had let it go on, or she would have let it go on,
> with still being mad about the situation then we wouldn't
> have been able to work. (Protégé, Reneé Miles)

When care is the basis of the relationship, it is much easier to deal
with issues that could turn into a conflict, such as when mentor and
protégé are communicating ideas to parents that are contradictory
or at odds. In another instance, one of Reneé's mentors, her current
principal, seemed to have gone around her and confided in the secretaries about who he was going to hire as the library clerk. Reneé
felt as if the search process was being subverted, and since it was
her responsibility, she asked him directly about the situation: "I said,

"I think the secretaries have the idea that you already know who you want to hire. Tell me about it.'" As it turned out they were able to discuss the situation, and the person the secretaries thought would be hired was not. It takes a good relationship for the protégé to feel comfortable approaching the mentor on difficult situations, but this level of honesty, communication, and trust seems to be critical.

Poor mentoring communication can also occur when the protégé is assigned or seeking mentorship that the mentor doesn't want to give. Assigning a mentor is not the same as finding a mentor who genuinely wants to mentor the protégé. Sometimes assignments, as in formal mentoring programs, are merely convenient, without being appropriate or meaningful for the people involved.

> When I became a teacher, they assigned me a mentor but that person wasn't a mentor, so I found one. I went and found one. Dale Priest mentored me. That really had a big impact on me. I still think about some of the things he said to me as a young teacher. And then the principal of that school gave me an opportunity to do some leadership things and I became assistant principal. And then Don Randall gave me my first principalship. (Mentor, Les Johnson)

When poor mentoring occurs, communication is minimal, there is a tentativeness to the relationship and the mentor does not feel free to give the necessary feedback and evaluation. In the following example, contrast the mentoring characterized by open communication, with the poor mentoring in the second case characterized by avoidance of issues and "treading lightly."

> We have had some discussion where she's [protégé] questioned what I've done. I know that's not the norm, but we have a very open trusting relationship, in contrast to my other protégé who is doing an internship with me this year, where I have to tread very lightly. (Mentor, Pat Sorensen)

In both cases the woman mentor is the same, but different relationships have been established. Clearly both parties play a role in helping establish the conditions and parameters of the relationships, and, in this case, communication would seem to be key.

In short, in some cases, interference with good mentoring occurs because of gender differences, irreconcilable differences of opinion or leadership styles, when trust is breeched, or where there are communication difficulties, for communication is at the heart of good mentoring. Situations to be aware of that are potential barriers to good mentoring include when the mentor's agenda takes precedence over that of the protégé's, or where the mentor does not recognize herself as a mentor, and conversely where the protégé does not recognize having a mentor. Additionally, poor mentoring occurs when the protégé is silenced or significantly constrained. Here the protégé is still benefiting from the mentor's guidance and advocacy, but there are problems arising in the relationship.

CONCLUSIONS

In good mentoring the mentor communicates and connects well on an emotional level, assisting the protégé with the physical, emotional, and logistical aspects of school leadership. Good mentors seek out their protégés and make them feel important, which helps develop a sense of competence. Part of the work of the mentor is to build a sense of pride in the protégé that what she is accomplishing is important and valued. Examples of the work of other women or people of color can be helpful here. People need to see themselves reflected in the leadership surrounding them, and for that leadership to be making a difference in tangible ways in the educational process. Good mentors also give access to the way that they do leadership, being able to reflect on their decision-making actions and communicate this to protégés. In addition, good mentors provide honest feedback and encourage their protégés to self-reflect and to engage in continual self-assessment. Good mentors also open doors and provide visibility in the school, school district, or at a state or national level. They have a change agenda, intent on promoting women and people of color into educational leadership. Finally, good mentors protect and buffer their protégés from harmful criticism, offering moral and emotional support as well as practical guidance. They encourage risk taking and mistakes which are opportunities to grow and learn, because they have provided a safe context in which to experiment and try out new ways of thinking and leading.

For the women in this study, mentoring that is part of caregiving leadership offers inclusion and new possibilities. Leaders who demonstrate care are likely to form connections with others and establish meaningful, long lasting relationships that strengthen the organization as a whole. Good mentors demonstrate caregiving leadership to their protégé by modeling caring behaviors in their mentoring and by providing opportunities to be caring. As a role model for caregiving, the mentor guides and nutures the protégés, using approaches that are constructive rather than punitive. The protégé learns by experience, being guided through key experiences and learning from their errors, not by being told by someone else how they did something, although that can sometimes be useful. A caring approach does not mean, however, that the protégé is coddled. The mentor has to have high expectations, and guide the protégé through the various processes, not do it for them.

A caring approach also means the mentor is a type of cheerleader, providing constant encouragement. In order to support and encourage a woman in educational leadership, a good mentor lends the verbal and other support that boosts the protégé's confidence to believe in themselves. This may be sending encouraging e-mails, notes, calling on the phone, and listening to the protégé's struggles and difficulties. Encouragement may also be in the form of the mentor's physical presence in the building, or taking the protégé out to lunch or dinners where they can talk in confidence, and the mentor can listen to any questions or concerns. For example, when Principal Elaine Bennett was having some difficulties in her school, her mentor offered a listening ear. Thus, the caregiving mentor is a model for the protégé, explaining what she is doing and why she is doing things, encouraging and providing opportunities for her to try out her own leadership. She listens to accounts of and observes the protégé's leadership, then offers honest communication, either in the form of cheerleading, or advice about improvement in certain areas. In the next chapter, we further develop what mentoring means to the participants in this study by detailing those specific mentoring behaviors and activities that characterize mentoring for educational leadership in K-12 public schools.

4

Specific School
Leadership Experiences

For women, beyond the relationship qualities of mentoring outlined in the previous chapter, precisely what specific opportunities in-school activities and opportunities did mentors provide and consider important for protégés to foster school leadership? In this chapter, we summarize the participants' points of view that mentoring should include activities designed for skill development and management training, opportunities for leadership, and gaining credibility in the school or school district or beyond. Our focus is to identify the kinds of activities that are helpful in mentoring relationships for school leadership. We also discuss conditions viewed as necessary for good mentoring to occur both for mentors and protégés. By identifying specific examples of mentoring in this way, we were led to specify stages in which mentoring relationships developed. These stages seemed useful to view mentoring relationships over time, noting the dynamic interplay between mentors and protégés. Finally, we discuss numerous questions and issues that emerged from our findings. This chapter is followed by three chapters on an issue for each of the individual states. The Washington state chapter examines conflicts that women experience as they are mentored into educational leadership positions. The Virginia chapter focuses on how mentoring for women is grounded in relationships of care. The Maryland chapter further explores what feminist mentoring means for educational leadership.

OPPORTUNITIES FOR SKILL DEVELOPMENT AND MANAGEMENT TRAINING

All new administrators need to develop expertise in tasks such as budgeting, personnel administration, legal, and student issues. Mentors can support protégés by providing management training, as well as enabling and encouraging their protégés to assume such tasks. One important task is managing school system resources. Traditionally, for many women in schools, their male superiors were responsible for budget concerns. As they have advanced in the system, they may have this responsibility within their purview. In the case of Director Maria Valdez not only did her mentor Barbara support her in learning the mechanics of budgeting, but she also provided emotional and moral support throughout the process. Moreover, her mentor provided a list of names of people she could ask for help, and made sure that she knew the people necessary to do her job well.

> Budget is a big part of the job. Five million dollars or so. So [Barbara] trained me very well, even though when she left she said, "You're not smiling anymore." And I said, "That's a lot of responsibility. I don't know if I can do this." And she just kept saying, "You can do this. And if you have any questions, these are the people you can ask, and call me." (Protégé, Maria Valdez).

Another specific managerial skill is handling personnel matters, from hiring new staff to professional development and training. In some schools districts, hiring of personnel is done at the site level, so the mentor has the responsibility to train her protégés in forming an interview team, reviewing files, writing appropriate interview questions, analyzing data from interviews, setting expectations for the team, and decision making.

> How to decide who the best person is for the building even though that may not be the best friend that we just interviewed. . . . A key role for principals is to be able to lead their

staff to choose good people to put into teaching roles. I appreciate that more because I've paid the sweat and tears for the poor hire that was done before. (Protégé, Diane Lynch)

Personnel matters can involve sensitivity and discernment, especially when handling dismissals as noted in this case of a woman principal. She had to be attentive to policies, while working through the process, the union, the appeal, and the court batttle. Her mentor advised her to only take on one teacher at a time, and he listened to her throughout the process. It was important to her that her mentor was experienced in such matters, having dismissed several teachers himself.

[My mentor] talked me through my meetings with the uniserve representative, which is the union representative for that teacher, and this particular union representative was an obvious male chauvinist, and he displayed a lot of emotional response. He'd say things to me to get an emotional response. So Les [mentor] gave me pointers on how to respond to that, which of course was not to respond. He checked with me to make sure my timelines were appropriate, because that's the first thing they do is look to see if you've missed a date or a time for a return conference or anything like that. (Protégé, Diane Lynch)

To conduct staff development is another critical experience in the personnel area. Sometimes the staff development may also be tied to evaluation, thus demonstrating for the leader the importance of the big picture, and overall planning for the school.

[I see it as important to] give her opportunities to do some staff development within the building and with teaching teachers. I had her give the reading recovery training, and so she always was looked on as someone who had knowledge of that program. (Mentor, Pat Sorensen)

In the education profession, it's important for people to be good evaluators. You need to be able to evaluate personnel. One of the things I always give my vice principal [protégé] is the evaluation of my classified staff. Sometimes I will give certificated staff. They're responsible not only for the observation and feedback, but they're also responsible for the in-service training. So as a result of what they see and observe, they need to make sure we have an appropriate staff development program for that group of people. (Mentor, Marcia Francis)

Mentors can encourage their protégés to sharpen their skills for staff development by facilitating their attendance at conferences and professional development programs that may be useful. "She always made sure that I attended a lot of staff development conferences that she knew would benefit me" (Protégé, Maria Valdez).

School administrators also need knowledge and skill in managing legal issues and implementing school policies. Some of this training the mentor may be able to provide directly, and other training may need to be from formal programs and classes, such as in a doctoral program. In any case, protégés need to be guided as to the importance of checking on all legal parameters on decisions made, and problems that might arise.

> [Protégé] is dealing with and learning about legal issues, and they have to be approached in context, so that there is a full understanding of what is going on, and the challenges facing the administrator and the school district. (Mentor, Joyce Stearns)

> How do you put together a schedule? Being aware of contracts as you schedule things, making sure that you're obeying the contract or following the guidelines of the contract, and that you're in compliance with the contract. (Mentor, Marcia Francis)

For beginning administrators in particular, student discipline issues can also take a great deal of time and energy. Specific mentoring on student discipline issues might take the form of the following:

> There's mentoring that goes on when I show how I approach certain problems like student discipline. We have a system in place where, before a student goes to the school board for disciplinary measure, we hold a show cause hearing with the assistant superintendent. Susan [protégé] has been able to see how I question parents, how I question students, how we look at what the rules and regs are from my

> perspective, not in a threatening manner but in a more open, objective forum. We're able to get at what the issues are, and if there were things that were not done. (Mentor, Jeff Stewart)

Thus, personnel, legal, and student issues (particularly discipline) are areas where protégés constantly sought and received assistance from their mentors.

Ultimately, protégés need to be placed in charge, having opportunities to manage the general school operations and demonstrate the day-to-day leadership. Women stressed the importance of learning through first-hand experience: "Jump right into it. It's just on-the-job training of day-to-day activities." (Protégé, Reneé Miles). Another aspect to management is that leaders also can't be always reacting to problems that arise, and "putting out fires" in their day-to-day operations. They need to learn the ability to plan ahead and anticipate any problems that might arise, and engage in leadership that is proactive rather than reactive.

> I provide her with day-to-day information so that she knows the operations, she knows the day-to-day administration of the school, and the problems you run into and how you deal with them. I also explain very carefully why I do things a certain way. She watches very carefully my interactions, and even though she is learning her own style, she can learn from mine and what works for me and why. . . . There's not much I need to develop in Eileen. She needs to learn the day-to-dayness of being a principal in an elementary school. She's fearful that she doesn't have enough experience. She feels like she needs more and that is what I'm providing at the building level. (Mentor, Pat Sorensen)

OPPORTUNITIES FOR LEADERSHIP

Instructional leadership.   Leadership is bringing people forward to be invested in the institution they are working in, and to take ownership for their part in an overall mission. A mentor is not a mentor if she simply gives the protégé "busy work," such as putting together manuals or file floor plans or school policies and preparation and paperwork. The mentor has to structure and provide opportunities for the protégé to learn leadership, and to learn to lead others. What is important is being a leader who can bring people together to work on improved teaching and learning.

> I make sure they're involved in staff training so that they are seen in a role where they can teach other people things. I personally think that a principal needs to be a teacher and able to teach teachers. (Mentor, Marcia Francis)

> The key thing you have to learn is dealing with other people . . . [As a mentor] you're willing to say, "I want you to work with the math teachers during this [curriculum] adoption, and I want them to change their thinking so that they're aligning with the [state] standards." So you've got at the high school the old crusty calculus teacher and trig teacher that's taught for fifteen years, and he is saying, "You're not going to tell me how to teach this!" And you've got to lead teachers, and motivate teachers into looking at it differently is the key part of educational leadership to me. It's easy to be an assistant principal and never have that responsibility. It's easy to be an assistant principal who sits in the office and handles discipline and makes master schedule and stands around at dances and games and doesn't truly share the instructional change and leadership part of the role. (Protégé, Meredith Koval)

In order to be an instructional leader and competent in staff development, good mentors encourage their protégés to be up-to-date, skilled, and innovative with their knowledge bases. As good teachers, mentors pay attention to the needs of their protégés, and where appropriate they continually recommend classes, books, and conferences. They make it a point to keep their protégés informed of the latest trends and possible future directions in education. They encourage them to become educational leaders: to be seen by others as leaders, to see themselves as leaders, and to lead in their own styles.

Earning advanced degrees.   Along with instructional leadership, good mentors also offer practical advice and encouragement for the protégé to earn the doctorate and administrative credentials and for continual professional development. Principal Doreen Ballard, an African-American woman, explains that her mentor, "recommends books, and she also recommends classes." Protégés and mentors describe how important entry or reentry into doctoral or credentialing programs is:

> Les [mentor] suggested strongly that I look at a doctoral program, and again I never wanted to really have a doctorate. I didn't know why I'd want such a thing. (Protégé, Diane Lynch)

> University degrees are only going to benefit us in the long run because the ideas that they bring back and the contacts they make are going to make it that much better for us. (Mentor, Jeff Stewart)

More than the attainment of advanced degrees, one mentor was instrumental in mentoring her protégé right through the entire educational process, from teacher's aide to teacher, which required the school district supporting and paying for her to get her teaching certificate, then later on for her administrative credentials. Maria Valdez, an Hispanic teacher's aide was, in the eyes of her white woman mentor, an extremely capable woman who had great potential as a future leader. With her mentor's encouragement, Maria, who came from a working-class family, went back to school and completed her certificate. The investment has paid off handsomely for the school district, but at the time it seemed rather expensive, given Maria's enthusiasm for learning and the additional classes that she enrolled in, once she had the opportunity.

> I wanted to finish [teacher training] in two years. I set my goal, two years, no more than that. At that time, our district had to train our own teachers in a career lab program. I just took as many classes as were available, and that very last semester I took twenty-four credits. I just wanted to be done before I did my student teaching. She [mentor] said I broke the bank that year because I took too many credits. She said she never thought to tell me I could only have a limit of so many. She says by the time it came across my desk it was too late, but I figured you really wanted to do it. So she let it go through. (Protégé, Maria Valdez)

It should also be noted that no mentor can push the protégé into doing something she does not have an interest in. For instance, Maria had had a chance as a teacher's aide to teach mini lessons in classes and a desire to become a teacher: "I loved it. So I thought okay I can do this. This is what I want to do" (Protégé, Maria Valdez). The protégé has to have her own idea of what she wants to do, and be receptive to the idea of growth and more education, then the mentor can help facilitate reaching her goal of leadership.

Participatory leadership.   Learning how to be a collaborative leader can be achieved through opportunities to chair different committees at a school, district, or state level. Protégés need experience as leaders of groups with members who have different interests and perspectives, such as a school site-based management team. Key to chairing a committee such as this is learning how to get people to work together collaboratively, for example, "involving teachers in decision-making" (Protégé, Eileen Hales), "putting together site-based leadership, site-based management in the school" (Protégé, Diane Lynch).

Women in this study argued that participatory leadership as demonstrated by chairing committees is predominantly about people skills (relating to people, how to interact with people), and that mentoring is helpful in facilitating one's success in these roles. It is seen as immensely helpful for them to see how their mentors deal with conflict, and how they motivate people. Then they can try on a variety of different approaches in order to find their own leadership style.

> So much of administration is 90 percent how you interact with other people, and graduate work doesn't prepare you for that. It prepares you academically but it never prepares you for that personal interaction with other people, and trying to please everyone or trying to make sure that we're following through on everything we're saying and we're doing. That's where I have found the mentorship role very valuable in helping me interact with other people more than how I deal with this situation that may be procedural or academic or administration wise. It's more the personal interactions that I need help with. (Protégé, Ramona Gonzales)

Negotiating skills and abilities, for instance, in dealing with external audiences, such as the media, or dealing with the union, are also critical, whether the woman is the union leader or the administrator negotiating with the union leader. One union president described how she worked with her protégé in developing leadership.

I taught her how to negotiate. The first time she was so uncomfortable she just sat in the room and watched. Then I gave her a piece of it and said, "Here take this piece and see what language you think we need to change. You can be in charge of this." "Oh, okay," she said, "I'll be in charge and you can help me with it." Eventually she became confident with it. She knew the knowledge of the piece, so that she could take it over by the time we were negotiating. (Mentor, Joyce Stearns)

Working with parents, hostile communities and outside constituents such as law enforcement agencies, and giving a variety of experiences, are also key to learning participatory leadership.

Working with parents and hostile communities, understanding how to deal with parents, how you work with that. Giving them opportunities to take care of situations that are hostile or not particularly comfortable, but coaching them through the process and acting as a coach in difficult situations [are essential experiences]. How do you deal with law enforcement agencies? What they can have and what they can't have. And those kinds of parameters. Giving them experiences in a variety of student, community, staff areas, so that they can build their repertoire. The more experiences you have gives you a better, firm foundation, so that decisions come easier and they're more reliable. They're more predictable and consistent. (Mentor, Marcia Francis)

For the superintendency in particular, school leaders also have to be able to present controversial ideas. A superintendent needs to not only be able to sell ideas with teachers at a particular school, but also to engender the support of parents and community, the media, and the school board. The mentor can play a critical role in setting the expectations, and teaching the protégé how she can best present and support her cases.

He [mentor] really helped me in how to present a very controversial idea, something that would push the system. So when I'd go in to talk to him about something I'd want to do in this building, I knew what questions he was going to ask.

And if I could answer those, I would probably get what I
wanted for the building. And if I couldn't answer and support them with appropriate data then don't bother coming
in. So his expectation was very high, and that taught me
how to meet those challenges. (Protégé, Diane Lynch)

GAINING CREDIBILITY IN THE SCHOOL
OR SCHOOL DISTRICT AND BEYOND

Crucial in the transition from inside the classroom to outside in
the school system is the role of the mentor in generating opportunities for exposure to others and networking with those in the larger
educational association. This might be especially true for assistant
principals who are often busy with responsibility for internal day-to-
day operations in the school building, and may not have many opportunities to meet with peers or others in the larger network. Many
principals described taking their assistants to conferences, inviting
them to present papers jointly, and the like. Credibility and visibility can also be enhanced in some of the following ways.

Chairing committee in larger system or association.   Beyond the
kinds of instructional leadership roles discussed earlier, public
speaking and presentations to the principals, school board, and to
the community are educative experiences for aspiring administrators, especially for those seeking the superintendency. At this level
in particular, women need to be good communicators, able to sell
ideas, argue competently, and bring people on board: "School board
presentations, presentations to the community are key experiences."
(Protégé, Diane Lynch)

> [Mentor] has arrranged for me to give presentations to the
> principal meetings and to the school board . . . so he's pro-
> viding me with visibility in that fashion. (Protégé, Susan
> Rembert)

In several cases, assistant principals spoke of their mentor's role as
assistant superintendents in instituting systemwide staff development for assistant principals. For Angela Patterson, an assistant
principal in her second year, encouraged by her mentor, linking with
the larger administrative association was now possible. She spoke of

moving beyond her own school and participating in the administrative association:

> So I feel like I'm starting to get more involved with other things that are not the responsibilities or roles of the assistant principal, going beyond that. You know, I'm trying to get more active in the county administrator's association. The first year I just really felt like I wanted to learn on the job and my roles and now I feel like I can take more of a leadership role in some other things like serving on committees in the county principals' association and doing things like that. (Protégé, Angela Patterson)

Networking.   Visibility is also connected with networking, and good mentors provide opportunities to encourage women as political people, understanding people and situations and focusing on building a network of people who will be invaluable support and resources. For women in particular, providing access to the mentors' networking and connections politically may be especially important. The mentor teaches and models the political aspects of leadership, learning the rules, playing the game, learning to navigate the politics. In networking, the mentor gives the protégé access to "their people." The protégé can use the connections of the mentor to achieve their own interests and purposes. Women may be new to this game, but they are learning to take advantage of networking, and to make it work for them. As an example, Ramona Gonzales, a female Hispanic Director of Special Programs, is given access to key people in the Hispanic community with whom her male Hispanic mentor is well connected.

> Part of my job is having excellent community relations . . . the other day I needed some thirty key people to attend a special function I was organizing, and I just called my friend [and mentor] and he knew ten of the thirty that I should have there and I didn't know them. He said, "If you like I'll call them or you can call them and tell them that you spoke to me and we would like them there." It's really helped. Certainly the meeting just went wonderful because all these people were there who wouldn't have been there if I'd called them on my own. So the networking piece has helped. (Protégé, Ramona Gonzales)

Women supporting women.   Another aspect of mentoring for women is women supporting women. Protégé Maria Valdez explains that her mentor specifically encourages such networking: "She also told me how I should be finding a network of women that could support me as I go through." An example is the conscious effort that a good mentor makes to inform the protégé of her responsibility to interact with particular individuals and to also present favorably the protégé to key people.

> [Mentor gives guidance on] where to be with certain people and who was there. Did you meet so and so? Well you go meet so and so. Introduce yourself. And she would do the same for me if we were out. She would specifically bring people over, "This is Doreen Ballard and she is one of the future." She always made it in positive terms. (Protégé, Doreen Ballard)

> She made sure that I knew who to network with . . . She really had me get involved and know a lot of the state supervisors. And I did. So I know a lot of people at the state office by first name. And I can get a hold of anyone I need to if I have a question. (Protégé, Maria Valdez)

> You have to introduce them to people. You have to say, "You need to connect with this other person." Seeking out women's support groups I think is very important. (Mentor, Gabriela Ramirez)

Mentors can also help introduce protégés to the necessary state-level educational administration associations and organizations, and encourage them to attend those meetings and get to know people: "It's important to belong to associations and organizations and attend those meetings. That's critical. And get to know people out there by their first names" (Mentor, Marcia Francis).

> [Mentor] always makes it a point of seeing me at state meetings, WASDA or all those acronyms, those places where you meet . . . always asks how I'm doing, and always has a big hug for me. Real supportive. (Protégé, Diane Lynch)

The women admitted that networks, particularly of women supporting women, are not always easy to establish, however, the desire to do so and mentoring that focuses on women mentoring women was found in this study. In contrast, S. Gupton and G. Slick (1996, 96) found that of the women leaders in their study "at least one-fifth of these highly educated women, with all their successes and experiences indicated that they saw no need to be part of a support group of women."

In the next section, we examine what it is that women protégés are looking for and seeking in their mentors. In turn we look at what mentors are looking for in protégés. We hope that these insights may facilitate further thinking about mentoring relationships, and how individual women, white and of color, may have unique and personalized needs that may be similar to or that differ from the ideas represented here from this study. In other words, given general qualities that characterize mentoring (chapter 3) and the specific activities of mentoring that a protégé needs (addressed earlier in chaper 4), how does an individual recognize and identify a mentor? What background, skills, experiences, and credentials does she need?

CONDITIONS NECESSARY (BUT NOT SUFFICIENT) FOR THE MENTORS

From the protégé's perspective, a good mentor is someone who is instrumental in the protégé's achieving her goals. Toward that end, first and foremost the mentor is someone who is knowledgeable, competent, and willing to provide the necessary information, training, and opportunities. The mentor has to be perceived as knowledgeable in all the important areas for educational leadership, and preferably experienced in the administrative role as well as the specific skills / tasks that the protégé is learning. Ideally, the mentor needs to have been through the system, and has held the position to which the protégé is aspiring. In addition, it is seen as a benefit if the mentor is not new to the system at the same time as the protégé is new, so that the mentor has institutional knowledge and memory that may be of assistance to the protégé: "I think it's critical that they [mentors] have been through what you've been through, and I think you can't be new at the same time" (Protégé, Susan Rembert).

Good mentors are also seen as problem solvers, investigators, and researchers who are a source of learning new things, whether grants management, interpersonal skills, public relations. First, the old approach for educational leadership where coaches who were political masters became educational administrators is seen as no longer valid. Second, perceived by the protégé to be important is that the mentor be a role model, advisor, confidante, competent professional, with relationship qualities such as trustworthy, caring, and committed. The protégé admires the mentor, and may have a desire to emulate the actions of the mentor.

> And I saw things in them that I wanted to emulate. When I saw [my mentor] run a meeting I thought, "Now that's a good idea. I can do that and see how he got from point A to point B. Now that makes sense. I'm going to try that at my staff meetings. I can do that." Or if he took me through a questioning time about why I wanted a certain program. Then I thought, "Now when staff comes in to me and they want new math cubes or whatever it might be I can ask those kinds of questions and that would make sense." (Protégé, Diane Lynch)

Protégés seem to learn by watching their role model, for example, observing how she leads the faculty or interacts with parents, and then finding their own style that is comfortable for them. Role modeling also means being a positive force in education, a cheerleader, and an advocate for education and their school(s). Protégés described how they learned by listening and observing their mentors at work and analyzing how they approached issues and situations, and then reflecting on whether this works for them or fits with their philosophy, personality, or style: "Modeling, she does a lot of modeling for me. I can't think of all the things she does, but there is a lot of modeling" (Protégé, Maria Valdez).

> I learn so much more from Pat by watching how she leads the faculty or interacts with parents than if she told me how to do that. You can learn some things from lecture, but administration, because it's so people oriented, you learn by seeing someone else do it and then trying on some of those behaviors to see if they work for you, and finding out what's comfortable for you. (Protégé, Eileen Hales)

Finally, protégés also appreciated that their mentor is also a role model / leader who is a person with a sense of humor, who enjoys work and shows the protégé the importance and value of humor to survive in a tough situation: "We both have good senses of humor, which is probably something I should have intertwined all the way through this interview. You don't have that, you don't get too far" (Protégé, Diane Lynch). The mentor plays a critical role in preventing the protégé from being discouraged by critics or questioning their competence, role or importance.

> There are lots of days where you wonder if you're doing things right because you hear from the small percentage of people who are unhappy most of the time. A mentor can help you deal with that and screen some of that, and keep you focused on what's going well, and allow you to work on things that can make productive change. (Protégé, Meredith Koval)

Thus, protégés' expectations for their mentor are that they do much more than promoting skill development and providing opportunities. Among these additional expectations are that the mentor is knowledgeable and experienced, a role model with qualities such as trustworthiness, and a caregiver, someone who advocates for women, and possesses a sense of humor and a leveled perspective on her work.

CONDITIONS NECESSARY (BUT NOT SUFFICIENT) FOR GOOD PROTÉGÉS

Perceived to be important by the mentor, were the following conditions necessary for good protégés: one who shares similar educational philosophies; one who is willing to put in extra time and effort to take advantage of the opportunities offered by the mentor; one who is motivated and demonstrates initiative; one who is seen as being a potential leader; one who is a good teacher; one who is willing to learn and share ideas; and one who is well liked by peers and community members and one who has good interpersonal skills. Protégés necessarily need to demonstrate capability. One mentor described her search for protégés in this way:

> When we're looking at selecting people or I'm personally looking at people that I would like to mentor, I look for those kinds of personality traits, but I also look for someone who has a strong knowledge base, has been involved in a graduate

program, has taken the course work that would enable them to understand what education in the twenty-first century is all about, and is willing to continue to do those kinds of things. These would be the teachers or the principals who always when you want someone to go to a conference, they're always there. "I'll go, I'll even pay for it myself." And then they'll come back . . . they'll go with the attitude that they're going to get something out of it good. And they'll bring back that positive thing that they got from it and they'll share it with everyone. (Mentor Clara Barnes)

When mentors connect with and begin the work of mentoring protégés, they are identifying the next generation of education leaders, people they want to continue their work in schools. While mentorship is considered important, mentorship only goes so far. That is, the protégé has to be seen to have an aptitude for administration. To some extent, it appears that reproduction does occur in that mentors typically select protégés who share a similar educational philosophy. We urge mentors that they also look for people who will add something different, a unique contribution to the state of education (more on this in later chapters).

Many mentors seem to be looking for the quality of caregiving and compassion in their protégés. People who are seen as self-interested or not possessing the "right" values in terms of focusing on others' success—teachers and students—rather than their own success, are less likely to gain mentoring. Those who give of themselves to others, and who appear to have the interests of children and public education as forefront in their educational philosophy, seem to be valued by mentors.

I'd like Meredith to take care of her people, have a commitment to the people that they are bringing up, no matter whether those are teachers or they hired a new secretary or they hired principals. They've got a commitment to those people. They've got to look them in the eye. I want them to feel some sense of responsibility for the success of the people they bring into the organization . . . I want them to care about people. . . . And I also want them to be proud of themselves and instill that pride in others, and then raise up the next generation of leaders. (Mentor, Les Johnson)

Combined with caring, mentors say they are looking for future leaders who are avid learners, good listeners, reasonable, objective and fair, not biased, people who base their decisions on best research and best practices. This new reflective leader is seen as able to bring schools forward by making decisions that are research-based, rather than political or idiosyncratic. The ideal protégé and future leader is an avid learner, constantly taking risks, and seeking new challenges and growth opportunities.

> If we are mentoring someone, we want to be sure that that person has the qualities, characteristics, and intellectual capacity to assume leadership positions which will influence many people, students, other professionals in a way it will lift up the profession. (Mentor, Glenda Alcott)

Like protégés, mentors say they also want future leaders to have a sense of humor, that this demonstrated quality of a joy in life and an ability to not take things too seriously is a valuable asset for an administrator.

> You've got to have good self-esteem because you'll constantly be put up against the wall, always, constantly. The other part is to bring a little humor into the situation. Be serious, but you have to be able to laugh. (Mentor, Gabriela Ramirez)

> I want them [protégés] to enjoy their jobs. Meredith kind of laughs. She just enjoys her work. I think that's a kick. We've got way too many serious people in our business, and I want them to enjoy their job, just have a good time. (Mentor, Les Johnson)

STAGES OF MENTORING RELATIONSHIPS

Broadly speaking, there are two distinct stages in most of the mentoring relationships in this study. The first stage occurs when the relationship is initiated and subsequently established. For the most part, this stage coincides with the early years of a protégé's administrative career. Most protégés in this study described this as the period during which they moved from teaching into administration. Many mentors supervise protégés at this first stage. They considered it to be crucial for the mentor and protégé to be in close proximity and that time to meet is built into the schedule. For some, the work day provided opportunities for mentors and protégés to meet and confer, but, for others, meetings took place after hours and on the weekend. If the relationship survives after the protégé enters administration or after the training for a particular job is completed, the relationship often evolves into a second stage. This occurs after a period of time when the relationship is maintained, although the initial goals of the relationship have been achieved. Face-to-face meetings are more infrequent than in the first stage, and contact is often made via the telephone or e-mail system. Participants described this stage as more collegial than the first stage. Many also talked of the mentorship developing into a friendship in the second stage. This stage is characterized by mutual support and understanding. Many protégés also broadened their experiences of mentoring by choosing other mentors, without abandoning the mentor that enabled them to reach this stage.

Initiation and establishment stage.   Most often, the mentor is a superior or boss who identifies the potential of an individual under her supervision. For instance, it is common to have a principal mentor her / his assistant principal, or to have a leader select an administrative assistant with potential for professional growth. Winoa, an elementary school principal, spoke of having numerous assistant principals over her thirteen years as administrator, but the individual who was currently serving in the assistant principal position was considered an ideal protégé, eager to learn and motivated to be the best she could be. Her initiative and motivation were valued by this mentor. A teacher-student relationship is another commonality in some mentoring relationships. A school superintendent recounted how her mentors had seen potential in her early in her career when she was a student teacher, still very shy and quiet. Two decades later, as superintendent of a suburban school system, she continues to call on her mentors for advice and support in her work.

At times, a protégé initiates a relationship with an individual whom they admire or seek to emulate. For example, protégé Denise spoke of an incident that occurred over twenty years ago when she was an untenured, classroom teacher. She noticed a racial situation in her school cafeteria and decided to complain to the administration. She pressed the matter beyond her school building to the central administration. The assistant superintendent came out personally to investigate the circumstances. Thus, began a long lasting mentorship and friendship between this teacher and her assistant superintendent.

However, it should be noted that mentors might turn down requests from admirers. An assistant superintendent, Clara Barnes, recalled those individuals who had asked her to be their mentor. Usually she asks them to specify what they mean by mentoring; often she does not take them on. In her words, "everyone can't be a mentor," because not everyone is into relationship building. When asked to elaborate, this mentor spoke of the need for a high degree of nurturing in mentoring relationships, and the need to care enough about the person for them to be successful.

Some protégés and mentors believed that the best mentoring relationships are ones where both people are in the same school district, and the mentor has a supervisory role over the protégé. Participants discussed the general worth of engaging in a mentoring relationship with people inside and outside the district. There are obvious advantages for the protégé in having both kinds of experiences. Carol Pierce argued vehemently for having an insider: "I think it's crucial and it's because of the dynamics of the system. It's knowing the system that you're in. It's not knowing education. It's knowing the system that you're in and what they want" (Protégé, Carol Pierce). Bobbi Reeves made a similar statement: "The advantage of a mentor within the county is if someone knows procedures and policy and you need help with that, someone here would certainly be able to advise you better than someone on the outside." (Protégé, Bobbi Reeves) These advantages are closely connected to the kind of influence the mentor wields in the district. This depends on the particular position the mentor holds and on the reputation of the mentor in the district.

> [My mentor Sarah] made an appointment to have lunch with [person responsible for hiring] when she knew I was going to be interviewing. [Sarah] had such a wonderful reputation in this county and when she came back from lunch, she said he was ready to hire me just from her recommendation. (Protégé, Bobbi Reeves)

> For [Sara Murphy] to get the training, I had to argue with the superintendent, and the area superintendent to get her in. The area superintendent and I had a great relationship

and he trusted me and so he went to bat for me too. Had he
not, she probably wouldn't have been accepted. (Mentor,
Marsha Poole)

I really prefer to be mentored by somebody who's evaluating
me. As long as they're honest, credible, and don't have a hid-
den agenda. (Protégé, Susan Rembert)

In the case of Principal Diane Lynch, while preferring mentoring
relationships to be supervisory, she has kept her main mentor Dr. Les
Johnson, despite his transfer to a larger school district across the
state. She would have preferred that he remained in her school district, so that she could have more frequent and regular contact, and
that he would know the inner workings of the district. His departure
brought this reaction: "When Les left the district I had a real sense
of loss. My rock was gone" (Protégé, Diane Lynch). This brings up the
issue of overreliance and dependency on a particular mentor, and
points to the need for multiple mentors and wider networks of people.

In contrast to those who insist on the value of supervision, others
argue for non-supervisory mentoring. Principal Pat Sorensen holds
the belief that when formal supervisory roles are involved, the protégé
is too sensitive to criticism, whereas a non-supervisory relationship allows one to be more productive, open, direct, and honest with the protégé. Still others (Protégé Ramona Gonzales, Mentor Meredith Koval)
argued that they appreciate having a mentor outside the district, so
that new connnections are able to be formed with an administrator
from another school or schools. The outside person is thought to bring
new perspectives and different approaches, and a more objective viewpoint on any leadership or educational issues, since they are not em-
broiled in the same sociocultural and political setting.

Selection of mentor or protégé occurs with mutual admiration.
The process seems to be that the mentor or protégé admires the
other, has come to know their professional work and capabilities, admires them, and sees in the other the possibility of a mutually beneficial relationship. Potential is recognized in different ways. For
example: (a) an assistant superintendent recognizes the potential of
a community member with whom she serves on a committee; (b) the
mentor and protégé were initially peers. When the mentor was appointed as assistant principal, she brought her friend along and then
the protégé was a subordinate and supervised by the mentor; (c) a
new principal is told about a "troublemaker" in the building. She

takes a special interest in her as a leader and facilitates this process. The principal then actively trains and mentors the would-be troublemaker; (d) an assistant superintendent takes on a protégé as someone to succeed her as Human Resource Director. This mentor recognizes the potential in the hiring process, not during the supervisory process. On the other hand, here is an example of the protégé first admiring the mentor, and getting an idea that she would like to do professionally what the other does.

> She was on the interview team when I was hired, but really I got to know her when she came in and modeled some lessons. She was a resource teacher at a district level, and she'd go into different rooms and model teaching for teachers and work with kids. And when she came in and did a lesson in the classroom that I was in, she was so dynamic and so motivational. I thought, "Oh, I would love to do what she does." (Protégé, Maria Valdez)

This first stage usually lasts while the protégé is entering administration or aspiring to the next level beyond classroom teaching or the school setting. Once these goals have been achieved, many relationships move into the second stage.

Maintenance Stage.   Loyalty and connectedness accounts for the long term nature of most successful mentorships. Rather than terminate when one leaves the job, mentor and protégé often remain in touch and connected throughout their careers. Interviewees noted that while they were not always in frequent touch with their mentors, they knew they could call when help was needed. Protégés spoke of long-term relationships lasting as long as twenty-six years in one case, with mentors staying in touch even as protégés advance in their careers.

This stage is also characterized by change in the nature of the relationship. As the protégés advance up the ranks in administration or move on to other districts, mentors view them more as colleagues than protégés.

> I don't know if I would still be considered to be mentoring Dorothy [protégé] as such now. I really think she has accomplished the levels, but I think I would still be an encourager to her. I think I still give a listening ear. Like with [other

protégé] who still calls me once in a while, "Joan, I've got this problem and I just don't know what to do with it." That is a continuation of a mentoring situation, but it has graduated. It has been elevated to a peer relationship. (Mentor, Joan Lewis)

As mentoring relationships change over the years, they shift to more equalized relationships, and in some cases the former mentor may seek mentoring and advice from the former protégé. The responsibility for maintaining relationships falls on both parties. Distance can occur if the protégé fails to keep up the necessary communication, even when the mentor is no longer needed. Of course, in some cases, the utility of the relationship has been exhausted, and the protégé simply moves on to be mentored by someone else.

There have been things where we aren't in agreement, where Meredith [protégé] pushes back at me, but that's my understanding of my role. At some point in the mentoring relationship the person is going to push back and that's not a negative. They say, "Wait a minute I know this better than you do." This comes sooner for some people than others. It doesn't mean the mentoring is over and the relationship stops. It means that they've arrived at a place in their growth that takes them beyond where we were. And then they start mentoring others. I see that happen. (Mentor, Les Johnson)

[A good mentor is] somebody who will let you move on when it's time. A good mentor designs the perfect helper, the perfect sidekick, and it must be a little painful to see them move on and have to start that again. (Protégé, Meredith Koval)

Furthermore, when the mentor lets the protégé move on, she typically also encourages the protégé to engage in mentoring of others who may need their assistance and encouragement. As Maria Valdez explains, "She said, 'Now it's your turn to be a support to someone else.' And not until she said that to me did I realize how much I had learned, because I always felt I was a full learner, and everyone knew what I knew" (Protégé, Maria Valdez). Of course, the potential also occurs at this stage for tensions and frictions in mentoring relationships as the protégé becomes equal or surpasses the mentor (Gupton and Slick 1996, 93; Welch 1993). As mentioned earlier, in the present study, some relationships were terminated for what were described as philosophical reasons, although we did not find direct evidence of jealousy in these relationships. Nevertheless, we suggest that mentors examine their motives, interests, and purposes in all mentoring relationships, and for ongoing examination of the basis of the relationship. Quality mentoring is based on the needs of the protégé, which includes their potential for progressing beyond their mentor. Most of the women in mentoring relationships in this study envisaged their mentoring relationships lasting a lifetime, with many other mentors and protégés also part of the web of interconnections. Maintaining an ongoing relationship with the women who have been critical to their career success is important to them.

The idea of multiple mentors was also common to women mentors and protégés alike. While they recognized that they had close, one-on-one relationships with their primary mentors, others concurrently were mentoring them, or they were mentoring others, or at different points of their career multiple mentors have played a significant role. While the women admired and respected their mentors, they did not believe that this was the only relationship that would work for them, or provide them with the access and opportunities they needed. The women were loyal and grateful to their mentors, but they did not put them on a pedestal, or vest them with authority or responsibility for their careers. There was much more the sense that these relationships were important, but that if the mentor was no longer able or willing to engage in critical professional roles for them, that the women would cultivate and find others to take their place, even while preserving the friendship with the original mentor. Here the mentor recognizes that the protégé needs the political and moral support of others at a particular time, and moves more into the background as a supporter, and a mentor in a different way.

CONCLUSIONS

Mentoring women for school leadership necessarily involves specific mentoring for K-12 public school settings in which the education of children also occurs. Leaders in schools today need: (a) skill development and management training, (e.g., budget experience, specific managerial tasks, personnel, legal, student issues; (b) opportunities for leadership (e.g., demonstrating instructional leadership, earning advanced degrees, participatory leadership), and (c) opportunities for gaining credibility in the school or school distict and beyond.

While there is no one-right-way to mentor, we found numerous examples of quality mentoring where mentoring is a reciprocal partnership, and where mentoring is built on a foundation of caring. What is important is that mentors are knowledgeable in all the important areas for school leadership, possessing the desire for the protégé to be successful, and taking the time to develop leadership capabilities in the protégé. Good mentors are considered by their protégés to be trustworthy, liked, caring, and committed. For women, mentors' advocacy and belief in women as leaders is also critical. A sense of humor is also valued in mentors and protégés alike. Women also saw it as critical that they develop and become part of a support group of women.

Mentors and protégés describe the stages of mentoring as progressing from the first stage of initiation and establishment of the relationship (where the mentor is clearly more powerful) through the maintenance stage (where the relationship becomes more equal, characterized by autonomy and interdependence). Thus, mentoring involves some chemistry to begin with, establishing comfort with each other, and good communication in the relationship, building trust and confidence to the point where the protégé can engage in risk taking and build leadership abilities of their own. Friendship may or may not be involved, but mentoring is different than friendship, because it is intentional, with a goal of the professional development of the protégé. As we have seen, women (and some men) are helping women to succeed in the predominantly male-oriented white world of educational administration. The journey is one where the thoughtful guidance of a mentor can make the difference between merely surviving and getting by, or leading with confidence, style, and a plan for improved schools and society. The next chapter, specifically reporting Washington state data, turns to some of the challenges and difficulties women encounter. The focus is on women's conflicts with leadership norms and expectations, and how mentoring can assist women in developing new strategies and new ways of leading that enhance a woman's whole life.

5

Women's Conflicts with
Leadership—Washington

The different perspectives of women, white and of color, in leadership may help bring about new forms of leadership, and necessary knowledge, understandings, and skills needed for teaching diverse school populations (Blount 1998; Edson 1988; Grogan 1996; Henry 1996; Pence 1995; Restine 1993). Yet for many women moving into educational leadership is not without its problems. As leaders, women are at once both powerful and oppressed in their professional lives (Chase 1995). We felt it was important to show some of the conflicts that some women experience, for this draws attention to the ways that mentoring can assist women in overcoming these difficulties. Mentors need to know and understand what women's lives are like, and their hopes, dreams, and aspirations. Mentors can help women in resisting dominant forces and seeking change, so that conflicts are a site for new ways of leadership. (Gardiner, Grogan and Enomoto 1999). Or as C. Weedon (1997, 5) puts it, "women's subjectivities and experiences of everyday life become the site of the redefinition of patriarchal meanings and values and of resistance to them."

It should be noted that in referring to women in this study, this is not to imply that all the women felt the same way, or that these voices in any way represent all women. There is considerable diversity amongst women educational leaders. While men superintendents are somewhat alike in their identities, there is proportionately more diversity amongst the 7 percent of women superintendents nationwide:

> Superintendents have not only been predominantly male they have been primarily Caucasian, Protestant, married with children and Republicans. Women superintendents are, more often than men, people of color, Catholic or Jewish, never married, divorced or widowed, and Democrats. . . . It is as though selection committees say unconsciously, "Since we've gone out on a limb to hire a woman, we might as well forget the other usual attributes as well" (Schmuck 1999, ix).

Thus, we need to remember that many women in school leadership hold different views and have different experiences. For instance, personal / family considerations were a dominant consideration for the women in this sample but may not be for many women reading this book. The voices included here are purposively selected as the most cogent examples of conflicts that the women in this sample recounted, but our focus was on the intersection of gender and race, not the many other identities of women. In addition, in examining mentor and protégé relationships, people identified as either a mentor or protégé in the narrative are also simultaneously engaging in the other role with others. However, the identification in the text as mentor or protégé refers to the pair relationship that was the focus of this study. (See appendix A for a description of the mentoring pairs and chapter 2 for methodological details of the study).

TENSIONS BETWEEN PERSONAL AND PROFESSIONAL LIVES

For some women, their aspirations for leadership positions seem to be tempered by a realistic assessment of what this is going to mean for them personally, and the costs involved. They ask, "Can I do this job and still be me, and hold onto the values that I have, such as a happy and fulfilling personal / family life?" Both private and public spheres have strong demands, what S. Acker (1983, 191) refers to as "two greedy institutions." Women in this sample talked at length about their desires and responsibilities for their personal lives, and the tension with contemporary work expectations and professional norms (also see Scherr 1995, 317–318). Partners and families of some women provide tremendous support for these women leaders, enabling them to pursue high profile and demanding careers. For others, families are less than supportive. Many women say that personal considerations are on their minds, and that they face additional difficulties because they are women who take on responsibility for much of the emotional and practical needs of children and family.

> The negative aspects of administration are the hours that you have to put in and how you balance the demands of such a challenging position with your family responsibilities and your personal life. I work ten to eleven hours a day with no lunch breaks and no coffee breaks from 7:30 A.M. to 6:30 P.M. every day. I don't take work home on the weekends. That's time that I've made a commitment to myself to keep for my family. You're everywhere all the time. I deliver things by hand. I'm up and down the halls. The hours are the biggest commitment, and how would you be able to do all that if your children were small? My youngest is now in high school, and I have a very supportive husband. (Mentor, Pat Sorenson)

> Everybody's pushing me in that direction [to be principal and later superintendent], but see my kids are young and there's a bigger time commitment as a principal than there is for a vice-principal, a much bigger time commitment. (Protégé, Reneé Miles)

Note the additional concerns of these woman leaders that career success may lead to changes and stresses in personal relationships:

> I think it would be interesting sometime to take a survey of the superintendents in the state and see how many have been married more than once, and how many have had some really tough relationships as principals. I'm one of two women principals in our entire district [thirteen principals in Lincoln School District] that hasn't had at least one divorce. It [the principalship] just really eats up time, and the emotional costs too, so I won't move into the superintendency until my daughters are old enough. I'm finding that they need me more now than they did when they were two and three years old in some ways. (Protégé, Diane Lynch)

> When I reflect back I did not have the support for my education and career from home . . . it caused a real gap in my marriage. And I did get divorced and I know it was because I was obtaining more education and moving up. I was not at home. I was maybe spending money frivolously in his opinion. (Mentor, Gabriela Ramirez)

A related conflict is that when women do choose to put family considerations first, they feel as though they are then looked upon as being unable to accept the challenge, that they simply can't do the job of leadership, and that family is an excuse to avoid taking on additional professional responsibilities. Thus, Principal Diane Lynch is concerned about time and timing. She knows that the expectations in her profession are that she will apply for and get the superintendency when she completes the superintendent credential, since she has been an effective principal for many years in a number of large schools. She is in her late forties, and the time is right for her to pursue this position. However, she is more concerned with time in terms of the potential loss of time for family life. For some women, while mentoring is welcome, the pressure that this can create for them to take higher level positions can create a conflict in themselves. They want the promotion and opportunities, but are afraid of the time commitment and the potential diminishing of the quality of one's personal life.

> I'm taking a real risk in doing that [deliberately delaying taking a superintendency] because in June I'll have the superintendent's certificate and the sage advice is, "You'd better go after a superintendency because you're going to have to explain why did you sit for so many years?" And my response is, "I want to be ready to do the job correctly." I feel I need more experience at central administration. But the paramount thing—my first priority—is my family, my second is to finish my doctorate. I know too many superintendents out there that have done all the class work for the doctorate but have never completed that final piece. My family has sacrificed a lot for me to go through this program and I'm not going to put that in jeopardy to go into a superintendency. (Protégé, Diane Lynch)

Some Hispanic women also talked about the conflict they experience between traditional roles and expectations, and women's professional roles and possibilities:

Conflict sometimes comes from spouses, and conflict can arise with parents. Conflict over different expectations for their wife or daughter. You know when you're looking at certain classifications or certain ethnic groups, education may not be the priority. So again it comes down to an awareness or sensitivity of that person's situation. Having empathy [is critical for mentors]. (Mentor, Gabriela Ramirez)

Mentors need to be sensitive to and aware of the struggles that individual women may be facing. Women agreed that personal support is essential if women are to be successful in leadership, and this needs to come from mentor(s) and from those who form the circle of significant others in their personal lives.

Women also are sometimes succeeding by fitting in and placing no special demands on the organization, and this comes at a cost to women individually and collectively (also see Stalker 1994, 367). Principal Francis stressed that work and family responsibilities must be "balanced," which she further explained as somehow "kept separate." This is an example of women treated the same as men in the partriarchal structures, and making no additional demands on the system. Other women in this study talked about their struggles to "balance everything" and minimize the disruption to the leadership position and the organization, rather than making the career and position responsibilities compatible with their whole life. Weedon (1997, 2) notes that women's inclusion in education and public leadership roles has "been on terms designed to meet the needs of individual men, unfettered by ties of motherhood, childcare and domestic labor. Women seeking inclusion have had to negotiate the conflicting demands made upon them by their dual role as best they could on an individual basis." Mentors who are sensitive to the multiplicity of women's lives, and this conflict between personal and professional lives can do much to help reframe organizational and individual expectations and support systems to be more flexible and compatible for women. Principal Sorenson's viewpoint that the principalship would be impossible to do "if your children are small" (her children are grown), contrasts with Principal Ballard's view that it is her "happy, busy small children" who give her the emotional energy to be a competent administrator. If we are to encourage the full range of diversity in leadership, women of all orientations, personal philosophies and lifestyles (those never married, widowed, divorced, with or without small children, single parents, gay parents, and so on) women need to feel that their differences and unique perspectives and situations are not only acceptable, but sought after and valued in educational leadership.

REDEFINING TOUGHNESS AS REFLECTIVE, ETHICAL, LEARNING-CENTERED LEADERSHIP

Some women in this sample see themselves as marginal to traditional educational administration. Since gendered identities and what is culturally appropriate are "socially produced and historically changing" (Weedon 1997, 4), women's perspective on gendered leadership demands attention. Women leaders say they often feel as though they "don't quite fit" the accepted pattern, and are constantly attempting to either fit into the mold, or change the system. The literature also includes some evidence of women feeling uncomfortable or not fitting in administrative roles. One study of why women leave the superintendency uses the metaphor of "dancing in red shoes" to explain the tension women experience being in high visibility, unsupported and "culturally inappropriate" positions, and the relief they feel to be able to take off the red shoes (Beekley 1999, 163). The metaphor is drawn from a story in Clarissa Pinkola Estés' book *Women who run with the wolves*, which includes the folk wisdom for women: "Look at your shoes and be thankful they are plain . . . for one has to live very carefully if one's shoes are too red." Red shoes have the power to make one dance faster and faster until one is no longer in control of one's life. The demands of leadership (likened to wearing the too-red shoes) includes the high visibility, lack of public support and credibility, and androcentric expectations for leaders.

As an example, some women in this sample argued that leaders are supposed to be tough and rational according to public expectations, and that women can appear more emotional than men, so they need some mentoring or coaching in how to present a logical and persuasive argument. They believe that women are not more emotional than men, but it is an appearance or perception. In this view, when men are emotional they tend to pout or get angry, whereas women tend to get hurt in a different way. Women can be taught, they argue, to fight with words, and get what they need by reason rather than emotion:

> The union representative was an obvious male chauvinist
> and he'd say things to me to get an emotional response, so
> [my mentor] taught me, gave me pointers on how to not re-
> spond instead of responding. (Protégé, Diane Lynch)

> Half our elementary principals are men and half are women
> and in watching them and working with them I have seen
> the women appear to be more upset easier than men. So the
> women need some coaching. I do some coaching quite a bit
> about how to not let that show, and to be able to fight logi-
> cally with words without letting the arrows come into your
> circle [refers to diagram to illustrate leadership that her
> mentor used to draw]. I was well taught. You have to learn to
> cope with it without losing your sensitivity or your caring.
> (Protégé, Meredith Koval)

While perceptions are changing, it seems that the idea that men are
more rational, and women more emotional persists. One woman said
that her leadership was described by a detractor as "leadership by
hysteria." Criticism such as this, even when a false accusation, can
erode a woman's self-confidence and her ability to lead.

Gender stereotypes about "women not being as tough as men," or
"women not being as able to understand fiscal matters or manage
money," have a negative effect. Women may challenge these stereotypes themselves, but nevertheless they feel that these public views
may serve to heighten a woman's concerns about taking on a high-
level leadership role. The woman leader who is reflective and self-
critical and holding herself to a very high standard, may question
whether she can really accomplish all the aspects of the position that
are expected of her.

> I think we [women] question ourselves more, have a ten-
> dency to be more reflective. Women in positions like this are
> usually pretty self-critical of themselves and have extremely
> high expectations. I know ahead of time that I will be ques-
> tioned about is a female tough enough? Does she know
> enough about money? All those silly gender questions are al-
> ways going to be out there for female administrators proba-
> bly until we are the majority at some point. I need to feel
> inside that I can do the job and do the job correctly, and this
> is too important. (Protégé, Diane Lynch)

Leadership in traditional terms has been defined as politics or management of such matters as facilities, finance, personnel, legal issues. Women in this sample feel strongly about the importance of ethical, reflective leadership that focuses on curriculum and instruction. As a result they sometimes will not take on higher level administrative positions, because of the belief that they will be unable to shape the position to meet their needs. Instead, too often, some women argue, the superintendency position is constructed and accepted in the public's perception as requiring an emphasis on politics, budget, building maintenance, and grievances. Thus, for example, a female assistant superintendent, who is being mentored for the superintendency, expresses some reluctance to enter the superintendency in particular, preferring other leadership roles. She argues:

> I'm more interested in the instructional side of business, and the superintendents spend most of their time with politics and the budget and maintenance and grievances. Maybe if I were younger I'd go for it. I figure I'm ten years behind men in administration. I was thirty-nine years old when I became an assistant principal and my mentor became one when he was twenty-nine years old. (Protégé, Meredith Koval)

Other women leaders complained that they do not like "playing games" or "spending time with politics." They believed their own work as an educator and leader should be enough. The important thing, in their view, is moral integrity, a strong work ethic, the capacity to lead, intellectual strength, and a commitment to children and education. However, this finding points out that mentors need to impress on women that politics is a part of leadership, but that does not mean one's integrity has to be compromised. Mentors of women also have a critical role as a sounding board in defusing some of these anxieties and encouraging women to redefine their leadership in ways that make sense to them.

Problems with Same Gender and Cross-gender Mentoring of Women

Recent literature addresses the problem of women not always supporting other women in leadership (Beekley 1999, 162; Gupton and Slick 1994; Klein and Ortman 1994; Woo 1985). One study found that some women superintendents deliberately distance themselves from other women. C. Bell (1995, 308, as paraphrased in Tallerico 1999, 142) explains that in male-dominated professions "pressure to disaffiliate from other women arises from women's need to prove themselves different from a negative stereotype of others like them." In the present study, since we only studied long-term established mentoring relationships, primarily of women being mentored by women, we found little evidence of women distancing themselves from other women. But we include this point here, because there was some evidence of women fitting in to the system and expecting other women to do the same. We also want to highlight the importance of women embracing women, rising above the stereotypes, and recreating the public's perception of the new woman leader in all her diversity.

A problem with women mentoring women in the literature is the relative weakness of the woman mentor's professional position. Compared to their white male colleagues, who dominate the power positions, women in administrative positions typically possess less security and networking potential (also see Aisenberg and Harrington 1988, 49, for a similar commentary on university settings). Women who are mentors may themselves be struggling for survival in a context where it is simply more difficult for them than for white males to achieve respect, position, and other support. The world of education is competitive, and women start the game with fewer role models, less visible and actual support for their ideas, and possibly for some, less confidence in their own abilities—having been socialized since birth that power and privilege belongs largely to whites, and in particular white males.

Male mentors of women are seen as disadvantaged in other ways, however, because they don't have the female perspective: "They don't see it from a female perspective and that has made it very difficult for me because they may brush it off when it may not be something that's so easily put away" (Protégé, Ramona Gonzales). For example, in situations where some women may be wanting a mentoring relationship of care, some male mentors may instead admonish them to be tougher or take a tougher stance on an issue, advice that may not always be considered helpful: "They handle situations a lot differently sometimes than females do" (Protégé, Ramona Gonzales).

Another one of the problems with men mentoring women into positions, particularly for women of color, is that if the mentor is a white male and he zealously recruits and supports the woman candidate into a position, he also needs to be cognizant of the fact that it takes more than one supporter for a woman administrator to be successful. The community in which the woman administrator finds herself also needs to be ready to acknowledge the contributions and ideas of a woman leader who may be operating from a different paradigm of leadership than in the past. Thus, for example, one superintendent recounted that:

> Les Johnson in Parrish School District brought over an African-American woman from the King School District to be Curriculum Director in Parrish city which is a mainly white community in South East Washington. He was clearly in a sponsorship mode and went out on a limb to get her into that position. But he brought her to an environment that was not personally rewarding for her and it hasn't worked out. (Mentor, Jeff Stewart)

The superintendent himself explains the mentoring implications of such negative experiences, and the need for systemic change.

> You have to spend time on reassuring minorities that the attitude or the beliefs of a few people cannot be allowed to break your spirit or your confidence in yourself and your belief in your training and in your own values and your experience. Sometimes people are outright cruel. Sometimes they're just stupid, and you've got to move through that and be reassured that you're doing it right. Don't worry about it. Those people don't get it. Racism is still an issue. From my perspective, my Hispanic background, and from seeing the reaction of the blue-collar community to a Black woman curriculum director, it's clear that it's still an issue. (Mentor, Les Johnson)

With all these pressures, women leaders in this sample say that they react by working harder to compensate for these difficulties, and to prove their abilities in the face of public scepticism and lack of support. Women are concerned that they feel they have to work harder than men to gain the respect and opportunities that men seem to garner so easily: "We still have to prove ourselves beyond what a male colleague has to do. There are a limited number of opportunities for women, a feeling of being kept in the lower level positions" (Protégé, Eileen Hales). Furthermore, women of color often feel that their benchmarks for success are even higher than for white women, and white males in particular: "You're always trying to prove yourself" (Protégé, Doreen Ballard); "Being a female I have to work harder" (Protégé, Ramona Gonzales). They feel they constantly have to prove themselves and work harder than anyone else simply to garner a modicum of support and respect. This finding emphasizes the need for purposeful mentoring to validate women's leadership in public settings, to encourage women to work less for more return, and to help overcome women's concerns that their own values and styles might not be validated in leadership.

FEW WOMEN LEADERS AND MENTORS

Finding mentors, male or female, at a level above that of the aspiring woman administrator is an additional problem, for there are still relatively few women in high-level leadership positions. For the state of Washington, men still outnumber women in gaining the most prestigious positions in public education: "This year there were forty-nine superintendent vacancies. Of the forty-nine new superintendents, seven were women, only one was an out-of-state candidate and four are serving as interim superintendents. (WASA Hotline, September 1997).

While the majority of the women in the Washington sample have women mentors, they nevertheless argued that it is not always possible to find a woman mentor with experience in the role to which they are aspiring.

> Even now as I look around there are not very many women that are superintendents. Ellen Waters is a great example of somebody. But a male has many more of those models and mentors along the way than females do, and although my main mentor is male, I look to Ellen Waters as somebody that is still a good model for me to look at. If I look around the state there are very few women . . . But there aren't many female mentors for females, and so those that we have are really important to us. (Protégé, Diane Lynch)

> If you only had females to look at, there aren't enough to look at. So you have to be able to cross-gender. (Protégé, Susan Rembert)

Many women currently have, or have had in the past, male mentors. Older male mentors may have a great deal to offer women protégés, such as their access to their power base, lengthy experience, and wisdom. In this study, women recounted how powerful men aided them in accessing the system. Similarly, C. Brunner (1999, 76) found that conditions necessary for a woman's selection as a superintendent included positioning in a district where a "prominent, respected male insider will support the woman's candidacy as superintendent." But women may prefer a woman mentor and this may be hard to find. Even if women protégés find women mentors, their mentors may suffer the typical fate of minorities and be pulled in many different directions, with multiple responsibilities as the "minority" participant in leadership, and many aspiring women at the lower levels all looking to those few women to provide mentoring. Nevertheless, the system will only change if the more established women make it a purposive agenda and way of leading to mentor aspiring women leaders. Women supporting women is a foundation for women to bring about systemic change.

An issue for women of color is that they have even fewer people to select as their mentors from the ranks of administrators of color. Minority women would like to have mentors of color, but they can't always find them:

> One need for women of color is just having role models and finding other women who are trying to accomplish what they are, and also seeing that their needs are met, their basic needs are met. Finding other peers or other women that they can connect with. And don't lose hope. Too often we've been burned and told that you should not be going for that. (Mentor, Gabriela Ramirez)

Some women of color have found male mentors of color, which they appreciate from the standpoint of having people who understand racism and cultural politics, but they also want women of color mentors, and feel that too few are available. More equal relationships do seem to be possible, with many women directors and principals able to find other women of color in their ranks that they can relate to and with whom to share things. As an example:

> There's a really good friend that I have that I tremendously respect and she's very professional as well. We communicate

a lot and I really admire her because she's an Hispanic female and that helps a lot. But it's not so much a mentor as much as sharing that this is going on, what do you think, type of thing, and helping each other out. But it's not so much as a mentor. (Protégé, Ramona Gonzales)

The equal peer type of relationship that Ramona has established with another Hispanic woman professional friend is seen by her as somehow different to mentoring. From our perspective this form of mentoring may be critical to women's success. The distinction for Ramona seems to be one of degree, that mentoring is more intensive, whereas the professional friendship is "not so much." The mentoring relationship seems to rely on the mentor having power, knowledge, wisdom, or opportunity beyond that available to the protégé, and these administrators of color at a higher level are so few, she argues, that mentor-protégé relationships of the same gender and race are not always possible.

Some women of color may also feel distanced from their white mentors, and may prefer to keep this relationship strictly professional, not personal. Ramona Gonzales, for instance, argues that women of color "personalize everything" more, therefore for good mentoring to occur it is critical that intimacy is there. And because women of color leaders may be more distanced from some of their white colleagues, and do not feel really connected, they may prefer to keep these relationships de-personalized. When women of color do not feel part of the white in-group, and do not share the high level of trust that is given when relationships are personalized, they may keep the mentoring relationships with white colleagues deliberately on a "professional only" basis.

Minorities sometimes, because they are not part of the in-group, may be feeling a little bit disenfranchised, and not have that personal / professional relationship that they want. It's kept strictly professional because it's kept that way on purpose. (Protégé, Ramona Gonzales)

For many women, the close mentoring which involves access to networking, a system or people, resources and assistance available has not yet been established: "Certainly minorities don't have a networking system that's already in place within the workplace. You just don't. It's a disadvantage because you can't discount that networking is incredibly valuable in administration" (Protégé, Ramona Gonzales); "We just don't have that network" (Mentor, Gabriela Ramirez). Women in leadership are a minority, and for many women the gap between their life experiences and the public expectations for leadership, combined with the lack of public credibility and public support, makes leadership difficult, and mentoring even more imperative. As we will see in the next section, the mentoring issue for women is confounded when race is also taken into account.

"Double Jeopardy" for Women of Color

In Washington state, K-12 public schools an overall gap exists between the percentage of the minority student population and the percentage of minority teachers and administrators in the K-12 system: 14.65 percent minority students and 5.10 percent minority teachers (USA Today 1997, 7d), and less than 8 percent administrators of color (OSPI 1998). Yet, in some areas of the state enrollment of students of color is 40–60 percent of the school population. While WA is still a predominantly white state, there are significant populations of Hispanic / Latinos, Native Americans, Asian Americans and African-American student in Washington schools, and few teachers and administrators who represent students of color. Thus, the state's teaching and educational leadership ranks includes insufficient teachers / leaders of color who represent students of color, and bring critical awarenesses to all students.

Furthermore, while needed by the system, women of color feel that they face additional conflicts with regard to educational leadership, what they call "double jeopardy" on account of being both female and a person of color. These concerns will be addressed briefly in the next section. Please note that in the Washington state sample, mentors and protégés were limited to Hispanic and African-American. Thus, in referring to women of color as a general term, the findings may not apply to other groups not represented in this sample. Where relevant we have indicated the ethnicity of the participant.

Women of color argue that with so few administrators of color in Washington state, the misperception persists that some people of color get their promotions and positions because of their ethnicity, not their competence. They also point out that while many white men are incompetent, no one questions their authority or capability. The very public confidence that is needed to carry out an administrative job well is undermined by the constant questioning and challenging of every decision made and every action taken by an administrator of color. Women of color argue that minorities are in a "fishbowl" and that this kind of intense scrutiny has a demoralizing and negative effect on performance, morale, and efficacy.

> We had a couple of administrators in our district hired because they were minority and I resent that so much because I want to be hired because I'm good and can do the job, not because I'm minority. It just makes all the other minorities have to work harder to prove themselves, and a lot of attention is called to these two people because they do screw up. Yet we have three or four white males within our district that are administrators that we accept and we tolerate and it's been like this for years, but they're white males so what's the difference. You have more of a spotlight on you as a minority and as a female. (Protégé, Ramona Gonzales)

When Doreen Ballard, an African-American principal engages in leadership, she feels that people are always ready to criticize or take complaints about her to the superintendent's office. The mentor's role is critical in helping women of color to believe in themselves, and not be discouraged by the demeaning and demoralizing effects of people thinking or saying that they gained their positions because of their color, not their competence. It may also be crucial that each person of color have at least one mentor who is a woman of color, or mentors who strongly identify with and understand the disabling power of racism. For instance, Doreen Ballard, an African-American woman principal, appreciates that her mentor, Othene Kirkland, is also an African-American woman who has been a principal for many years and has faced racism herself (e.g., a staff member telling her she got her position because of her color). For Principal Ballard, her move from the eastern United States to a predominantly white city in eastern Washington state was a "shock." Her mentor who has lived with the racism that she sees as widespread in Texas, helped her to deal with the trauma.

> The lady who is mentoring me had been a principal for fifteen years; she was from Texas, and she had grown up in the era of Civil Rights. See I was from back east, so I think my

background was different. But coming to [city] and being subjected to some of the racism, discrimination, was really a shock to me. (Protégé, Doreen Ballard)

Through shared experiences and an empathy built on trust and friendship, her mentor is able to motivate and inspire her to believe in herself, despite the discouragement of others.

Being considered a "novelty" and typecast into stereotypical roles. Women of color leaders say they also face the situation that they are considered a "novelty," and must deal with the hardships and difficulties of being considered different and unusual in a patronizing way. White teachers, staff, administrators, and parents don't necessarily bother to learn about the minority administrators' language, cultural, and ethnic heritage. Women of color appreciate their male mentors of color because they are at times also victims of this patronizing white world view, and they understand what it feels like to be marginalized by the dominant white culture.

> Part of my mentorship [with my Hispanic male mentors] is helping me through that and helping me respond to that. Once I opened my mouth and they saw that I knew what I was talking about, it was semi-okay, I guess. You still have to prove yourself. But I was a novelty and that was very uncomfortable for me. I think they understood that, being Hispanic males. I think they find themselves in that particular situation as well. (Protégé, Ramona Gonzales)

Another example of institutionalized racism is that women of color say that they are frequently typecast into the role of ESL / Bilingual or multicultural specialist, and overlooked for their competencies as a specialist in other areas that are more broad-based and mainstream. They feel that just because they are people of color doesn't mean they have an interest and desire to always be the authority on diversity issues.

> I don't want to be just categorized as that. I try to be more mainstream as well, because I don't want to be locked into a box that this is all I can do. For example one of the programs that I manage is bilingual ed. I don't want to be locked into a box that that's all I can do. I can also analyze

curriculum. I can also do various things that go along with that. So it's very important that I communicate that just because I'm Hispanic and I speak Spanish doesn't mean I can be locked into bilingual ed. That happens a lot with our teachers and with our administrators. (Protégé, Ramona Gonzales)

If women of color are channeled into the so-called diversity positions, they feel that leaves them on the margins yet again, with only infrequent opportunities to make complete and systemic changes to the system. A woman of color who is assistant superintendent for instruction or curriculum, for instance, may have more opportunities to make significant changes to the school system's culture through the curricular and instructional changes that are introduced, whereas the ESL Bilingual person may only have influence over a smaller percentage of the school population.

Undermining of leadership.   At times, the challenges and obstacles to success in leadership are blatant, and at other times they are subtle. Women leaders of color recount numerous conflicts that have arisen from individual or collective racism. For instance, Doreen Ballard, an African-American elementary principal in a predominantly white city, is experiencing staff and parents going around her to a higher authority, the white female area director, in order, she believes, to undermine her efforts. In addition, complaints are taken to the Education Association. As a leader she feels her work is constantly undermined. Instead of coming to her directly to solve conflicts and problems, she sees staff and parents "going downtown," taking the issues to other leaders, actions which challenge her leadership. As a leader, she has been trying to develop relationships of trust, but she doesn't feel that others are giving her a chance.

Somehow they don't trust, have faith, I don't know what the word is. Somehow they question you more. You're always on the firing line. I've been here four years [as principal] and they're easy to judge, easy to accuse, and not so easy to communicate with. Only certain people, like some of the comments they made to [city union]. My area director said, "These are just petty, these are not major." But why don't they come to me? If they came to me we could talk about it. I feel they don't come to me because some of these statements are not true. . . . When I go to them they say I'm targeting them or they've also used the word fear, like they fear me. I said, "Why do they fear me?" (Protégé, Doreen Ballard)

When this principal questions these end-runs around her, people say that they "fear her," which is also part of the discourse of racism. Principal Ballard believes she is a good leader, yet when complaints keep going to the union and to her area director, she begins to question her own competence. Other principals have downplayed her problems, and made comments such as, "Everyone has their year, so it's your year this year" [to be on the firing line]. But she is tired of the constant challenges to her leadership and has promised herself that if it continues it will be abuse, and she is not going to let these difficulties affect her health or family: "If it was unbearable, like it would affect my health or my family, I would get out of it. I thought I would not stay in here to take the abuse. You know my ancestors were strong, but I don't know about that" (Protégé, Doreen Ballard).

Throughout all the challenges to her work, her husband and two children are her foundation and support. While it is difficult to balance family, young children, and work, this has not been a problem for her. Unexpected additional obstacles, arising from racism, have caused her to set some limits on what she is prepared to endure for her job. She confides, "Sometimes I stay awake at night and think, why is this happening to me, knowing that I'm a strong leader, and that everything I'm doing is for kids' achievement and for teachers doing their jobs, and people are just challenging me" (Protégé, Doreen Ballard). She has tried questioning her white female area director and seeking her support, and while she has this support in words and verbal commitment, she does not feel this carries over to substantive support.

> My mentor [a retired high school principal, African-American] had lots of problems because there was no support. I have a little more support, more than she, because I just went to my area director and said, "Hey, I'm an African-American female. I have different needs. I need more support. I need you visible. I need the staff to know and I need the parents to know that you support me." So she said, "Well how does this look?" And I just told her, I said, "Listen, you are born and raised in [city]. Open your eyes. This is what's happening." (Protégé, Doreen Ballard)

While Principal Ballard has been able, through her own persistence, to gain some of the support she needs from her white woman area director and the district, this burden might not have been put on her shoulders. Why did she have to go to her area director and ask for support? With experiences such as these, some women leaders of color may not be retained in their positions, or potential leaders may not aspire to leadership positions, with a subsequent loss of talented people from leadership. We also see how critical the mentor can be in understanding, sustaining belief in oneself, providing emotional and practical support, and negotiating conflicts and tensions.

White man's rule: Activist plan to help our people.   Women of color also talked about their commitment to "helping our people." Particularly in central Washington state, where many Hispanics are employed in agricultural farm laboring positions, it is disheartening for Hispanic women who are progressing in their careers to look around themselves and see their people in poverty, with few prospects for professional improvement. Ramona Gonzales came to Washington state from New Mexico and was surprised to find so few Hispanic middle class in Central Washington, and it renewed her passion and commitment to social activism.

> It was literally cultural shock for me coming here because I had never seen Hispanics so downtrodden. And it has made me a better person because I have become more passionate about helping our people, whereas in the past I thought about it, but now it's become a vocation to help our people. And they've [Hispanic male mentors] instilled that in me, both of them, because they have been here before and gone through that. (Protégé, Ramona Gonzales)

Women of color also displayed an awareness of the politics of race and consciousness about whiteness as an invisible hegemony. They spoke about the need to understand and teach about "white man's rule." For women of color, knowledge of this political situation is necessary to strategize and move up in a social world that accords more success and privileges to whites, particularly white men (also see McIntosh 1989; Jensen 1998).

> If they are a person of color they have to be aware of what I call the "white man's rule." . . . These cultures have been in

place for a very long time. But I still face those barriers today. Learning to know the rules. I'm to the point in my life now where I know the rules and so I can kind of play with them now and poke fun at them and I'm actually more verbal about it. What is a white man's rule? What is a white man's world? It's a mirror image of who or what they are, meaning, tall, thirtyish, now these are stereotypes, white, Caucasian, education, Ivy League, good salary, knowing sport statistics, knowing how to play golf, driving a nice car. But these are just a part of it. Part of it is how men connect and in these fashions. Sports is a real big metaphor, if you want to say how they do, their connectiveness, how they do their business and how they're promoted. It's been established for hundreds of years now. Well you can learn to play golf, you can learn to speak their language, sports, whatever's happening with business efforts or something like that. Then maybe they can learn to speak your language. In most cases, the school board is based on a white hierarchical type of system. Then it is important to know the rules of this white hierarchical system and it will definitely have an effect. (Mentor, Gabriela Ramirez)

For Gabriela Ramirez, an Hispanic woman mentoring an Hispanic woman, she sees part of her role as a mentor to teach her protégé about the historical and contemporary situation, as well as strategies to cope with white privilege. She believes that you can't simply change the system, you have to work from within in order to be effective.

> You don't want to be revolutionary, definitely not. Nothing turns people off quicker than anything when you become very serious, what they depict as violent behavior. As a woman of color, I've always felt we needed to go beyond the policies, work from behind. . . . I don't want to call it Uncle Tom, but you have to play along with it, just go with the flow, be flexible, be collaborative. Now this is also stemming from women, go with the flow, being flexible, being more collaborative. (Mentor, Gabriela Ramirez)

At the same time, Gabriela believes that women must be prepared to stand up for what is right and name oppression when they see it, and demand change from within. If necessary, women must go above the ordinary chain of command in order to seek justice.

I can remember one instance where another white male had done something which was wrong and it put me in an awkward position. So I brought the issue to my white male boss and he said, "Well forget it because that is just the way the guy is." Well I said, "No you don't understand. I'm here telling you calmly that I don't like it and if he does it again I'm going to go over your head." He could get away with these things, but I had to stand up in a corrupt system. (Mentor, Gabriela Ramirez)

Women of color in this sample displayed a strong sense of justice and social responsibility, and a belief that if they could only be supported in ways that they need, that they can help change the system from within.

Mentoring Women

To further explore the implications of these findings of women's conflicts with leadership, some specific to women of color and some experienced also by white women, we turn now to the mentoring process. Many women in this sample say that they are still hesitant about taking on higher level leadership roles, and this is where mentors can provide critical guidance. Women may hold themselves to a very high standard, and want to prepare themselves fully before taking on leadership roles. Their male counterparts they see as less prepared; that men simply jump into higher level positions even if they do not seem to be fully prepared. Men are willing to learn on the job, and may feel publicly supported in doing so.

Gail Shelton, one of the first women superintendents in the state of Washington, described it best when she said, "When a female goes after a position such as the superintendency, she wants to make sure she essentially has all her ducks in a row, that she has all the skills that are needed to experience before they step into that role. A male, on the other hand, will say, "Oh yeah, I can do that," and jump into it and do it without all that preparation ahead of time. (Protégé, Diane Lynch)

At times, women may experience conflict between their own high standards and expectations of themselves as a leader and their own critical assessment of their performance. The women in this study sample say they need additional and specific mentoring beyond what they are currently getting. These women say they often feel inadequate and unprepared as leaders, despite extensive background in teaching, and academic preparation. Thus, one of the critical mentoring needs of women is for extensive support and advocacy. Men already have a very strong institutional and cultural support base for their leadership roles. There may be less need for men to be looking for any kind of validation from superiors because it is embedded in the institutional norms and expectations. As one woman director explains:

> I don't think you feel so successful as maybe a male colleague would. It's almost not as accepted for a female to screw up than it would be for a male. This is true for minority / non-minority persons and it also transfers over to females as well. (Protégé, Ramona Gonzales)

Women leaders are often more highly criticized than males, and leaders of color are also under more scrutiny with less support than whites.

Women leaders in this sample say they sometimes feel as if people are watching them with a "wait-and-see if they can prove themselves" attitude. This situation puts women in a position of defensiveness; they do not feel that they can trust people. As Principal Diane Lynch explains, she wanted to be successful, and had the feeling that the other principals were in a competitive relationship with her. Therefore the mentor's role was critical in providing an avenue for testing ideas and getting feedback that she felt she was unable to get with the other principals.

> It was really hard for me to go to the other principals in the district because I felt that I was playing catch-up and that I was being watched to see, well can she really do anything with that building or is it going to stay the same? And so I needed him [mentor] to give me that feedback because my very competitive nature did not allow me to call the other principals probably as freely as I should have felt I could. But I used him, then, for that feedback piece rather than my colleagues. (Protégé, Diane Lynch)

Part of public support is the network of people to assist you in your work. Women leaders need to be aware of the importance of networking with all internal and external groups in the community (Beekley 1999, 171). But as women move up to a higher level, they can become isolated with fewer and fewer people with whom to discuss plans, ideas, and approaches. This is where mentors' encouragement and support is important in assisting women as they take on leadership challenges, and providing critical access to networks. Mentors can also benefit in their networks from the affiliation with a promising new leader. The protégé also serves a useful thinking partner to the mentor. Mentors are someone professionally that the protégés can talk to frankly, without having to feel that they have to put up a front that they always know what is going on, or what to do. Key people with access to information and resources, and the wisdom of experience, are essential if a woman leader is to feel that she is not "making it alone," which is impossible to do anyway as a leader:

> I'm sure when I have my first superintendency or assistant superintendency I"ll call [mentor] and either go visit him or give him calls, that kind of stuff, or if I want to bounce it off somebody. Because as I move up this chain of command, from school and being a classroom teacher to a principal to central office or superintendency, in a way you have fewer and fewer people to talk to. So those mentors that you have along the way become really important people. (Protégé, Marcia Francis)

> And there was always this next step. She [mentor] was saying, "You can do this." I don't think there was anyone in our family [in leadership positions.] I look back at anyone I'm related to, people don't have management positions. We're the basic blue-collar worker, and so I never thought beyond that. So having someone push me was really good. I think that a lot of my success was that she had a vision that I could be there and I achieved it. A lot of it is her credit. (Protégé, Maria Valdez)

Women in this study also argued that women need to learn to take the initiative and shape and create their own mentorship, rather than waiting for a mentor to "rescue" them, because it won't happen.

A person creates their own mentorship too. A person has to decide what are your strengths and what are the areas that you need to work on and design their own program. If you have excellent competencies in certain areas you don't want to spend your time on that. You want to just spend your time on areas that you want to develop. The mentor needs to get direction from the protégé in this regard. My mentor is so supportive, and any time I need anything I just need to say, "I need to have you do this and this." (Mentor, Marcia Francis)

I think my responsibility [as a protégé] is also to voice where I would like to go. Is it feasible? This is something I want to do. I'm learning to ask questions because I didn't do that early on. (Mentor, Gabriela Ramirez)

Furthermore, mentors have to be aware of and support their protégés to deal with and challenge sexist and racist practices and situations. When some women are faced with conflicts and challenges to their leadership, they describe how they have reacted as involving three stages: (a) disbelief, (b) personal distress, questioning oneself, and (c) cultivating an attitude of bravery, to do the job to the best of their ability (Protégé, Doreen Ballard; Mentor, Gabriela Ramirez). Initially, they are surprised that this is happening to them, because they enter educational leadership with a focus on children and a commitment to improving teaching and learning, a certain idealism and energy associated with their new roles.

Women leaders argue that in order to survive these challenges they need a number of support mechanisms, and to develop certain qualities within themselves. First, they need the support of a mentor who understands their struggles: "She [mentor] was from Texas so the things that went on in [city], some of the racist things she just dealt with it, and she was able to come in and survive. She's a survivor" (Protégé, Doreen Ballard). Second, women talked about having and needing a spiritual, and / or emotional support system, that can come from the church, one's partner and children, and close friendships. Such support is not usually found within the school or school district, with the exception of that provided by mentors, who may or may not be in the school district.

Women, particularly women of color, also talked about the obligation they have to mentor other people of color, and how important mentoring is in opening up the possibilities and opportunities, particularly for those with lowered aspirations. Women understand how limited one's opportunities can seem when one does not have white privilege or the class background to see possibilities for oneself as a leader, for example, if no one in your family has ever held a professional or leadership position. Some women argued for the need for mentor and protégé to be matched in race or gender so that they can share experiences. Shared understandings means that the mentor is better able to prepare the protégé to deal with difficulties and challenges that arise. Mentor Gabriela Ramirez explains, "It stems back from a culture or experiences, or gender experiences which are two different situations. I think it's very important that those are matched."

Finally, women advocate having multiple mentors, not just a reliance on one mentor. As Gabriela Ramirez puts it, "Different mentors can offer different things." Mentors might be women or men of color who can identify with race issues of women of color, or mentors might be white women who have the "gender piece," and possibly also some empathetic white men who may be gatekeepers in allowing access and entry to positions, and have the advantage of experience and public credibility.

CONCLUSIONS

The literature tends to support the notion that women, white and of color, who aspire to educational administration positions are somewhat more likely to advance beyond their highest goals (Edson 1995, 43). But many women do not aspire to administration, or the level of administration they are capable of, because of the conflicts involved and the perceived costs to themselves and their personal goals in life, and the additional difficulties they face.

This chapter shows a number of women struggling with conflicts between the public role of leadership and the desire to preserve their personal priorities and values. Mentors can play a critical role in showing how women can successfully be an educational leader while also enjoying a full personal life. And changes need to be made to the workplace setting to accommodate women leaders of all situations, including those with small children. As we move to the new century, it makes no sense to see women struggling to minimize disruption to the system and avoiding high-level leadership roles because inadequate support services are available.

More experienced women need to mentor and support younger women in this quest. Older women may assume that because in their generation no services were available (such as quality daycare available on-site at the workplace) and it was less likely that one could be a public leader with small children, that today that is also acceptable. Women of all situations and experiences have much to offer in public service and public leadership.

This chapter also shows that women may have perceptions of themselves as "other," different, and at odds with traditional administrators and administrative norms, yet they are trying to make a difference. For instance, some women in this study saw themselves as reflective, caring people who valued people and relationships over traditional leadership practices. They argued that this focus on learning-centered leadership and a personal ethic of care meant they were different from traditional administrators who may strive to engage in power politics and use a transactional style of leadership. For their own particular leadership style to emerge, they felt they had to constantly shore up their efforts, with their mentors' encouragement.

The feeling was also expressed that women suffer from a lack of public support and credibility necessary for effective leadership. The women describe situations in which they are scutinized, challenged, and undermined. At the same time, we see strong, pioneering women who are accepting the challenges and persevering in an adverse environment, because of their belief in their contributions and abilities, and with the necessary support of their mentors.

Finally, racist practices and attitudes are revealed that women of color face in working within a conservative predominantly male, predominantly white culture of educational administration, what one woman calls "white man rule." Mentors can help boost their protégés' confidence and develop a sense of connection and identity as a leader. Examples of the work of other women of color can be particularly salient. Thus, for an African-American leader, if her mentor is an African-American woman who is clearly making a difference in education and doing well, this can help build a necessary sense of possibility and connectedness. People need to see themselves reflected in the leadership surrounding them, and for that leadership to be making a difference in tangible ways in the educational process. We see a strong desire for social and educational change / critical consciousness, particularly amongst women of color. The women's gendered, race, cultural and class experiences came through in these interviews. Later chapters further develop some of these issues, and draw out in more detail the complexities of race and gender for women in leadership. Chapter 6 explains how mentors can provide caring mentoring relationships and assist their protégés in offering practical guidance, intellectual support, and also emotional and cultural support as they deal with issues of leadership. Mentors can greatly shape women's growth and potential in school leadership. As we have seen, it is not enough for women to be trying to "prove themselves" and "working harder" than anyone else. As their mentors can show— women also have to learn the rules and then bend them to their advantage—to be smart and have political savvy, able to change the face of educational leadership.

6

Mentoring for Women as Relationships of Care—Virginia

Of the many themes that emerged in the Virginia data, care for one another best characterized the relationships between the mentoring pairs. Participants used the term often and they used it to refer to various aspects of their relationships. This chapter analyzes care as it is presented in the data and places it in the context of leadership. Using feminist moral theorists C. Card (1995), V. Held (1993, 1995), A. Jagger (1991, 1995), N. Noddings (1984, 1992), and J. Tronto (1993), the mentoring relationships, all of which are intentional ones, have been probed for their illustrations of care as the literature defines it.

Leaders who adopt a care perspective are more likely to enter into meaningful relationships with others in the organization especially with their emphasis on creating communities (Beck 1994; Sergiovanni 1992; Starratt 1994). Such leaders demonstrate care by forming connections. In deliberately connecting with others, leaders form relationships that can strengthen the possibility of collectively achieving the organization's goals. Noddings (1984, 1992) and Tronto (1993) define care as both a sensibility and a practice. "Care as a practice involves more than simply good intentions. It requires a deep and thoughtful knowledge of the situation, and of all the actors' situations, needs, and competencies" (Tronto, 1993, 136). Noddings (1992) stresses the importance of being engrossed in the other's concerns.

127

"When I care, I really hear, see or feel what the other tries to convey" (16). Important elements in a relationship of care from the perspective of the care provider include: a focus on the other's needs as the other expresses them, an emphasis on the other's projects and not on one's own, and a level of competence that can translate into meeting the other's needs successfully. To complete the relationship, those receiving care should also recognize the outreach as care.

The extent to which care is a dimension of unequal relationships rather than equal ones is an interesting question. In our private lives, we are most familiar with expressions of care associated with relationships in which one member is dependent on the other. Examples include: parent / child, teacher / student, nurse / patient, priest / parishioner and so forth. Educational leaders can find themselves in relationships of both kinds. As supervisor or disciplinarian on the one hand, they interact formally and authoritatively with those they supervise or discipline. On the other hand, leaders are also in relationships that are more equal with peers and community members. While care can develop in both kinds of relationships, it is less likely to develop in a formal, unequal relationship unless there are personal dimensions to the relationship. To achieve this, educational leaders should get to know others on a personal level as well as on a professional level: "When administrators see themselves as connecting with others instead of controlling others, the possibilities for collaboration and creative problem-solving increase dramatically" (Grogan, 1998, 27). In reasoning this way, what becomes most important is that leaders see themselves in relationship with, rather than as aloof from, those around them.

This chapter looks first at the relational context within which care has developed. Then, using the framework discussed here in the introduction of the chapter, the relationships are explored to see whether or not they are examples of relationships of care. The third section looks at the organizational advantages of building and maintaining collegial relationships. And finally, care is discussed as a desirable principle upon which good leadership practices are based.

FORMAL AND UNEQUAL RELATIONSHIPS VERSUS INFORMAL AND EQUAL RELATIONSHIPS

Relationships can be characterized as formal or informal and as unequal or equal. The latter distinction defines the relationship as a

hierarchical one or a peer-to-peer one. The former distinction traditionally refers to the difference between public and private relationships. Claudia Card (1995) makes the point: "Different kinds of
relationships have been differently distributed among women and
men in patriarchal society: a larger share of the responsibilities of
certain personal and informal relationships to women, a larger share
of the responsibilities of formal and impersonal relationships defined
by social institutions to men" (p. 80). Work relationships then, on the
whole, tend to be formal and impersonal, while private relationships
are often more personal and informal. However, mentoring offers the
possibility for blurring this distinction. Since the study included only
examples of informal mentoring pairs, there was certainly an informal element to most of the relationships. However, all the relationships originated in a formal, professional context. In the Virginia
sample, there were no examples of peers mentoring each other at the
initiation stage of these relationships. Thus, all were hierarchical relationships. Mentors held positions ranging from assistant principal
to assistant superintendent. Originally, protégés either were teachers
or were hired as subordinates to the mentor. Although not all mentors continued to supervise their protégés, when they did supervise
them, the relationships were formal and unequal. However, paradox-
ically, for most of the pairs the supervisory aspect of the relationship
was the catalyst for growth into a deeper, personal relationship.

> I think if you're in a supervisory role, you're prone to have
> more contact with an individual and as a result of having
> that contact, I think it's easier to really get to know the per-
> son and what he/she is capable of doing. If you're not in that
> position, you just see her/him on a sporadic basis, I'm not
> sure that you can really make that true evaluation. I'm not
> sure he/she can make a true evaluation of you—whether
> he/she wants you to be part of their professional life or not.
> (Mentor, George Street)

> [Supervising the protégé] helps. . . . When I was working
> with her on a daily basis able to see not only the products of
> what she was coming up with and to tell her that she needed
> certain experiences, but also to give her assignments to
> broaden her array of skills. . . . It was much easier to be in
> the role (of mentor) when I could work right with that per-
> son. (Mentor, Pam Egan)

Therefore, supervision allows mentors to get to know their protégés well and to tailor their mentoring activities more specifically. But supervisory relationships do not always turn into relationships that are more meaningful. Looking back on a relationship she had with her supervisors, one of the participants, who is now a superintendent, said:

> I wanted to be a principal, although people that I worked with here advised me, "No you don't want to be a principal, you want to be supervisor at the central office,' because that was for women and administration was for men. And because of that even though the people I worked with, my principal loved me, thought I was a wonderful teacher, never had complaints about me, the people at the central office loved me, I was well-regarded in the school division, but no one thought I should be a principal. And even though I had a good working relationship with the man who supervised me, no one was willing to help me get a job as an assistant principal. (Mentor, Sarah Anderson)

Thus, it seems what makes the difference is whether or not supervisory relationships become mentoring relationships. There is added responsibility that both individuals accept under these circumstances. When the supervisor chooses to become the mentor, the mentor's commitment to support the professional and personal development of a protégé realigns the pair. Their relationship becomes more specifically focused on the needs of the protégé. It is still a relationship where one member is dependent on another, but there is a personal side to it that helps both mentor and protégé reach their goals. This is because of the particular interest the mentor takes in the success of the protégé and because the protégé feels gratitude for the assistance of the mentor. Although bosses can also develop warm relationships with subordinates they are not mentoring, the intensity of the mentoring experience crystallizes the advantage of a professional relationship that is deepened and broadened by personal knowledge. This personal side was characterized in a number of ways. However, none of these ways suggested that the relationship became inappropriately informal.

Most of the participants agreed that there is a difference between mentorship and friendship. Many said the distinction becomes blurred over time. Some talked of the relationship evolving over the years. "It's more of a friendship now . . . I feel like [Sarah] has elevated me to a point [almost] as an equal" (Protégé, Bobbi Reeves). Factors that have to do with a change in the relationship include: protégé achieving the position to which she aspired; one of the members moving out of the district where the relationship was initiated; and both growing older. However, despite the realization that a mentorship can become a friendship over time, there are strong beliefs that mentorships and friendships cannot be the same and should not be the same.

Certain elements of a friendship are identified as not being appropriate in a mentoring relationship. Many equate friendship with social activities.

> A friend is a person with whom you can casually go out, eat lunch, and talk about all different kinds of things, other than professional duties. A mentor is a person who really . . . shows interest and wants to help you succeed, and become more entrenched in your profession. (Protégé, Julia Dawson)

> When I use the word friendship, I truly mean there's a friendship between [Anderson] and I. . . . It's not this social thing where, you know, she's my best friend and we talk every day. It's not that. But there's certainly a bond that I believe will always be there. (Protégé Bobbi Reeves)

But even if there is a sense of social friendship, for some of the protégés, in particular, it is still a friendship with some distance. Beverly Thompson made this clear in her discussion of how the relationship has developed. She said, "I knew Dr. Burns before I was in education. So the bond was already there. When I came into education, the bond became stronger. Our friendship never dissolved. . . . but we're not so close" (Protégé Beverly Thompson). Brenda Monroe explained it like this:

> Actually,[Pam and I] were social friends. It worked for us. Not like best friends, where we were on the phone every night or shopping or whatever. We'd go out to dinner sometimes or I'd go out to her house. Her children called me Aunt. . . . I'm afraid that [Pam] will probably tell you I'm one of her best friends, but we just see friends as different. (Protégé, Brenda Monroe)

Indeed, Pam Egan did see the relationship somewhat differently. She believed that, "the friendship part helps the mentoring part and vice versa. . . . the mentoring part becomes better because you relate to that person on a friendship basis" (Mentor, Pam Egan). She saw the relationship with Brenda as especially meaningful: "It's like somebody becomes so meaningful to you . . . because you've gotten to know them—they become known to you not just professionally, but personally—that you don't want to let them go" (Mentor, Pam Egan).

Curiously, for those in mixed-race mentoring pairs, a sense of closeness accompanied a sense also of distance in the relationship. Both members of the pair described the relationship as a friendship, but, it was also most often expressed as a qualified friendship by the African-American protégés. The white mentors did not phrase their sense of the relationship in the same way. Only one mentoring pair, Eve Farley and Vicky Fletcher, both acknowledged their distance. Farley saw it as a consequence of their hierarchical relationship. "[Vicky] and I, we're sisters, I'm the bigger sister, more directive . . . wanting to help. Friendship is more equals" (Mentor, Eve Farley). Fletcher brought up the issue of race. [Eve] and I were different, she was white and older and had a different life experience than I did. And . . . we were friendly to each other, but we weren't socially friendly, you know" (Protégé, Vicky Fletcher).

Like Pam Egan, though, most of the participants acknowledged the value of the personal dimension to the mentoring relationship. Many felt that it made the mentorship more successful. George Street made a useful distinction between the two kinds of relationship.

> I think that if you're going to be a true mentor, then you've got to pretty much keep it on a professional level and not let the personal come in, although I think it has to come in to a certain extent—because you've got to know who the real person is. But I don't think you let it get to the point where you're friends to the extent that you go out together to parties and things of this sort. . . . I think you have to go to a certain extent to make sure there's some friendship feelings present, but I think you have to just sort of cut it off at that. (Mentor, George Street)

Street's reasons were rooted in his belief that it would be difficult to "discipline someone who is a dyed-in-the-wool friend" (Mentor, George Street). Marsha Poole also alluded to the supervisory nature of the relationship when she commented that, "You have to be careful. I would prefer that the [protégé] get to the position they're looking for before it develops into a friendship. It's just cleaner" (Mentor, Marsha Poole).

Thus, to talk of a personal dimension to a supervisory relationship that is also a mentorship is to highlight the extent to which both members of the relationship know and like each other. It is not to suggest that the appropriate professional dimension is lost. As some of the pairs in the Virginia sample acknowledged, over time, some of the relationships did develop into friendships, but none of those that retained the supervisory aspect did. It is important to make clear this distinction. In advocating for closer relationships in the professional working world of educational administration, one does not encourage inappropriate relationships. Leaders cannot effectively supervise employees if they become their friends. A supervisory relationship is first and foremost, a dependent and unequal one. Yet, supervisors do not have to remain distant and impersonal. All working environments improve when bosses make an effort to connect with their subordinates. However, the Virginia data further indicate that if the supervisory relationship develops into a mentorship, which involves personal connectedness, then the individuals involved receive great benefit, as does the organization.

These mentoring relationships are formal in the supervisory sense described above. (They are not formal mentoring relationships that are imposed on novices or administrative interns, for instance, for the purpose of training or teaching particular skills.) However, it is their informal nature that really allows the personal dimension to evolve. It is when mentors and / or protégés extend their professional day to engage in mentoring activities, that the members come to know each other as human beings, not just as members of the profession. In mentoring relationships, the members go above and beyond the call of duty to teach and learn specific tasks and expertise. These opportunities are often provided outside the regular day or in addition to designated responsibilities.

> [Beverly and I] have formed a pattern of an informal relationship so that she can call me at home, ask questions whenever she needs to, can leave me notes and I will call back and will set up a meeting based on whatever the issues may be. (Mentor, Patty Burns)

The three of us [Egan was mentor to both] would make a conscious commitment to go out to lunch at least once a week and catch up on everything. . . . Those lunches became very important to us because at that point each of us knew exactly what had been going on. I think I created the freedom for each of us to question the other on what was going on or to give suggestions about a way that it might work even better. . . . and so those lunches became not just reporting but also arguing and laughing and, I think, the freedom to really feel like you're part of the team. (Mentor, Pam Egan)

One time when I asked Marsha if I could go to this conference, she said, "Oh, are you going to present?" I said, "No." She said, "What do you mean no?" . . . She said, "I can help you, go ahead and do it." So . . . we started meeting at breakfast time, it was like Saturday or Sunday. . . . We'd talk about the strategy I could use, she came [into my classroom] and modeled a couple of strategies, and then, I had a presentation. (Protégé, Sara Murphy)

All the stories above illustrate the advantages to the members of a mentoring pair of meeting and talking informally. Had the mentors remained locked in to the limited opportunities to interact with their protégés that most structured work days provide, little would have been achieved. Therefore, of all the characteristics of mentoring relationships examined in this section, the most significant one is informality. Informality generates personal knowledge, which enhances the mentor's capacity to help the protégé. The fact that many of the relationships remained unequal was seen as less important in terms of how worthwhile the connections were between mentor and protégé. In addition, it was the personal dimension that was gained through the informal aspect of the relationship that contributed to the second stage of several relationships (see chapter 4 for a discussion of these stages). Once one of the members of the pair had left the district or once the protégé had reached the position to which she aspired, the relationship evolved into a more equal and less dependent one. Indeed, many protégés became fully independent of their mentors and yet, they remained close to the mentor and described her or him as a mentor still.

Mentoring as Care

Explicit references to care were made by mentors and protégés. Janet Cochran expressed it simply, "I probably care about Dr. Street as much as anybody on the earth, and I think he cares about me" (Protégé, Janet Cochran).

> I look at mentorship as working with someone, taking a genuine interest in helping that person develop professionally and personally, in that profession. You care about the person, the character, the judgment, you know, the professional savvy, as well as getting a job done. (Protégé, Brenda Monroe)

Many protégés, for instance, interpreted their mentor's actions as prompted by care.

> The relationship evolved into a mentorship. Pam became more than just boss, supervisor, evaluator. . . . I certainly experienced a real caring, you know this is someone who really wanted me to succeed—and I certainly wanted to too. (Protégé, Brenda Monroe)

> I think the friendship that developed put more emphasis on the trust and the respect that we had for one another. Sarah wasn't just a person that could give me advice, she was a friend, who was a caring person . . . who went beyond the call of duty, to help me in my career advancements. (Protégé, Bobbi Reeves)

One of the protégés equated mentoring directly with caring. She said, "[Mentoring] means that there's someone there who cares. They kind of believe in you even though you question yourself" (Protégé, Beverly Thompson). Indeed, offered as a motive for mentoring, for some, care seems to be a prerequisite. Many suggested that in the absence of care mentoring would not take place. Care is also used rather loosely to mean kindness, and caring is used, at times, to describe a leadership style. However, broadly speaking, there is evidence that both a disposition to care and a practice of care were present in the discussions. But to what extent were all the elements of caring present? Specifically: (a) Were the mentors competent to help the protégés achieve their desired goals? (*b*) Did mentors see the protégé's needs as the protégé saw them? (*c*) Did the mentor focus on the protégé's projects instead of his or her own? And finally (*d*) Did the protégés perceive the actions as care?

Were the mentors competent to help the protégés achieve their desired goals?   A simple answer to the question is yes because all the protégés achieved success. But perhaps a more relevant reason for believing that mentors were competent, is that none of the protégés would have entered the relationship had they not perceived their mentors as being competent to guide them. In other words, the women in this sample argued that there would be no mentoring if protégés saw the potential mentor as incompetent.

Competence and expertise were the most often cited reasons for both members of the pair to connect. In many instances, experience as an administrator rendered the mentor competent to prepare the protégé for that particular administrative position.

> Mary Ellen would look at my resumé, she would tell me exactly what I needed—I guess because she had been there before. I think experience always helps. She would tell me how to phrase a letter . . . that you need to mention that you have this background. (Protégé, Julia Dawson)

> When Sarah came, she was the optimum of what I thought an administrator should be. I felt like all the things I believed that you should be and do as an administrator, she came in and did them. (Protégé, Bobbi Reeves)

> Mary Ann knew how to do things and get things done, and at that time, I didn't realize what I realize now. She had a political savvy to her because she knew how to work the system. (Protégé, Carol Pierce).

No amount of goodwill would have made up for a mentor's lack of expertise in the eyes of the protégés. Mentors too, saw themselves as most helpful to their protégés, because they had learned a lot and knew that they could teach it. Many participants likened mentoring to teaching. Some saw it as training for a specific job based on a mentor's skills and experiences.

Mentorship, to me, is a relationship between two persons, one of whom has experiences and training or qualities that could be beneficial to the other person's career goals. And the mentor voluntarily shares the benefit of her experiences, training, and qualities with the person being mentored. (Mentor, Sarah Anderson)

Mentoring to me is really devoting yourself to helping that person know everything that you know about a particular field. (Mentor, Pam Egan)

You are talking to (protégés) about what their needs are and you discuss with them where to take those needs, and you model for them the pieces that they don't know themselves, and then, eventually they take it over. (Protégé, Sara Murphy)

Although protégés were drawn to their mentors because of the professional skills and aptitudes mentors demonstrated, gradually a sense of trust evolved that cemented the relationship.

Trust building is important, with mentors, so that you really believe what they are saying to you. And you usually trust what they say to you because you've watched them operate as they make a difference in the lives of children and the community. . . . I have only connections with people that walk their talk. (Protégé, Vicky Fletcher)

Part of being perceived as competent is the capacity to inspire trust, and if competence is an integral factor of caring, then these mentoring relationships are good examples of caring relationships. They appear to be founded on the teaching and learning of specific skills and expertise. Mentors were actively engaged in providing relevant opportunities for protégés either to become educational administrators or to advance up the hierarchy. However, were the mentors engrossed in their protégés' concerns?

Did mentors see the protégé's needs as the protégé saw them? Most did, but some did not. Those mentors that did were aided to some extent by choosing to mentor women with attitudes and beliefs similar to the ones they held themselves. This choice enabled mentors to filter a protégé's needs through their own experiences.

> When things got difficult for Carol to take classes and she had to back up, I'd just call her in and say, "Wait a minute," I'd say to her kiddingly, . . . "I picture you in here [the principal's office], now you need to get out there and get those courses." . . . and I'd say, "Let me tell you, these are some things that worked for me." (Mentor, Mary Ann Chase)

Similarities in race and gender facilitated this capacity also. Many mentors felt that they could better identify with their women protégé's situations, because they had faced gender issues of their own in the past. None of the five African-American protégés in the Virginia sample were matched with mentors of the same race. However, several of them spoke of deliberately choosing other African-American mentors to complement the experiences they were having with their primary white mentor. Several expressed needs that their white mentors could not satisfy (see chapter 8 for a fuller discussion of this).

> I found strength and wisdom from other individuals that have had the racial experience. Personal friends that I've grown up through school, that we shared the same education and family background. . . . [name] who was director of instruction many years before Dr. Farley. She is an African-American leader and outstanding educator in our city. She also promotes me as an individual. . . . She has helped a whole lot, to move me along, and she has the whole cultural experience that relates to what she knew about me. (Protégé, Vicky Fletcher)

On the whole though, the protégés in the study felt that they had been very well understood. Some of them expressed surprise and frustration at times, because, occasionally, the mentor seemed to disregard their needs. There are stories of mentors insisting that course work be taken, even though protégés felt that they could not manage it at that point in their lives. There are examples of mentors pushing their protégés to do something the protégé did not feel ready to do, like confront a difficult colleague or speak in public. But all those involved describe these experiences as positive ones. Most of the protégés argue that the mentor knew better than they did what would be good for them. Only one exception stands out. George Street mentored Janet Cochran into the position of assistant superintendent. And although that seemed to be the logical development of her career, for personal reasons, she soon became aware that it was the wrong move. Because the relationship had been so tight, so deep, this conflict nearly tore it apart.

> Giving up the assistant superintendency was the hardest professional decision I ever made—anyway I did it. . . . In some ways, I think I really broke Dr. Street's heart. I think he was really very disappointed. I don't think he fully understands cause he said to me . . . "Every decision you ever made careerwise in the past, has been good for you and for me and this one is not good for me." (Protégé, Janet Cochran)

Cochran goes on to explain that she did not "have this burning ambition to run the school district. I was there to support Dr. Street and as long as I could support him and support my family as well, we just had this great relationship" (Protégé, Janet Cochran). In this instance, it is clear that the protégé needs were subsumed within the needs of the mentor himself and the needs of the school district. Street, like two of the other mentors in this sample, said outright that one of his primary motives in mentoring individuals was to serve the needs of the school district. This belief provides an answer to the next question that helps to distinguish relationships of care from other relationships.

Did the mentor focus on the protégé's projects instead of his or her own?   The majority of the relationships were formed to serve the protégé's needs and wishes. Therefore, the answer to this question confirms that, according to the definition provided, these mentoring relationships are also relationships of care. Nevertheless, some of the mentors focused on both the protégé's projects as well as on their own. Joan Lewis knew that the success of her curriculum plan depended on her protégés' quality of work.

> You see, these positions were not budgeted, so that first year I was not able to put anybody in until we were able to get it into the budget. . . . It was absolutely critical that they succeed because if they didn't, the whole thrust of what we were

trying to do in the school division was not going to be validated. (Mentor, Joan Lewis)

However, none of the women who were protégés in this sample expressed a feeling of being exploited. The relationships were all described as mutually beneficial. Still, it is useful to probe more deeply
the consequences of such mutual benefit. A discussion of this aspect
in the third section of the chapter asserts the relationships leaders
build and maintain with other members of the organization are good
for the organization.

Did the protégés perceive the actions as care?   Finally, looking at the
last question, the answer is yes according to the participants. All of
the interviews with protégés revealed that they believed their mentors to have been instrumental in the protégés achieving their goals.
They also believed that their mentors were motivated primarily by a
wish to see them succeed. Because of that, these relationships were
highly valued. If good mentoring relationships are characterized as
achieving their purposes, and if protégés believe that good mentoring
relationships are largely prompted by a mentor's care for them, then
the outreach associated with mentoring is seen as care. Whether this
would be so if the mentoring relationship were not described as successful is an interesting question. To what extent is mentoring in and
of itself an expression of care? It certainly depends on how much the
mentoring is focused on the protégé and not on the mentor. This point
will be considered further in the last section of the chapter.

ORGANIZATIONAL ADVANTAGES

It is argued that leaders who make the effort to connect with
others in meaningful relationships are better able to help generate
productive organizational energy. This suggests a synergistic approach to finding common goals to work toward. In contrast, leaders
who remain distant and aloof from their colleagues and from community members are less likely to gain the support necessary to
achieve shared organizational goals. As Vicky Fletcher puts it:

> A mentor has to share some common goal, or a vision that
> you have, they have to walk the talk that seems progressive
> to you. It's an advisory type of guidance that you get and a

support that develops as a result of being involved in the same type of work or experiences that help move some type of organization or business along. (Protégé, Vicky Fletcher)

The Virginia data have provided some insight into that claim. Although none of the participants was asked to comment specifically on the organizational advantages of mentoring, many made reference to them in describing their motivation to mentor.

One organizational benefit that surfaced in the study is continuity of well-qualified personnel.

> The mentorship role was something that Pam wanted to do for me. She actually said, "I want you to know everything about human resources, the work is fascinating work." . . . because her idea of being not only a supervisor, but a mentor, was that you train someone who could do your job. The phrase she used was, if you were run over by a Mack truck on the way home, you know somebody would need to carry on. (Protégé, Brenda Monroe)

It is clear here that both the women and the school district gained from this relationship. Indeed, although it was not planned, Brenda Monroe eventually, after a stint in the principalship, held the same position that Pam Egan held when she first began to mentor her, in the same school district. Similarly, there were other protégés who later held the exact same position as their mentor had held when the relationship was initiated. Few mentors set out to have their protégé succeed them. George Street was delighted that Janet Cochran proved to be as apt in the area of finance and budget management as he was himself. He put it like this:

> I saw a person with lots of potential and I wanted to do everything for her to fulfill that potential. Plus it helped me a great deal. So I guess that ulterior motive was there. One of the things I found out about myself over the years since I've been in administration, is I'm not easily satisfied. I'd rather do it myself if I have to depend upon someone to do a task and not do it correctly. [Janet] can do a task and do it correctly and I had lots of confidence in her and as a result of having that level of comfort, she just got more and more responsibility. (Mentor, George Street)

Ultimately, almost seventeen years after their relationship had begun, Cochran became an assistant superintendent in that district. By that time, Street had moved into the superintendent's position from an assistant superintendent's position. However, as mentioned earlier, Cochran's tenure as assistant superintendent was short lived. Despite Street's pleading with her that she stay, she left the position because she was not happy in it.

Two other protégés, Vicky Fletcher and Carol Pierce, also took positions in the school district that their mentors had held at one time. In both cases, it was after the mentor had left the district. Fletcher's mentor, Eve Farley, had not trained her for this specific position, but Fletcher's close contact with Farley, gave her the confidence to apply for it.

> When this job [Director of Instruction] description came out, it was like thirty some items. I just kind of said, "Who could do that?" I just laughed it off. . . . But, having worked with Eve on so many of the areas, you know I had better training than a lot of them. I thought well, it's worth a try. . . . She shared with me what the job responsibilities would be and I had watched her so I knew what the job was going to take. (Protégé, Vicky Fletcher)

Mary Ann Chase was a little more overt in her wish that Carol Pierce and another protégé would take over as principal of the alternative school that she had created. She explained it in these terms:

> This was a program I had conceived, it was my baby, and I wanted to make sure even though, I couldn't . . . pick my successor, I wanted to do all that I could to prepare somebody who would take it and who understood it and would do nothing but improve on it instead of throwing the baby out with the bath water later. (Mentor, Mary Ann Chase)

To this end, Chase chose two protégés, one who was further along in her academic preparation for the principalship, and Carol Pierce who had only been in education three years when she was hired by Chase. As Pierce put it, "I think Mary Ann saw herself as being able to mold a leader . . . I was ripe for the picking . . . I wasn't one of those people who had been in education and had figured out this is the way to do it" (Protégé, Carol Pierce). As Chase had hoped, both women succeeded her as principal of the school, one after the other. Pierce had moved out of the school to take an assistant principal's position in another district, but as soon as the first protégé moved on, she applied for and got the position. She was pleased, "I had been here (at the school), knew the philosophy and had bought into it" (Protégé, Carol Pierce). But she also made the point that Chase's ideas would live on.

> In addition to Mary Ann making a contribution to me, she has made it to education also, through me. You know so much of what she believed in, I'm sure is engraved in me, in the way she works. (Protégé, Carol Pierce)

There were certainly instances, where the mentor's ideas or visions were transmitted very clearly and adopted by the protégé. Thus, mentors benefited from the relationship in the sense that their educational philosophies and beliefs were reproduced in the next generation of educational leaders.

> I look for people who are willing to take risks, who are anxious to try things, who believe fundamentally in the child and who I know will, bottom of the line, think of what will be best for the children regardless of the situation . . . and who are very much trying to work with others. (Mentor, Patty Burns)

However, equally as important, for many of the mentors in this study, the school district benefits directly from their mentoring efforts. In the broad context, education benefits because mentors believe that what they contribute is good for children:

> If you are interested in your own district, which I have always been, [mentoring] allows you to see good people promoted into positions where they could be more effective and it allows you to keep good people I would hope. (Mentor, Mary Ellen Remington)

> I felt a sense of gratification in that . . . we had come from nothing to really something to be proud of for a school district of that size. And lots of [my protégés] were invited to lead workshops in other schools. (Mentor, Joan Lewis)

A clear focus on organizational advantage is repeated throughout these stories. It is not at the expense of the protégé, however. There is obviously mutual satisfaction in that these organizations gained quality, trained individuals to carry on in the wake of highly respected mentors, and the protégé achieved career advancement. Relating back to the issue of care, though, one sees that in these instances, the mentor's projects appear to have been equally as important as the protégé's. The mentors were getting reliable, well-trained help to do their own work. Nevertheless, the mentor's motives cannot be seen merely as personal gain. Street describes gaining valuable assistance from the protégé as an "ulterior motive," but, put in context, he is primarily serving the organization, not himself. He said "I think [mentoring] helps the organization and that's really the whole purpose of everything that you're doing in this" (Mentor, George Street).

There is another kind of advantage for the organization, although caution must be exercised that it does not become a part of exploitation. White mentors who mentor individuals of color learn a great deal from this relationship. Like all the white mentors, Patty Burns had the advantage of coming to appreciate the different perspectives that her African-American protégé could contribute. Burns acknowledged it openly as did Eve Farley who actively sought Fletcher's help with reaching some of the African-American community when she was assistant principal of a city high school. Fletcher saw the relationship as mutually beneficial.

> I learned a lot from watching . . . Eve in her role as assistant principal. . . . Then I think she learned a lot from me . . . I could give her a different perspective. I've always taken on the role of not fearing a discussion when it came to race issues or anything. . . . And you know there were times when I was like on five, six, seven, nine to ten committees . . . there's a lot of things I've been involved in in this city. . . . So being a resource sometimes for another perspective, that's a role I've taken on. And Eve appreciated that and so . . . I think we learned a lot from each other. (Protégé, Vicky Fletcher)

Beverly Thompson agreed, "[Patty, mentor] gets, first of all, a friend—knowing someone of a different culture, learning about another culture, . . . I want to think that she is broadening her knowledge." (Protégé, Beverly Thompson). While several of the

African-American participants in this sample pointed out that their mentors were attracted to them because of their race, they did not feel exploited. They emphasized that they saw their relationships with their mentors as mutually beneficial. In particular, the African-American protégés argued that their white mentors provided crucial access to the system and insights to assist their rise as educational administrators.

Therefore, connections such as those developed through the mentoring process are worthwhile ones from both an individual and an organizational perspective. From the viewpoint of those in leadership positions, the organization gains good, trusted people, and from the viewpoint of those aspiring to leadership opportunities, protégés get the necessary support and know-how. Most of all, in receiving information from a trusted insider, they learn how the system works. Of course, there are instances where protégés gained the knowledge and skills to move into leadership positions in districts other than the one in which they were trained. Informal mentoring, as it is described in the study, is not designed to keep individuals within the school district. Questions such as to remain in the same district or to relocate to another are decided, depending on how well-suited the protégé would be. Above all, the purpose of mentoring is to facilitate the protégé's career.

Central to the process is that skills, attitudes, and beliefs are passed on—skills, attitudes, and beliefs that many school districts value highly. In this narrative, competent, well-respected administrators trained others to be competent, well-respected administrators. Many participants in Virginia asserted that not only did their own school districts benefit from their mentoring activities, but so, too, did education itself. This claim is based on the belief that what makes them competent and well-respected is that they work hard for the welfare of the students and communities that they serve. For example, protégé Sara Murphy talked of the resources she was able to garner for her school as a result of what she learned through the mentoring experience.

> [Marsha] talked to me about how to push an issue, how to be a nudge, how to force the issue, . . . and how to go out and fight for it. . . . It was something I could admire, and something I could copy. . . . If I'm known for anything, I'm always able to get things for my school. (Protégé, Sara Murphy)

And as these mentors explained:

> I am always on the outlook for people who are really child-centered and I found [Beverly] to be very child-centered and so I began to recruit her into our school system. (Mentor, Patty Burns)

> Peer acceptance was important if protégés were professionally judged to be competent to handle that kind of administrative job. Being an exemplary teacher, which Dorothy was, is important . . . I mean the kids, she just was a favorite of all of the students as they came through her classes. (Mentor, Joan Lewis)

CONCLUSIONS

In this chapter, informal mentoring relationships are seen as good examples of caring relationships between educational leaders and their colleagues. Caring relationships have been advocated as being good for education in general. The reasons for concluding this are embedded in the nature of the relationships themselves.

Leaders who care enough to share the kinds of information necessary for mentoring and who are generous enough with their time to follow through on the activities that are required to train others are good for schools. They demonstrate that they value being connected to others in ways that are good for others. Students benefit from this perspective. And child-centered mentors have deliberately chosen others who share the same values and attitudes.

This reproduction of values and attitudes can benefit children only if the attitudes and values are centered on children. Many participants entered into the mentoring relationship because of such attitudes. The mutual respect that characterized the relationships grew out of working with others who cared about children and their communities. Mentors mentioned being wary of potential protégés whose focus was not on children, and protégés spoke of avoiding mentoring relationships with mentors whose priorities were self-serving. This confirms the importance of shared values in a mentoring relationship. Mentoring highlights the potential for educators to work together. In the end, those who are not connected to others cannot serve the needs of others.

In addition, there is a gender issue that has not been raised thus far in this chapter. In the past, women have not been mentored into educational administration as frequently as men have. Again, it appears to be a feature of the mentoring relationship itself. Mentors choose like-minded individuals to train, and women do not always share the same attitudes and beliefs as their male colleagues do. Studies show that many women lead differently from men, and many women come into administration with educational backgrounds that are different from men's. This does not mean that women have not been mentored by men: they have. It does mean, however, that if women mentor other women different kinds of leadership approaches may be produced. In this narrative, it is clear; the most valued leadership approaches were ones based on care and connection. C. Gilligan (1993), and N. Noddings, (1984, 1992) both associate women's experiences with developing an ethic of care.

This then lays claim to a moral position. A. Jagger (1995) sums up the views of many that advocate an ethic of care. She says it is regarded as "a distinctively human way of engaging with others that produces morally appropriate action" (p. 181). One is able to do the right thing by others because through connection to others, one empathizes with the other's life situation. Examples of what has been argued is morally appropriate in this chapter include serving the needs of the other through mentoring her into educational administration and benefiting the organization at the same time. However, the mentoring relationship does also illustrate one of the weaknesses attributed to adopting care as a moral perspective. It is criticized as too particularized to address the needs of the wider, unknowable public.

Some argue that care relies on individual efforts to meet individual needs which obscures the necessity to address the larger social structures that create many of the injustices in the first place (Jagger 1995). This raises the issue of whether it is likely that leaders who have benefited from such individualized help can translate their ethic of care into more diffused action. On the one hand, such leaders cannot do worse than those who have operated out of a universalistic, detached sense of justice. For that has been the preferred mode of operation to date observed among traditional educational leaders who have not served the needs of all children.

On the other hand, connections offer the possibility of learning and growth. One of the major findings of the study is that mentoring is about developing new ideas and gaining different insights. The openness and curiosity that accompanied many of these experiences promises to encourage leaders who have benefited either from mentoring or from being mentored to look beyond what is known. They have been women, in particular, who have struggled to reach their goals, who have not had easy paths in becoming administrators. The chances that this next generation of leaders will reach out in response to others needs, in general, is strong. To be connected to others in a caring relationship is to know best how to learn from others, and how to work with others to become mature, interdependent individuals. That is why the experiences of mentoring and being mentored described in this chapter promise to be so valuable for educational leaders.

The next chapter looks more specifically at how leadership itself is generated through the practice of mentoring. The Maryland data provide us with an opportunity to consider how the mentoring of women into educational administration suggests the possibility of new ways to lead. Many women have learned ways of leading that are different from the traditional ways. Therefore, the liklihood that change will result from women choosing to mentor other women is strong.

7 Cultivating Feminist Leadership Through Mentoring—Maryland

One strand of research on women administrators takes a feminist orientation to studying women's experiences "on their own terms" (Tetreault 1976, 51) and validating the importance of women's perspectives on their work lives as school administrators in a profession that has traditionally been male-dominated. Some examples are studies by L. Beck (1994), Maenette Benham (1997), S. Chase (1995), M. Grogan (1996), M. Henry (1996) and M. Tallerico and J. Burstyn (1995, 1996). Generally the studies emphasize that "women as administrators are more democratic, caring, and reform minded than their male counterparts" (Shakeshaft, 1999, 115). Women's contributions toward both administration and leadership offer alternative ways of interpreting the work in educational organizations as more nurturing and relationship-oriented than had been characterized by traditional forms of administrative management. According to Grogan (1996), "such approaches to administration invite nurturing kinds of activities and decisions that are child-centered. They also highlight the relational aspects of school communities working together" (p. 138).

Identified as feminist leadership, these alternative approaches can be categorized in three kinds of leadership: instructional leadership, participatory or shared decision-making, and caregiving leadership. The first kind emphasizes the purpose of educational leadership as child-centered and instruction-oriented. Seeking to promote excellent opportunities for students to learn, a leader must attend to the importance of teaching and learning as well as her or his administrative functions. Second, a leader engages all members of the school community in the process of participatory or shared decision-making. This approach to leadership amplifies the importance of collaboration and engaged action in the process of achieving a successful school organization that meets students' educational needs. The third kind of leadership is based on the philosophical premise that caring and caregiving underlie all decision-making, policy, and practice. "Caring does not mean that standards are lowered, but that the educator acts in the interests of the other, and proceeds based on intuitive, personal ways of knowing, rather than simply on linear, rational ways of knowing, (Belenky et al, 1986 as paraphrased in Henry, 1996, 182).

Collectively these three kinds of leadership contrast the typically corporate managerial and bureaucratic functions of school administration. Traditional administration is not sufficient in the current school reform and restructuring context for several reasons. First, more attention must be placed on how students are learning and how teachers are educating in efforts to not only improve student achievement, but also promote the activity of learning in more informed ways. The vast body of empirical evidence on student achievement and effective school organizations needs to be taken into account. Second, with greater tension and adversity among different groups, all competing for limited school resources, educational leaders must engage more collaboratively and partner with the business, government, and community sectors. A school principal cannot operate effectively without connecting with the larger community and school system. Attending to administrative paperwork alone, without working with inside and outside constituents, is not sufficient. Third, new problems demand innovative solutions and change. Administrative leadership tends to foster routinized and regulated action that is inadequate in dealing with the complexity of contemporary problems. Drawing from a multiplicity of educational partners can encourage new thinking and potentially better solutions. Fourth, a hierarchical, top-down organization commanded by an administrator cannot respond as quickly or as adequately to the changing times. This is true not only in educational organizations but in business and government as well.

M. Grogan (1996), H. B. Regan (1990), P. Schmuck (1995), and M. Tallerio (1999) propose that feminist administration offers useful reform and revitalization in current management practices with more women entering the profession of educational administration. An early advocate of a feminist leadership, Regan (1990) stated:

> Feminist administering . . . is an inclusive mode of leadership in schools practiced by people who understand the necessity of the both / and as well as the either / or ways of being in their work. Its inclusiveness requires that both teachers and administrators participate in the decision making in schools, and thus it conceptually overlaps with several thrusts of the current reform movement: teacher empowerment, shared decision making, school restructuring. (Regan 1990, 576)

In examining the Maryland data in this chapter, we begin with the proposition that women administrators bring a different alternative to the profession, "one that views administration in its original meaning, 'to minister'" (Schmuck 1995, 215). We look at how our interviewees in this study are promoting alternative leadership styles not only in their administration, but also in their mentoring relationships. To what extent does the practice of women mentoring other women as educational administrators cultivate such alternative feminist leadership? What links are there between mentoring relationships and feminist leadership? And lastly, what can be learned and applied to our understanding of educational leadership as a result of this examination?

As was the case with the other state chapters, we restrict our discussion to data from the transcripts and field notes of the state of Maryland. These data include twenty-one interviewees, totalling fifteen discrete pairs of mentor and protégé. See appendix A section 3 for a detailed description of each Maryland pair. Among this sample, there were twenty females and one male respondent; eight who identified themselves as African-Americans, thirteen who were white; and eleven mentors, ten protégés, among whom there were some who spoke from their experiences as both mentor and protégé at different times in their careers. There were 3 superintendents, 5 deputy or assistant superintendents, 9 principals, 2 assistant principals, and 2 who held staff positions.

EDUCATIONAL LEADERSHIP

In conducting this study, we were clear about our intention to describe mentoring practices of women educational leaders. In so doing, we examined whether those interviewed for the study demonstrated what might be considered new or alternative feminist leadership aspects as evident in the literature, namely: instructional leadership, participatory or shared decision-making, and caregiving leadership. How did they describe their own leadership styles? How did they relate mentoring experiences with these leadership approaches? The findings will be presented in this section.

Instructional leadership. Focusing upon teaching and learning, this approach to leadership acknowledges the administrator as the instructional leader within the school organization, not simply the manager or director of the corporation. The role of the administrator is as much an educational role as managerial, involved directly with the teaching activities of students and professional development of staff. Half of the twenty-one respondents recounted the importance of this instructional component to their work as school administrators. An elementary school principal, Winoa Chambers, spoke adamantly that her work as administrator involved student learning:

> It's not just that somebody has to be the principal of the school and make sure that it all runs smoothly but that children learn. And I think the bottom line is that. The children's learning. . . . And I guess the reason I'm going back on this tangent is because it gets back to classroom instruction. I feel a very strong sense of obligation to the parents who entrust their children to us everyday to provide them the best that this school can provide. And regardless of where that is. And so that's something that I feel very very strongly about. (Mentor, Winoa Chambers)

Dr. Chambers contrasted her previous bosses, two of whom had been managerial types, but the third, a woman principal, reflected the same belief in instructional leadership. Different from the two men, this woman was the first to actually mentor Winoa and teach her about the work of being an instructional leader.

> The very first principal that really . . . that I had was very much the manager. So I felt that under his leadership style, I learned an awful lot about managing but not much about instruction. And then I went to another principal who was another manager. Both men ironically. He was another manager and I felt that I learned an awful lot about what NOT to do under the second person. So then when I transferred to the third principal—I had a woman—it had to be the most wonderful mentor experience I had had. She was such a strong instructional leader and she was a good teacher, which I felt was very helpful to me. She was very patient. (Mentor, Winoa Chambers)

In one mentoring pair, mentor Chuck and protégé Sharon spoke individually about sharing the view that instructional leadership was necessary in building successful schools. For Chuck, his vision of the importance of instruction to school improvement was validated by protégé Sharon. Likewise, for Sharon working as an assistant principal, her interest in instructionally related activities was supported and promoted by Chuck who, as high school principal, was her boss.

> Chuck allowed me to get away from just the management kinds of duties that (the) assistant principal normally does and moved me into areas that are very tied to instruction. (Protégé, Sharon Perta)

When asked how educational leadership was changing, most respondents said that managerial leadership was no longer sufficient. Past practice of being an efficient manager was adequate to be a successful school administrator. However, the recent thrust for school reform and standards-based education has required more than administrative expertise and skill. Rather, the knowledge of curriculum content and teaching pedagogy is crucial for school and district level administrators to be champions for change. In the words of this school superintendent:

> I think there's going to be changes in educational leadership. There really has to be kind of champions for that effort and champions who see the need to change. I think there's . . .

somewhat of a change in terms of the importance of instruction and curriculum rather than just administration. People are really looking at truly instructional leaders, rather than just good administrators. (Mentor, Constance Lee)

Participatory leadership.   This leadership approach can be identified by its emphasis on sharing ideas, philosophy, and information among the various stakeholders participating in the educational process. It necessarily draws other participants into the school or school system and values the multiplicity of perspectives elicited for often better and more informed decision-making. It strives for consensus and community building, with less emphasis on competition among those with different interests and functions. Describing her own leadership as participatory and facilitative, retired assistant superintendent and now private school principal Nanette Morrison said:

> Well, I'm the kind of leader that likes participation, participatory leadership, wherein everybody is involved as much as possible in the decision-making, in developing agendas, for instance, and the associate superintendent and I had directors and assistants working with me, I didn't set the agenda. You know, we decided jointly what are the issues that we need to discuss. There was always a segment on the agenda for me to give an update on school system issues or whatever, but I believe that a leader must be involved with those who are the so-called followers. You're not a dictator, you know it's not autocratic, you're a facilitator, that's the kind of leadership I like to think that I have. (Mentor, Nanette Morrison)

At times, one must balance facilitative leadership with a more directed kind of leadership as noted by Dr. Constance Lee. As superintendent, she felt it was important to distinguish being directed and task-oriented in specifying goals and implementing them for her school district. However, she did value what she called "the people part of the process" and caviled herself for sometimes forgetting that aspect. Dr. Lee acknowledged those around her who would encourage her to talk with and listen to others.

> I think it's important to have focus and to have clear goals in terms of what you want to have done in the system and very

clear ways to evaluate what's happening. So in that sense, I think it's very important to be directed and to be task-oriented. But you still have to understand the people part of the process and the importance of the people part. Sometimes I get so focused on getting the job done that I forget the people part, but I have good people with whom I work who'll say, "Hey, you need to go have a cup of coffee with the maintenance men." (Mentor, Constance Lee)

Participatory leadership is demonstrated in mentoring, as noted by the many interviewees who commented that a mentoring relationship was about having someone, either a protégé or a mentor, with whom to share thoughts and ideas. This can be seen from this mentor's perspective of protégés calling her to share ideas and being a sounding board to get advice or other viewpoints.

They're (protégés) not always calling to ask for information or to ask for help. Sometimes they call just to bounce ideas off of you. You know, "I was thinking about doing so-and-so, what do you think about that?" Or, "If I did this, who should I involve in this activity or who should I contact?' Or, "Do you think this is a good idea?' (Mentor, Clara Barnes)

Conversely, a protégé values the information sharing given by a mentor in a committed relationship involving teaching based upon the mentor's experiences in the profession. The mentor knows something that needs to be shared with the newcomer. Further, she demonstrates through mentoring how one can be a participatory leader, gaining others' support and consensus. The protégé learns by observing the mentor in action and eventually trying it out for herself in leading school groups.

Collegiality is that you're sharing ideas with somebody. You might work on a project with somebody. You have conversations about pedagogy. There might be all kinds of opportunities for you to have a collegial experience but a mentorship relationship means that actually there is an understanding that one person is teaching the other. And that one person knows something that the other person needs to know. That's what mentoring means. (Protégé, Cassie McHenry)

> There are situations that I could make my staff feel more comfortable with me, and also win their approval—if you want to call it approval—win their approval by letting them in on the decision-making process. And that's something that Roberta (mentor) did all the time. . . . I really watched her closely and didn't even know that I was watching her closely, because at that point I had no earthly idea I was ever going to become a principal. It wasn't until actually the last few years that I decided that I might want to do that. But I did learn a lot from her, as far as her leadership style. She's firm, direct, fair, consistent, and I think all those are good qualities that a leader needs. (Protégé, Elaine Bennett)

Besides sharing ideas and information, participatory leadership can be thought of as a team-oriented style, where not just the administrator is involved in the school or system management, but there are faculty, staff, student, and community members involved and empowered in the decision-making process. With school improvement teams, more administrators spoke directly about team building in their organizations which they felt resulted in stronger schools (mentor Winoa Chambers) and greater ownership among the faculty and staff in making school decisions (mentor Chuck Donnelly; protégé Sharon Perta). Reflecting on her experiences as an elementary school principal, Dr. Paulie commented about the collaborative team effort that was involved in making decisions for school improvement and change. She did the same thing later in her work as superintendent.

> As a principal, I had chairpeople, teachers who were chairs of different committees and a school improvement team, and clearly there were some decisions that have to be made by the principal. But there are also many decisions that can be made as part of collaborative team effort, and where they can, they should be. In this role [as superintendent], I do the same thing. I have a wonderful management team and I rely very much on their input and I will run ideas by them constantly. In a mentoring I think I probably promote that team concept. (Mentor, Roberta Paulie)

Caring and caregiving leadership. The third kind of leadership emphasizes the ethical basis of care and caregiving. Premised on the notion that relationships form the basis for any organization, caring is viewed as fundamental to fostering and sustaining the connections between individuals within the organization. These relationships can be between a student and teacher, two colleagues, faculty and staff, a mentor and a protégé. For principal Dr. Chambers, there was no distinction in her role as an educational professional and caring friend. She extended the same care and concern for everyone in her school, be they children, parents, teachers, and staff. In her words,

> It's hard for me to separate caring for someone as a profes-
> sional and caring for someone as a friend because that's
> something that's very important to me as a principal . . . that
> people see you as someone who is a friend also. (Mentor,
> Winoa Chambers)

Her protégé Angela concurred with this appraisal, saying that Dr. Chambers extended care and support to many individuals in the school, not just to her as the assistant principal.

> In that capacity Winoa is clearly my mentor, but it's not just
> me. She has other people. She had another teacher who did
> her fieldwork under her, and I know that she would say that
> she is her mentor as well and her coach and her cheerleader.
> All those things. (Protégé, Angela Patterson)

Between mentor and protégé, relationships were grounded in caring and caregiving as exemplified by spending extra time to-gether, working on special projects, debriefing an activity, and lis-tening to personal concerns that affected the individual. Further, mentoring relationships could be examined in terms of level of in-volvement or intimacy, with greater involvement between mentor and protégé than in most supervisory relationships (Burke, McKenna and McKeen, 1991). Despite this greater connectedness, most of the interviewees characterized their mentoring relationships as more professional than personal in nature. They were more apt to view their connections as professional ones, rather than as social or intimate. That is, mentoring relationships were clearly directed to-ward the profession with career outcomes in mind. At the same time, the professional relationship did not deter an evolution of a closer, more personal relationship over time. Indeed friendships did develop in the association between mentor and protégé. For instance, two mentoring pairs (mentor Chuck Donnelly and protégé Sharon Perta; mentor Paula Jenkins and protégé Constance Lee) began as boss and subordinate. They had worked in the same district, and over time became close personal friends, involved with each other's social lives to the extent that they shared vacation times together. Constance viewed that the mentorship had evolved into a friendship:

> Well to me friendship . . . just goes beyond the job. And I mentioned before about (Paula) who was a mentor for me and is now a close personal friend. And our relationship is more than worker-job related and has continued when she retired. I see that as friendship, as opposed to mentorship. Although the friendship grew out of the mentorship relationship. (Mentor, Constance Lee)

Similarly, protégé Marion Bateson spoke of how she was included in her mentor's inner circle, transforming what had begun as a professional relationship into a more personal one.

> It clearly began as a professional relationship because I met (mentor Martha Ellison) as a result of working in the County. But she's the kind of person that goes beyond. She makes that effort to go beyond the professional interest. And she does that by inviting you into her inner circle, meaning, there are times when she's invited me to her home, or invited me to some family gathering. And that was clearly a signal to me that she saw me as a friend. (Protégé, Marion Bateson)

What had been initiated as a professional relationship had become more personal and intimate. As with all relationships, there was the foundation of caring for the other, beginning with the mentor noticing the protégé as a talented young teacher, as in the case of Ellison and Bateson, and taking the time to get to know about her. Being singled out as a teacher was an important beginning in Bateson's mentoring relationship with Martha Ellison and made a significant difference in her professional life as well as her personal life: "So I was very excited that someone would care so much about a teacher, and actually actively seek out knowing me and getting to know something about my interests and so that was the beginning" (protégé Marion Bateson). Without the ethic of care, there can be no relationship and certainly no mentorship. Mentor Clara Barnes expressed the sentiment in these words:

> It reminds me of this saying, "People don't care how much you know until they know how much you care." . . . I don't know that the experience would be that valuable to me if there was no relationship between me and the person. And, I don't mean that it has to be purely, purely affective in that they just lavish me with compliments and all of this kind of thing. I guess for me, I have to recognize in that person leadership qualities that I want to emulate. (Mentor, Clara Barnes)

Interviewees tended to identify their mentoring styles as caregiving and coaching, more commonly than other approaches such as "tough love" or "sink or swim" where the mentor might take on a more detached stance. According to superintendent Paulie, her style was a combination that aimed at collaborative team building.

> I would describe my style as a combination of caregiving and coaching. My style is very much team-oriented. And everything I've done, I've tried to do [collaboratively] . . . I've tried to build a team and I've tried to function as part of a collaborative team. (Mentor, Roberta Paulie)

As with other kinds of leadership, protégés learned how to give care and support to others by observing their mentors in the school setting. A caregiving leadership style was validated, reinforced, and modeled by the mentor. Roberta Paulie's protégé acknowledged that she learned this approach from Dr. Paulie.

> I think you've probably gotten it—it's not tough love at all. It was very caregiving, it was coaching, it was [mentor Paulie's] philosophy that I got from her. (Protégé, Elaine Bennett)

While fundamental to relationships, a caregiving approach can pose problems such as familial ties, patronage, and favoritism as recounted by some interviewees. These were exceptional cases, which serve to suggest cautions necessary in cultivating caring and trustworthy relationships. Among the pairs, protégé Elaine Bennett commented that her relationship with Dr. Paulie was at times like a "parent-child kind of relationship," and that Elaine as protégé felt the pressure of meeting the high expectations held by her mentor. Similarly, protégé Grace Holly expressed her uneasiness in relating to her boss-mentor who, Grace felt, acted on occasion as if they were mother and daughter. Interestingly, in an earlier interview, mentor Constance Lee had spoken of Grace being the same age as her own daughter. Given these similarities in age and relationship, it was not surprising that an individual would transpose one relationship (mother-daughter) for the other (mentor-protégé). Grace described the situation in this way:

> It's like a mother-daughter relationship. She cares enough to say things to me that she wouldn't necessarily say to other people. I don't think she's mean. I don't think she, by any means, means to hurt my feelings or upset me. I just think she thinks she can say things to me that she doesn't probably say to others. She couldn't possibly say what she says to about me to other people. So there is a difference. It's definitely that kind of a relationship. (Protégé, Grace Holly)

Another problem arising in the caregiving approach involved the perception of favoritism resulting from having a close, caring relationship between mentor and protégé, especially when the latter is seen as having privileges or career advancement bestowed by her mentor. Favoritism and privileging can be problematic in mentoring relationships because mentors are often the supervisors and can be crucial in providing opportunities for personal growth as well as career advancement for her protégés. In some cases, mentors were directly involved in suggesting whom their successors as school principals or unit heads might be. Thus, the question arises: Is the mentor playing favorites? When her mentor became superintendent of their school system, protégé Elaine Bennett acknowledged a concern about being favored in the hiring process. Her strategy was to remain somewhat distant from her mentor during the year following her appointment.

> And I wouldn't want anybody to say that I got here because Roberta [mentor] put me here. I mean she put my name in front of the Board. But I'm here on my own merits too I believe. And I really didn't want anyone [thinking that] . . . so we really did stay away from each other this year. (Protégé, Elaine Bennett)

By contrast, mentor Nanette Morrison spoke proactively about how she selected protégé Ellie over the others because Ellie was a recognized leader and thus, the most qualified person for the job. It should be noted that in their relationship, the protégé had to prove herself capable and hard working in her position as curriculum specialist. Likewise, her boss-mentor was highly regarded in the school system and considered extremely ethical as assistant superintendent.

> I think people saw that, yes, I did play favorites. And I think Ellie also didn't want folks to see her, you know, as the favored person. . . . I didn't really have to confront it because I had loved everybody. I gave everybody the opportunity to capitalize upon each person's strengths, gave them a particular task, a leadership role that I knew they could handle very well. And there were times when Ellie was clearly the only one that I had assuming the leadership. (Mentor, Nanette Morrison)

In summary, we characterize a feminist alternative to educational leadership first as instructionally oriented, rather than strictly administrative or managerial. Many of the respondents spoke of the importance of this instructional leadership in building successful schools where children's learning was optimized. The second kind of leadership is a participatory, facilitative one which emphasizes sharing ideas, philosophy, and information with the members of the school organization. Beyond simply information-sharing, this type of leadership is team-oriented, involving members to work collaboratively and act out of consensus and shared decision-making. Third is a caring leadership which values caregiving as necessary and fundamental in educational organizations. There were clear connections between mentoring relationships and caregiving, but also some problems which arose from close, intimate connections between individuals. We turn now to the links between mentoring and these feminist leadership approaches.

MENTORING LINKED WITH EDUCATIONAL LEADERSHIP

Mentoring relationships were closely identified with at least two of the three alternative approaches. Mentoring could be thought of as directly related to being participatory in sharing one's ideas, information, and experiences, and to being caregiving toward one's protégé. In both cases, mentoring takes place through information sharing and caregiving, and as some noted, mentoring does not occur when there is little care and support. The qualities of being participatory and caregiving lend themselves to being a good mentor and friend.

However, mentoring is not necessarily linked to instructional leadership partly because a mentoring relationship is aligned with career advancement or personal development irrespective of one's profession. In chapter 3, quality mentoring is distinguished as that which is active, engaged, and intentionally directed toward professional needs of the protégé. There is little mention of focusing upon teaching and learning which are key to instructional leadership. While some interviewees spoke of teaching and learning in their schools or systems, not all spoke about this kind of educational leadership related to their mentoring relationships. At the same time, it could be argued that good teaching is linked with good mentoring practices, that is, a good teacher makes in turn a good mentor. Many interviewees commented about this aspect of their mentoring relationship, where mentors taught protégés new skills and encouraged them to engage in opportunities for learning something different. Like a good teacher, the mentor sees the potential in the individual and seeks to promote their personal and professional growth as much as they can. Taken in this light, instructional leadership can be seen in mentoring relationships.

HOW MENTORS CULTIVATED THESE APPROACHES TO LEADERSHIP

In exploring how mentors cultivated these approaches to educational leadership, protégés seemed to follow the example set by their mentors. Frequently they spoke of their mentors as "role models," demonstrating how to become an educational leaders in schools and school systems. Observing how their mentors acted was often cited as the way in which protégés learned, especially when a mentor was also the boss or supervisor in one's school or educational unit. Likewise, mentors viewed themselves as consciously demonstrating and modeling for those who might follow in similar careers, particularly as women in positions which were primarily held by white males.

Notably, there were two respondents (mentor Chuck Donnelly, mentor Paula Jenkins) who did not see their roles as mentors and expressed slight surprise at being identified as a protégé's mentor. These exceptions suggest that while not defined as mentors per se, these individuals did engage in activities that achieved the outcomes of mentoring, namely, career advancement, personal development, and professional integration. Another explanation for these two cases is the long-term association that existed between mentor and protégé. Both pairs (mentor Chuck Donnelly and protégé Sharon Perta; mentor Paula Jenkins and protégé Constance Lee) had known each other for many years and shared close personal friendships as well as professional relationships. The maturity of the relationships might explain the mentor's reluctance to consider the association currently a mentorship.

Role models were not exclusively women mentoring women. There were numerous examples of women having been mentored by men, especially those in senior positions such as high school principal, assistant superintendent, or superintendent. Speaking of their experiences as protégés, the women in the study who held senior level positions, for example, superintendent, deputy, or assistant superintendent, frequently identified a male administrator whose vision for career advancement had encouraged them to seek administrative offices in their school system or had opened doors of access to other organizations. There were also examples of minority women whose advancement was promoted by white individuals, both male and female, who held supervisory positions. With the changing composition of educational administrative officers and steadily increasing numbers of women and minorities entering the profession, it is more likely that there will be mentors and protégés who are similar in gender, race, and ethnicity as well as other factors such as philosophy, personality, and interest. In the future, role models might indeed be more alike than different.

Furthermore, the traditional dyadic relationship of one mentor linked with one protégé might not reflect the reality. Most interviewees in this study commented about the numerous mentors they had had throughout their careers, some for shorter periods of time and in different job assignments. While the designated pairs of mentor and protégé were probably the most significant mentoring relationship, these were not exclusive relationships. For instance, African-American protégé Ellie Carlye identified two African-American women administrators in her district as well as two white male superintendents from neighboring school districts, all of whom were important to her career development. In chapter 8 on women of color, more is said about the importance of multiple mentors and alternative support systems.

In weighing the impact of the mentor upon the protégé, it is not possible to say whether mentors transmitted their values to their protégés or whether in fact, protégés followed those individual leaders whose values and styles complemented their own views and approaches. It is likely that both of these explanations are valid. Mentors influence the kind of leaders their protégés become by role modeling and nurturing the professional development of these novices. Conversely, protégés are drawn to and chose to emulate those whose leadership they value and believe in. From the mutuality, reciprocity, and friendships noted in these mentoring relationships, we might infer that both mentor and protégé were influenced by each other, as well as supported and encouraged in their work as educational leaders. In the words of one mentor,

> You don't become a clone of the one person who has been the strongest person in your life. You adapt from the different people that you work with to develop your own style of leadership. And I think that's what I want Angela [protégé] to make sure she's experiencing as well. It's not just me, you know. It's other people. (Mentor, Winoa Chambers)

The long duration of successful mentoring relationships, that is, ten or more years, was evident in all of the pairs, even when mentors and protégés took different positions or moved to other school systems. Rather than terminate when one leaves the job, mentor and protégé often remained in touch and connected throughout their careers. Interviewees noted that while they were not in frequent touch with their mentors, they knew they could call when help was needed.

Cultivating Feminist Educational Leadership

Having explored the mentoring practices of women in educational leadership, we consider what lessons have been learned about mentoring relationships which cultivate feminist educational leadership. We return to the proposition that women mentoring women are cultivating new alternatives in instructional, participatory, and caregiving forms. First, we find that the proposition is not so clearly evident because there are men as well as women mentoring in these alternative ways. Historically, this was the case because there were so few women in administration. At the same time, men did provide needed opportunities for women as described by the more senior interviewees. The lesson is to acknowledge all supporters, irrespective of gender, race, or other seeming differences and to consider the availability of opportunities for learning and growth. A cautionary addendum is that power and authority must be acknowledged. In a mentoring relationship, does the mentor strive to empower, rather than overpower and control her or his protégé? To what degree must the protégé become a clone of her mentor? What attention is given to the protégé's needs and personal growth? These are important questions to consider as a protégé draws upon a mentor's support.

Second, while there are traditional mentoring relationship pairs, there are also more than one mentor at times. In some cases, there are peers, mentoring each other as they work together in school systems. There are mentoring clusters where individuals succeed each other as administrative leaders. For example, mentor Chuck served as high school principal and directed protégé Sharon, who in turn became a secondary school principal. Later, Sharon mentored Frances who was the assistant principal. The protégé credited Sharon for being instrumental in her promotion as middle school principal. From Chuck to Sharon to Frances, there was a succession of principalship. The lesson is to look at the multiple ways in which mentors and protégés connect and can support each other in leadership. Especially in school systems, individuals connect at the school level, between school and central office, across schools, and within neighboring school districts. In a small state like Maryland with twenty-four school districts in relatively close proximity, administrative protégés benefited from connections across these different systems. For example, protégé Ellie Caryle spoke about interning under a superintendent in an adjacent school system, more affluent and suburban than her own urban school district. She benefited from observing a different leadership style in a different context.

Third, we identified at least participatory and caregiving leadership styles as evident in mentoring relationships. Both mentors and protégés spoke of sharing ideas, information, and experiences as colleagues, and of fostering caregiving relationships with each other.

However, instructional leadership may be more difficult to link with mentoring in part, because the practice of mentoring can occur in any profession. While it could be argued that to be a good mentor is to be a good teacher, the focus on teaching and learning with attention to a child-centered, instructional leadership is not a given. The lesson here is to attend to the importance of instructional leadership and good teaching as directly related to mentoring in educational leadership. Today's school reform agenda demands this kind of leadership and mentors need to direct their protégés toward the curricular, pedagogical and professional development of the school organization.

Fourth, in caregiving leadership, there were tensions related to closely connected familial ties where mentor and protégé related as parent and child. Such tensions suggest the intense nature of a mentoring relationship beyond that of boss and subordinate, inferring perhaps a greater level of intimacy and involvement. The lesson is that such tensions and potential conflicts in caregiving need to be addressed. One side might be unaware of the other's feelings. If indeed caring occurs as L. Beck (1994) suggests, when one individual cares for the other as one's self, then difficulties and misunderstandings must be shared openly and freely. It will not an easy task, but given the importance of honest and open communication between mentor and protégé, these tensions need to be resolved.

Fifth, the concerns about favoritism were expressed in cases where the mentor took an active role in advancing a protégé. How then do women mentors demonstrate their caregiving while retaining consistency in all of their relationships? How do women protégés demonstrate their qualification for promotions to dissuade opponents who might object because of perceived favoritism? In dealing with favoritism, interviewees suggested several strategies to respond to such questions: (a) that leaders provide a variety of opportunities for any individuals who demonstrate desire and motivation, not exclusively those individuals who are selected by the leader; (b) that mentors encourage protégés to advance their own levels of expertise and knowledge, making them the "best" qualified; (c) that protégés gain greater visibility in their schools and school systems to demonstrate their competency and qualification to others; and (d) that individuals draw from a multiplicity of sources for information, support, and guidance. The lesson is to be proactive as suggested by these four strategies.

CONCLUSIONS

Much has been learned about how mentoring relationships cultivate and promote feminist alternatives to educational leadership. But there are numerous questions yet to consider in exploring women mentoring women. Among these are the following: First, are there alternative educational leadership styles not yet identified? With many varied women entering the profession and several generations of mentors, we might expect greater variation in approach, style, and even interpretation. Considering these variations over time might also be useful. Second, what can be said about how women and men might differ in their orientation toward leadership and mentorship? C. Shakeshaft (1999) comments that in examining women's practices without comparative data from males, there is little to support why there might be gender differences in administrative and leadership styles. Further exploration may be possible with more comparative data on women's leadership. A related third question is whether anything can be said about race, age, religion, and other kinds of differences that might be related to leadership and mentorship. As well, we might examine how the differences are bridged by other commonalities such as one's educational philosophy and values. In addition to individual similarities and differences, we might consider the environmental context of school, school system, and municipality. Finally, if we as educational administrators and faculty in leadership programs are to be informed by the diverse perspectives from which we speak, how can we incorporate these perspectives into our understanding of mentoring relationships and leadership? This concludes the section of this book examining key issues in this study, with data from each particular state. We turn now to the larger study for a consideration of issues of race and gender related to the mentoring experiences of women of color.

8 Mentoring Relationships for Women of Color

According to Homer's tale of the adventures of Odysseus, the Greek goddess of wisdom Athene is responsible for the mentoring of the youth Telemachus while his seafaring father Odysseus is away. Disguised as Mentor, a loyal friend of Odysseus, Athene aids and guides the young man. She acts as trusted friend and counselor in all aspects of the boy's life. Thus, originates the English word "mentoring" (Stalker 1994).

From a feminist perspective, this narrative is illustrative of the dilemma faced by women of color who serve as mentors in institutions that are androcentric or patriarchal. They are regarded for their wisdom as depicted by the supernatural Athene, but they must in some ways disguise themselves, acting as dominant white males in leadership roles. In this way, women of color are often misrepresented for both their gender and their racial identification. These misrepresentations and mistaken identities can erode their sense of self and cause doubt in their abilities and competencies. However, as these women of color attain success in educational leadership positions, they like Athene as mentor, can aid those who follow in their footsteps.

We describe in this chapter the ways in which mentoring provides the means for women of color to gain entry and access into educational administration. Briefly, we sketch the mentoring relationships of our

respondents of color, fourteen African-American and four Hispanic educational leaders, in their roles of either mentor or protégé. We explore how issues of race and gender might have affected their career
paths in educational administration, and how mentoring aided them
in successfully negotiating their way within organizations that have
been largely male and white. Given the challenges of these situations,
we identify the needs and desires of protégés aspiring to careers in
educational administration. We present these notes to Athene in an
effort to provide insights for those mentoring particularly women
of color.

As authors, we felt it was important to acknowledge that our
own viewpoints would be different from that of African-American or
Hispanic woman administrator perspectives because we were writing about ethnic groups that were not our own. Respondents in this
women of color sampling are minorities of either African-American
or Hispanic origins. None of the authors are African-American or
Hispanic. Ernestine is an Asian-American; both Mary and Margaret
are Australian immigrants to the United States. But as women faculty members in educational administration, we share concerns
about issues of equity, social justice, and affirmative action. It was
our intention to write this chapter to highlight the concerns of race
and gender expressed by our interviewees of color.

Further, we note that these interviewees are not all the same. As
women of color, they are individuals who do not speak in a singular
voice. In their interviews, these women expressed differences in
their needs, desires, histories, and career aspirations. They formed
unique mentoring relationships with others who were similar as
well as those who were different from themselves in attaining educational leadership positions. In the chapter, we describe their challenges as well as the advantages derived from their mentoring
relationships.

Study Sample

The chapter draws exclusively from the interviews of women of
color in the three states: Washington, Virginia, and Maryland. We focus closely on the issues of race and gender raised by these respondents as they described their mentoring relationships. Our dataset
consists of a total of eighteen women, of whom fourteen are African-
American and four are Hispanic-American.

Usually mentoring relationships were initiated by mentors who recognized potential in prospective protégés. For example, while serving as a district officer, mentor Martha recognized an exemplary middle school teacher whom she encouraged to pursue graduate studies. Her protégé eventually become a school principal. In another example, protégé Beverly did not have a teaching license at the beginning of the relationship. Her mentor was proactive and supportive of her career development. Beverly was successful in attaining the presidency of the educational association.

On occasion, protégés initiated contact with a prospective mentor. Carol Pierce, as an aspirant to the superintendency, sought the advice and encouragement of her mentor in academics as well as in specific career related areas. But several mentors spoke of being wary of those who might approach them, especially if the prospective individual was not clear about her career objectives.

At times, mentoring relationships were mutually established. For instance, mentor Othene Kirkland and protégé Doreen Ballard were both African-American women principals in the same school district. With few minorities in the district, the two women were drawn together in friendship. Kirkland coached Ballard through difficult times in her principalship. The two women remain in close touch, even though Mrs. Kirkland has since retired and moved out of the state. In another case, two Hispanic mothers Gabriela and Leticia met on a bus trip as they journeyed to advocate for their daughters' college admission. Both mothers had daughters who were the same age and enrolled in the same classes. Their friendship developed from mutual concern for their daughters. Mentor Gabriela encouraged protégé Leticia to complete high school, obtain a teaching credential, and enter school administration.

TABLE 8.1.   Study Sample by Race and Role.

	Total	Washington	Virginia	Maryland
Women of Color	18	5	5	8
African-American	14	1	5	8
Mentors	4	0	0	4
Protégés	10	1	5	4
Hispanic-American	4	4	0	0
Mentors	1	1	0	0
Protégés	3	3	0	0

Ties between mentor and protégé were generally long term, the least being 5–8 years with the longest relationships lasting ten or more years. During these years, mentor and protégé roles changed and occasionally reversed. For example, mentor Monique Avery and protégé Ellie Carlye were first acquainted when Carlye was hired as a curriculum specialist under Avery, then the assistant superintendent of instruction. Later, Dr. Avery took a position as a high school principal. When Carlye was appointed to the position of director of curriculum and instruction, the protégé became her mentor's boss, and their roles were revised. This case was an exception.

Mentoring relationships can be crucial for women in succeeding in administration, as evident in chapter 5 on women's conflicts with leadership. In the next section, we describe the further challenges faced by women of color and examine how their mentoring relationships aided them.

CHALLENGES FOR WOMEN OF COLOR

Being a minority among a white majority. Six interviewees spoke about their unique place in organizations or systems where they were one of few persons of color in leadership positions as mentoring pairs like Othene Kirkland and Doreen Ballard, or Nanette Morrison and Ellie Carlye, or individuals like Carol Pierce and Ramona Gonzales. As director of human relations, Clara Barnes described joining a mid-Atlantic teacher staffing organization where there were only a few persons of color and in her words:

> You talk about a good ol' boy network. This was a good ol' boy network, I mean, at its finest. And it took them some getting used to, diversity in this organization. (Mentor, Clara Barnes)

Barnes was subsequently nominated to be the first female African-American president of the organization. But she was only the second African-American and one of a few women ever to hold office in a thirty year span.

For some women, being a minority was to their advantage. For example, Carol Pierce took the opportunity to get a teaching position in her hometown, but she remained the only minority at her school for a long time. As a well-educated Hispanic woman, Ramona Gonzales experienced more career opportunities in central Washington state than in her home state of New Mexico, where competition for positions was greater among middle-class Hispanics. This advantage came at a cost. Ramona left a "very, very strong support system" of family members to take a job far from home. She left a situation where she was in the majority to live in a state where her educated Hispanic background was considered a novelty.

Being a minority in a predominantly minority organization. Women of color were not always in the minority. Several of our interviewees experienced either living in states or working in educational organizations where as persons of color, they were not the minority but the majority in their school system. An assistant superintendent of curriculum and instruction remarked: "within the ___City public schools at least, until very recently the leadership— the top level of leadership—was very heavily African-American (Protégé, Ellie Carlye). Mentor Clara Barnes reported on the African-American educators who made up the majority of her urban school system. Despite the fact that the white males were no longer in leadership positions, African-Americans were still looked upon as minorities. Similarly, Beverly Thompson, the president of an educational association, remarked that African-Americans are in leadership positions where "it's an all minority program or group. . . . But if it's an integrated group, you'll never find a Black in a leadership role" (Protégé, Beverly Thompson). The comments raise these questions: What does it take for persons of color to gain recognition in their school systems? How can they gain leadership positions in their organizations? How long will they remain a "silent majority?"

Mistaken identities. As minorities in predominantly white male organizations, many individuals spoke of being mistaken for the subordinate in their schools or offices. The same Hispanic protégé who had moved from New Mexico recounted being mistaken as the secretary, which she resented very much. One assistant superintendent laughed as she recalled episodes of mistaken impression, where the woman behind the desk is assumed to be someone's secretary, not the boss. An African-American elementary school principal related a story of a parent who mistook the white secretary for the principal, and assumed the African-American principal was the secretary. Unlike the assistant superintendent whose response was laughter, this principal voiced her frustration with the mistaken identity and perhaps even anger over the stereotyping and discrimination.

A parent came in and was talking to the secretary [whom] she thought was the principal. [The parent] had talked to my area director, she said. And she thought I was the secretary. You know this is the 90s, almost the millennium, the year 2000, some of the stereotypes and discrimination should not be happening. (Protégé, Doreen Ballard)

Racial intimidation.   Mistaken identities when based upon racial stereotypes can be particularly malicious and harmful. Moreover, there can be a carryover into the community as noted in protégé Ballard's comments about the racism present in her community.

You can't please everyone and they do look at you as an African-American. They do. And one of my teachers said to me, "I never thought there was racism in [city] until I saw how people react to you." They react to you. So you need someone [a mentor] to be there to say, "Hey, this is normal, so forget about it and go on with life, you know you can't dwell on it." (Protégé, Doreen Ballard)

Race confounding one's gender.   Difficult as it might be to distinguish race from gender or remove gender from race, respondents spoke of viewing themselves first as persons of color and second as women. Protégé Vicky Fletcher contrasted white women and minority women where she believed whites view gender to be more prominent than race:

I find that white women [consider] the sex thing, the gender thing is so much more important to them than it is for a black female. We can't put a whole lot of energy into the male, female, because we are dealing with the race issue first. So even though we know it's an issue, it doesn't take top billing for us. It's mainly the racial things that we have to contend with first. (Protégé, Vicky Fletcher)

Many of the interviewees echoed similar sentiments regarding their dual role of being a woman and a minority as "two whammies" or "double jeopardy." Protégé Doreen Ballard said it in this way: "I have two whammies. I'm a female and I'm an African-American and I'm the only support." Her comments suggest the struggles of both race and gender as well as the lack of support available for someone in her position.

Self doubt and needing to prove one self.   The "double jeopardy" of being a women of color takes its toll in terms of an individual's self-esteem as a leader. For instance, elementary school principal Ballard said that she was always having to prove herself as competent and capable. What perhaps might appear to be a "small complaint" directed at her seemed to find its way to the central administration downtown.

Discouragement can come not only from the school system, but may also come from the home. According to mentor Ramirez, women are too often discouraged:

> And it's just difficult to break. Sometimes in a relationship mentoring women of color, where the spouses are not receptive to this, you really are dancing on a fine line because they [protégés] want to do something with their lives and they don't have the support from home. (Mentor, Gabriela Ramirez)

To summarize the challenges faced by women of color in our study, interviewees recounted the difficulties of being in the minority, where they were often the first or one of a few in administrative positions in their organization. Notably there were some career opportunities to being the first or the only one of their kind. In some urban school systems, persons of color were in the majority, rather than in the minority. Overall however, persons of color remain minorities in a predominantly white society, and in a white male educational administrative system. The women of color in our study related incidents of being mistaken for their subordinates, regarded as the secretary rather than the boss. They also spoke of the racism present in their larger communities. Mentors and protégés alike spoke of "double jeopardy," being both women and minorities. Both race and gender factored into feelings of self-doubt about their capacity to do their work and be successful as educational administrators. If mentoring is to be useful for women and minorities who have not been prominent in educational leadership, we need to examine how mentoring relationships have benefited especially women of color in successfully negotiating their way in predominantly white male administrations.

MENTORING RELATIONSHIPS OF WOMEN OF COLOR

Generally the role of mentor was that of supporter, guide, protector, and advocate, as noted in earlier chapters on quality mentoring and specific school leadership development. This role of supporter and cheerleader enabled the protégé to meet the many challenges and self-doubts accompanying the job of administrator. According to one individual:

> In order for someone, a female or someone of color to be successful, they have to have a good support system, a good mentor who is willing to take the time to mentor them, to listen to them and to guide them, give them advice and be there for them. (Protégé, Doreen Ballard)

Faced by the challenge of being one of few persons of color in their school system or organization, interviewees spoke of their personal experiences under the tutelage of white male mentors. As an African-American female administrator who was in the minority in her organization's leadership, Ms. Barnes recalled:

> I have to say that I was mentored by men. At the time that I moved into personnel work, personnel in school systems historically had been dominated by men, particularly middle-aged, white men. And I was fortunate though to have the opportunity to work with a couple of people who took responsibility for my development. I don't know that women didn't want to do it, it's just that there weren't any there. (Mentor, Clara Barnes)

As associate and later deputy superintendent, Martha Ellison was first mentored by a white supervisor who had been promoted to district superintendent. Subsequently she was hired away to work in a suburban district under an African-American superintendent. An African-American herself, Ellison spoke of learning much from both men in terms of educational leadership and politics in the different school systems. However, she eventually returned to work under her first mentor, explaining that she felt more compatibility with him despite their differences in race and gender. Both Barnes and Ellison sought and received guidance from those who were in positions of power. They were selected for their competence and demonstrated their capacity for leadership.

For protégés of color, regardless of race or gender, it was important that the mentor believe and value them. In the words of an African-American protégé whose mentor was white:

> I'm convinced that [mentors] have to care about the other person's success and well-being as an individual and as a professional. I say that because I know that's what motivated Pam [mentor]. She didn't try to make me into a Pam Jr. That wasn't it at all. But she wanted me, Brenda, to succeed and to do well and she knew that I wanted that also. So it was kind of easy to mentor me, you know. (Protégé, Brenda Monroe)

Relationships of care were important with mentors providing support, encouragement, and thus nurturing the newcomers. Echoing sentiments regarding the importance of caring, Clara Barnes recalled: "I don't know that the experience would be that valuable to me if there was no [caring] relationship between me and the person" (Mentor, Clara Barnes).

Mentoring relationships were mutual and reciprocal between mentor and protégé. Although the protégé gained much in terms of skill development and leadership opportunities that aided in career advancement, both sides benefited from their relationships. If mentor and protégés differed in racial-ethnic backgrounds, the other offered a look from a diverse perspective. For example, with a mentor whose upbringing was easier than her own, protégé Beverly learned what it might be like coming up "on the easy side of the mountain." She recounted:

> I have enjoyed hearing [mentor Patty's] background and comparing it. It's nice to meet someone who came up "on the easy side of the mountain." I already know the tough side of the mountain. I've already been there, done that. Don't want to do it again. (Protégé, Beverly Thompson)

Besides an individual's perspective, protégés could offer a community perspective as evidenced by protégé Vicky Fletcher who held long-standing ties with the African-American community. Her mentor, a white assistant principal, appreciated the perspective Vicky could bring about the community served by the school. Likewise, protégé Reneé Miles, a Hispanic assistant principal who spoke the language and communicated with other Hispanic families, felt she offered her white principal a different insight and invaluable connections to that community.

Mentors also acknowledged the perspectives provided by their protégés. For instance, deputy superintendent Dr. Ellison mentored others by advising them in their careers and felt that her protégés in turn served as a "pulse" on what was happening out there. As teachers and administrators, they offered her a different perspective on education occurring in her school system. Another assistant superintendent drew upon her protégé, Lauren Kente, to serve on various committees for the district. The protégé brought her perspective as an assistant principal while benefiting from the opportunity to demonstrate her leadership capability for a wider audience in her school district.

Beyond information sharing and providing different perspectives for mentors, protégés often served as confidante and friend particularly where there were few women of color in the organization. They support the mentor in personal as well as professional ways. Protégé Denise Oscar commented in a general way that: "Quite often we don't realize that there's something in us that's fulfilling the need of that mentor" (Protégé, Denise Oscar). Personally she felt her mentor Martha Ellison had been there for her during graduate school in a time of family crisis:

> Martha was there for me. There were times I didn't even feel like coming to school and she would come by my home and pick me up and bring me to school (Protégé, Denise Oscar).

Many interviewees described their ties to either mentor or protégé as very close and personal ties. For mentor Mary Chase, there was a strong bonding between her protégé and herself built upon similar experiences of struggle and hard work, despite differences in background and race.

> [Protégé Carol's] belief that I'm going to be real straight with her [is important] . . . that I've been able sometimes to claw my way and she herself is somebody who's had to do that. . . . She could see that maybe there was a perception that

white people had it easier, white people had it better. But I
was a white woman who had been a free lunch kid, who
came up through the ranks, who did what it took to get into
administration. So I think that served as a bond. (Mentor,
Mary Ann Chase)

Much of what has been described in the quality mentoring relationships of the women of color in our study can be applied to all
novices in educational administration irrespective of race and gender. Like the Goddess Athene, the mentor serves as a guide and advisor to the novice, providing opportunities for learning and
feedback on experiences to aid in professional growth and advancement. Relationships are based on care and concern, mutual trust,
and respect. There is reciprocity between mentor and protégé in associations that often last a long time.

Additionally, there are specific considerations placed on mentors
and protégés who are women of color in their mentoring relationships. We highlight four that are derived from the feminist framework of this study. First is the power relationship on which a
mentoring relationship is based. Often the mentor is the boss or supervisor of a subordinate who gains access and privilege as a result
of the mentoring relationship. Both mentor and protégé need to consider how their relationship is supported by such privileging. Many
of the mentoring pairs in this study are of a boss and a subordinate.
This is further complicated when there are race and gender issues
involved, as for example with a white male boss and an African-
American female subordinate. In one such case, the interviewee
spoke of having more opportunities and consequently responsibilities given to her because of a white male boss. Were these really opportunities or simply more work? According to the interviewee, these
were opportunites because her boss had relieved her of more routine
duties. Support and recognition should follow increased responsibilities and workload.

A second concern is that of support and caregiving. As has been
indicated, the role of the mentor as supporter is vital for the protégé
to succeed, especially given the many challenges of being a woman
and a minority. However, one must be cautious when support turns
into patronizing actions that create dependency rather than independence and self-reliance. Relationships of care should be based
upon an understanding of the protégé's needs and aspirations.
Without this basis for mentoring, caregiving is not seen as beneficial

and satisfactory. Ultimately, relationships between mentors and protégés ought to evolve into mature relationships which are more of
equals than superior and subordinate.

A third concern in mentoring relationships for women of color
arises from being under constant scrutiny, especially if they are one
of few persons of color in the organization. Others might ask
whether they are being selected for their experience and expertise or
whether they are in a favored position with a supervisor or mentor.
In response to this concern, mentor Nanette Morrison was clear that
she chose protégé Ellie Carlye because of Ellie's performance and
ability to do the work. Formalizing the arrangement they had as supervisor and subordinate helped to document Ellie's capabilities to
be the designated leader in the curriculum and instruction.

Lastly, those who choose to mentor persons of color should attend to their role as advocates. Empathizing with those who have
been outsiders to predominantly white organizations, these mentors often take on an affirmative action agenda that seeks to promote equal access and opportunity for all. For example, Ramona
Gonzales spoke of her mentor, a white woman who passionately advocated for the representation of all women, and particularly
women of color, in educational leadership throughout the district.
In taking on the role of advocate, mentors need to understanding
the historical, social, and political context of persons of color, which
can be challenging for those who enjoy white privilege, but should
be expected nevertheless.

Protégé Needs

All women aspiring to educational administrative positions
regardless of race and ethnicity require certain skills and opportunities for leadership. However, we identify six needs that are especially important to protégés who are women of color. These needs
address the challenges of being a minority who experiences her difference in the organization as well as in the wider community. There
are tremendous tensions and conflicts being a minority in a white
majority organization as well as being a female in a male-dominated
network. To combat these challenges, our findings suggest that
prospective mentors and women of color who seek to be educational
leaders attend to the following: (a) gaining political savvy; (b) ac-

cessing networks; (c) finding mentors who are similar to their protégés; (d) seeking mentors who are different from their protégés; (e) having more than one mentor; and (f) securing alternative support systems. It should be noted that we make no distinction between protégé wants and actual needs. In some cases, these needs are expressed as desired by the protégés and might not be fulfilled.

Gaining political savvy.   Many respondents spoke of the highly political environment in which schools and school systems exist (protégé Denise Oscar; mentor Martha Ellison; mentor Gabriela Ramirez). For example, protégé Ellie Carlye spoke at length about her school organization as being in a highly volatile situation, affected by the politics of the metropolis and the state, and subjected to much media scrutiny.

Understanding how to maneuver and manage is crucial for an aspirant in educational leadership. From her former superintendent and mentor, Martha Ellison learned the politics of the school district as well as survival skills in "shark-infested" waters where people were not as "honest and above board as you are." For protégés Ellie Carlye and Carol Pierce, having mentors who demonstrated personal integrity and political savvy in highly charged political environments, was encouraging to them. With the politics of the school system and government bureaucracy, educational leaders need political savvy in order to survive and retain a sense of integrity. Protégés and mentors alike commented on the importance of this knowledge in order to succeed in the profession.

Accessing networks.   As women of color, interviewees expressed the need to gain access to networks and organizations. Opening doors and gaining access are probably as important for women aspirants seeking to enter an "old boys network" but as our protégés reported, it is even more important for persons of color who must negotiate entry into a white male-dominated hierarchy.

One African-American administrator benefited from contacts made through a university graduate program. Her advisor, a white male and former school superintendent, aided her in making contacts outside her own urban school district to secure an internship. The protégé was able to gain access to a different school system and was given different opportunities as a result of this access. Similarly, protégé Carol Pierce acknowledged that her white mentor provided what she would not have gained from a mentor who was similar in race, a different perspective and access to the educational system:

> I don't think it's good or bad but I think having Mary Ann as opposed to another African-American gave me some insights, I would not otherwise have and I think it gave me access. (Protégé, Carol Pierce)

Finding mentors who are similar to their protégés.   For the most part, interviewees desired mentors who were similar to themselves in race and gender, noting reasons such as ease of communication, greater affinity, and desire for role models. Given the importance of good communication in fostering effective mentoring relationships, it follows that having similarities like gender and ethnicity would potentially facilitate communication. Protégé Denise Oscar felt the common dialect she shared with her African-American mentor enhanced their relationship. Her comments suggested an ease of being herself. Likewise, Ellie Carlye felt a greater affinity with her African-American supervisor despite the benefits gained from her previous white male mentors.

As African-American principals, Doreen Ballard and Brenda Monroe sought the counsel from mentors like themselves, knowing that their mentors had experienced and endured similar hardships. According to Monroe:

> I knew [mentor] had some experiences that no other principal there had or would have simply because of his color. I knew that and that was important for me. So he and I could talk about things that other principals couldn't talk to me about, because they didn't have the experience, you know, and they would not have been treated in that particular way. (Protégé, Brenda Monroe)

Several mentors spoke of providing guidance to those persons of color irrespective of gender. Mentor Gabriela Ramirez provided guidance to men of color with whom she shared cultural background. The mentorships were aided because "we both knew what ground we were from and knew some of the barriers that occurred and how to get over those barriers." Likewise, mentor Martha Ellison, a deputy superintendent in a large suburban county, was an advocate for minorities in her job. Early in her work as a human relations counselor, she had been an advocate for Affirmative Action. Later as she assumed more prominent positions in the school system, Martha remained an active spokesperson for minorities.

Seeking mentors who are different from their protégés.   What a protégé desires may not always be possible. With few women of color in administrative positions, there may not be the role models or mentors who are similar in race and gender as protégés. Interviewees spoke of seeking mentors who were different from themselves but who were nevertheless invaluable in their career development. Despite a desire to have a Hispanic female as a mentor, Ramona Gonzales spoke of having two Hispanic men in administration who gave her a male perspective. Their connections in the Hispanic community also fostered opportunities for Gonzales.

In one case, the protégé met her mentor because of a racial incident that occurred in her school. Recognizing the empathy felt by the white administrator over the incident, this protégé said: "It would be possible to have a good relationship, but it made all the rest of it so unnecessary, because we met each other under hardship and she was there . . . that helped me put race to the side early" (protégé Denise Oscar). By contrast, protégé Dorothy Hunnicutt was asked to speculate about how she might communicate with her white mentor about a racial matter. Her remarks suggested an openness with which mentor and protégé were able to relate and share with each other.

> I don't think I would have felt uncomfortable sharing something for instance if I had experienced some kind of racism or someone had resisted something and I perceived it was because I was Black. I would have had no problem sharing that with Joan. I may have shared it in a different way with an African-American. I probably would be more attentive a little bit or would have been with Joan. (Protégé, Dorothy Hunnicutt)

Other respondents considered differences other than race or gender that might distinguish a mentor and a protégé. Among those differences were age, education, work experiences, marital or family status, sexual orientation, upbringing in urban, suburban or rural settings, personality, philosophy, and religious affiliation. Often one's experiences can make someone who looks physically different actually be quite similar according to protégé Doreen Ballard.

Conversely, those who share physical similarities may differ in background, philosophies, experiences, and so on. For instance, protégé Denise Oscar who is a fair-skinned African-American, believes that shared culture and common values are more important than skin color in drawing mentor and protégé together.

Having more than one mentor. To counter the difficulty of finding a mentor who might be similar in all aspects, one strategy is to seek several individuals as mentors. For instance, protégé Brenda Monroe recommended that an individual secure more than one mentor, suggesting at least two: "One who looks like you whether it's color or gender or both. The other whose experiences are in the area that you want to move toward. So we need to factor in all of that" (Protégé, Brenda Monroe).

Protégé Ellie Carlye's mentoring relationships also reflected more than one mentor. The two women who were interviewed as her mentors were similar to Ellie; both women were African-Americans who had been assistant superintendents. In addition to these two women, she identified one university professor and one school superintendent, both white males held in high regard in the education system. Ellie credited her current position with the mentoring of these men who guided her, made contacts, and wrote letters of recommendation on her behalf (Protégé, Ellie Carlye).

Securing alternative support systems. Beyond arrangements for formal mentorships in educational organizations and informal relationships between mentor and protégé, many interviewees commented about having alternative supports such as family networks (protégé Doreen Ballard; protégé Vicky Fletcher; protégé Ramona Gonzales; protégé Maria Valdez), personal friends outside of their work organizations (protégé Ramona Gonzales); and religious communities and faith (mentor Martha Ellison, mentor Nanette Morrison, mentor Gabriela Ramirez, protégé Ellie Carlye, protégé Doreen Ballard). In the words of one African-American protégé,

> People can survive when they have a strong support system, someone they can communicate with . . . and my husband. I have a support, although my husband travels a lot. I have a strong support in my husband. . . . Just hold on to the Lord, you know, just pray; and my church. I think my religion has helped me through this. (Protégé, Doreen Ballard)

CONCLUSIONS

Our chapter began with the narrative of a disguised Athene, Greek goddess of wisdom, whose mentoring of Telemachus aided him in all aspects of his young life. Her disguise as the elder man was a useful one because it provided access into a world dominated by men. But after all, Telemachus was a young man, thus appropriately being prepared for his role in such a world. Suppose Athene were to prepare a woman for the world of work? How can the many Athenes in the world of educational administration prepare these women of color?

There are numerous challenges for persons of color attempting to enter into these unknown waters. As non-white minorities in a white majority culture and profession, women of color are often the first or one of only a handful within an organization or community. Many are still viewed as "novelties" though this is changing. Race compounds gender, doubly plaguing women of color who seek leadership positions. It is not expected that the head of the division or school system be a woman of color. Often mistaken as subordinates rather than bosses, they become frustrated and sometimes angry. These misrepresentations can slowly erode their sense of self, causing doubt in their abilities and competencies.

Fortunately, there are many Athenes to guide their career paths. Some of these goddesses are women of color like themselves who have successfully achieved positions in educational leadership and can offer ways to negotiate the difficulties along the path. Other Athenes are different from the protégés but nevertheless are empathic, white women who share their concerns, or male administrators who provide guidance, direction, and access to educational networks and associations by virtue of their power and position. They, too, need to be acknowledged for their work is important and they can take an active role in bringing forth the most talented leaders for our schools.

In advising these many Athenes, our study identified six expressed needs and desires of protégés of color seeking to move into educational administration. First is understanding the highly charged political dynamics of school systems and specifically enabling persons of color to develop the necessary skills to walk the "fine line" as both minorities and women. Along with this understanding comes a second need, gaining access into networks within and outside of school systems. Third, protégés desire and would benefit from mentors who

are similar to themselves. Those who have succeeded in entering educational administration are urged to never forget the pioneering
women on whose shoulders they stand, and to make it a part of their
daily work to reach out and mentor the next generation of women of
color leaders. With few women of color who are in positions of power,
protégés also need the mentoring of those who might be different
from themselves. Relatedly, a fifth need is to have more than one
mentor or guide, at least one female and one person of color preferably. Finally, there is the need for alternative support systems beyond
the formal and informal mentoring arrangements established in educational organizations. In attending to these various needs, we suggest that mentoring can become an activity which allows for diversity
and difference among the leadership in educational organizations
and can promote the advancement of those who might lead differently. Our final chapter draws these threads together, examining our
findings, and suggesting ways that mentoring might be reconstructed
in new ways.

9

Mentoring as a Transforming Activity

Despite the optimism of this book suggesting that women are doing things differently, we need to be aware that the practice of mentoring, steeped in the masculine tradition of reproduction of self, dominant values and attitudes, is likely to reinforce a discourse of educational administration no different from the one we have always had. "The existing mentoring process is designed to perpetuate the status quo" (Cline and Necochea 1997, 142). Just because women now have more opportunity to engage in mentoring does not guarantee that the practice itself will be a transforming one. However, we believe that it can and should be. In this concluding chapter, we outline, first of all, why the traditional model of mentoring can fail women, white and of color, in various ways, and then, we explain why and how it is possible and desirable to use mentoring as a transforming activity. The two dimensions to mentoring that may not serve women well are revealed when we consider mentoring as a power relationship. Both the practice of perpetuating the "Good Old Boys" and the abuse of the position of mentor cautions us against embracing mentoring uncritically.

187

MENTORING AS A POWER RELATIONSHIP

Perpetuating the "Good Old Boys."   Stories throughout the book re-
mind us that, in administration, mentoring practices have been traditionally designed to keep the dominant white male in power. As an
activity, mentoring privileges a few and excludes many. Not even all
white men who wished to reach the upper levels of administration in
K-12 settings have been mentored. And, needless to say, few women,
and, fewer women and men who are also minorities, have been mentored into principalships or superintendencies. Therefore, mentoring
is associated with power, privilege and social stratification.

When the term networking is used, it refers most often to "the
old boys network"—an invisible network of sponsorship whereby
older professionals groom younger versions of themselves for leadership positions. They have typically been white men who promoted
other white men. Women and marginalized others who have gained
entry into these networks are rarely accorded full power and authority within them. They are always included at the invitation of
the men who have been established as the "good old boys." However,
the mentoring and sponsorship that accompany these invitations
cannot be disregarded lightly. Such mentoring determines access to
principalships and superintendencies. Yet, to participate, even with
the best intentions, often means to perpetuate this highly exclusive
process.

Thus, women and minorities are caught in a dilemma. Traditional mentoring may have been their only means to enter the
ranks of administration, but once they are within the network, how
do they keep themselves from succumbing to the same attitudes and
beliefs that discriminate against so many others like them? Certainly, there are African-American, Asian-American, Hispanic and
other networks out there that engage in the same practices. It is not
only the privileging that is based on race, class, ethnicity, or sexual
orientation that is at fault here. Equally insidious is the notion of advantage that is reserved only for those who are part of the network—
whatever network. The power to include or exclude potential
administrators, to reward or punish them, lies not in the hands of individuals within the networks. As Michel Foucault (1980) argues:

> Power must be analyzed as something which circulates, or
> rather as something which only functions in the form of a
> chain. It is never localized here or there, never in anybody's

hands. . . . Power is employed and exercised through a net-
like organization (p. 98).

Power is felt in the effects of participating in the network and in
the outcomes of the activities that sustain it. A solution that some
women suggest is to organize a parallel network of women administrators as more women reach the superintendency and serve on
school boards. However, this will simply reproduce, in other forms,
the privilege of networking. There will still be those who are in and
those who are out. It does not address the weakness of having to engage in networking and sponsorship in order to enter and move
through the ranks of educational administration.

Abusing the position of mentor.   When mentoring is viewed as a relationship of power, there are other conditions of which women,
white and of color, need to be aware. Because mentoring often grows
out of a supervisory relationship, there is the potential for the mentor to abuse the power that comes with mentoring. The invitational
aspect of mentoring puts protégés at a disadvantage particularly if
they feel the mentor is exploiting their services or exhausting them.
While there were relatively few instances where the women in the
study felt truly exploited, some protégés spoke of being "worn out" or
"driven too hard." In these cases, too many extra "opportunities" or
duties were assigned and mentors, too often, relied heavily on the
protégé when others were equally capable and qualified. In addition,
a protégé's gender and race can exacerbate the situation since traditionally women and people of color have served as subordinates to
white men.

In the breakdown of professional administrator / teacher or boss /
employee relationships that have not been elevated to the level of
mentor / protégé, there are some possibilities for the subordinate to
extricate herself. There are voluntary transfers, for instance, reas-
signments, appeals to a higher authority and in the last resort, of
course, resignation. However, although a protégé still has recourse
to all of these solutions, the situation is much more difficult once the
privilege of mentoring has been extended. For the same reasons as
cited above, because traditional mentoring is associated with favor
and promise, protégés risk exclusion and punishment if they reject
the patronage of someone who has influence in the system.
Particularly for a novice, being mentored adds another dimension to
a hierarchical relationship that is already a relationship of power.

Yet, protégés are also vulnerable in situations where their mentors are not their immediate supervisors. There were several cases where the mentor held a prominent position in the district but did not directly supervise the protégé—examples include an assistant superintendent mentoring an assistant principal or a superintendent mentoring a teacher. Protégés who experienced this spoke of an ambiguity with respect to power and authority that surrounds such a relationship. In one instance, the protégé experienced great discomfort. She reported to the director of secondary schools who in turn reported to her mentor, the associate superintendent. When the director was less attentive to her needs than she felt he should be, she was torn between two options. Should she approach her mentor about this situation? Should she talk more freely with the director and risk a poor performance evaluation? These were possible courses of action for her to take. Although she believed in going through the correct channels, she also felt that she would not hold back from talking to her mentor if the need arose. However, since supervisors do not like subordinates to go over their head, this latter course of action brings added risk. Therefore, it is clear that while traditional models of mentoring have served many well, these models also have built-in flaws that may heighten the difficulties women, white and of color, face. Nevertheless, rather than advocating the abandonment of mentoring, we encourage using its formidable power to transform educational administration itself. The key lies in the fact that it is a relation of power which has the potential to change people's lives in a positive sense. One way to see this is to contrast the position of mentor and protégé.

MENTOR VERSUS PROTÉGÉ

One of the major strengths of this study is that because we have drawn upon perspectives of both members of a pair, we have had the opportunity to crosscheck members' impressions. In numerous instances, both members of a particular pair recollected similar events, (unprompted) and many interpreted incidents similarly. At the same time, there were some telling differences in the way one member of the pair perceived the same event. Nevertheless, despite some tensions and conflicts both members of the pair regarded the relationship as highly significant in their professional lives. It was obvious to both members of the pair how vital the mentoring process was for the protégé to move into a position more powerful than the one she had previously held. To recognize the potential of mentoring as a transforming activity, perhaps the most valuable aspect of studying pairs is that we get a clear sense of what mentoring is like from the different positions of mentor and protégé. As mentioned, all the participants could and did speak from both positions when they discussed general issues, but they spoke most often from one position in a particular relationship. The notion that mentoring can be instrumental in redefining one's subject-position is most helpful here.

Mentoring as Offering Different Subject Positions in Administration

From a feminist poststructuralist viewpoint, to focus on the idea of subject position, brings certain insights. Feminist poststructuralism, as C. Capper, 1993, B. Davies, 1994, and C. Weedon, 1997 argue, explains the idea of subjectivity. Immersed in different discourses, we are all subjectified by those discourses according to how the discourse molds our minds, bodies, and emotions. Thus, our sense of self and our expectations of what we can achieve are shaped according to the rules and regulations of the discourse. There are various subject positions available to us in any given discourse, but they are gendered positions and race appropriate ones. In other words, each discourse offers ways of being that are appropriate for men and other ways of being that are appropriate for women who are subjects of that discourse. None of these is fixed; subject positions are constantly being re-negotiated. But, the parameters within which they can be re-negotiated are determined by the discourse.

White, middle-class males have traditionally dominated the discourse of educational administration. Whereas individual women have periodically been successful, Ella Flagg Young, for instance, the numbers clearly indicate that women are still positioned less powerfully in the discourse. One of the ways to perpetuate the attitudes and beliefs that constitute the dominant discourse is to pass them on through mentoring. In the past, men have most often mentored other men into educational administration. They have also mentored some women who share their traditional values and attitudes. Mentoring like-minded others has always been an effective means of reinforcing the dominant discourse. It ensures continuity of ideas and ways of thinking that keeps those who do not share the dominant values at the margins of the discourse. As R. Hall and B. Sandler (1983) put it, "Members of professional . . . systems tend to choose persons like themselves as protégés—but to overlook (or actively exclude) newcomers who are 'different'" (p. 2, quotation marks and parentheses in the original). Z. Cline and J. Necochea (1997) reinforce the point from another angle: ". . . individuals who are predisposed to different philosophies and attitudes from the referent group often self-select not to participate in the process of becoming an administrator" (p. 150).

For all the women in the study who did choose to participate in the process of becoming an administrator, it is easy to imagine there are many others out there who might not have liked the models offered or who might not have found a helpful mentor. Race and gender issues certainly complicate this. As explained in chapter 8, women of color often feel the need to disguise who they really are in order to become administrators in predominantly white settings. Not only are women, white and of color, sometimes asked to lead in ways that are not comfortable, they are also only encouraged to aspire to positions that are traditionally open to women in administration, supporting roles such as assistant principal, administrative assistant, coordinator of curriculum, and assistant superintendent. The administrative ranks held by women are relatively low and the range of leadership styles is curtailed by expectations influenced by gender and race.

What is interesting about women being mentored into educational administration is that the activity offers women access to a different kind of subject position in the discourse. Looking at it from a historical viewpoint, simply gaining access to administration has provided women educators the means of being different; that is, becoming principals rather than teachers, or becoming superintendents rather than assistant superintendents. However, more important now is that women's entry and continuing presence in administration offer women the possibility to renegotiate the terms under which women are subjectified as administrators. This is how mentoring can transform educational leadership. Mentoring can achieve this ". . . in destroying the sexual stereotypes and myths . . . in helping women to become more independent, self-determining people, in offering an alternative view of a intellectual discipline, and / or in conveying a more radical view of the society and the potential of feminist action to change its underlying structure" (Fisher 1982, 57).

In this study, we have heard many women speak of holding their own ground and leading in ways that differ from traditional examples. Embedded in their discussions of how they lead and what they admired in a mentor or protégé, many participants highlighted collaboration, participatory leadership, community building, an ethic of care and an unwavering focus on teaching and learning. They celebrated a diversity of ideas and did not shy away from dissensus. There are women principals, women superintendents, and women who aspire to the superintendency who are not limited by the formerly constricting notion of women in educational administration. They are seeking influential posts instead of remaining in the background.

RE-SHAPING EDUCATIONAL LEADERSHIP
OR COLORING OUTSIDE THE LINES

In a mentoring relationship, a protégé is learning to reposition herself with the help and guidance of a mentor who can transform practice if she uses the opportunity as we and others suggest (see also Cline and Necochea 1997; Stalker 1994). Indeed, from a feminist poststructuralist viewpoint, re-positioning is often seen as a process that is difficult to achieve without help. While those who occupy a subordinate position in a discourse can and do resist the power of the discourse in order to gain more access to it, without support, those efforts of resistance are often less than successful. Therefore mentoring provides the means by which individuals who wish to lead differently can be successful. Particularly, informal mentoring practices like those described in the study provide a structural means of assisting others to reposition themselves.

One can argue that simply getting more women into educational administration is a desirable goal in and of itself. However, more important are the possibilities for women to lead differently from the ways they have been encouraged to lead by the traditional discourse. Along with different subject positions in a discourse comes the power to reshape the discourse itself. The study suggests efforts on the part of mentors and protégés to create a new discourse, what we have called coloring "outside the lines" in this book. Our participants reveal attitudes and beliefs that promise to have a major impact on leadership in the future, thus changing the image of educational administration, as outlined in the introduction. Because mentoring is

so powerful, the process encourages the transference of highly regarded values and attitudes. For instance, in observing and inter-
acting with their mentor or protégé many women identified
leadership priorities that they, too, embraced:

> [Marsha] was very much a hands-on principal, . . . very
> much a teacher first, and that's what I believe in. . . . Her
> way of solving problems was to get people together, and
> have them talk about what happened. (Protégé, Sara
> Murphy)

> [I learned] . . . Joan's . . . way of running a meeting, . . . be-
> ing sure that people left feeling that they had gotten some-
> thing done there, but yet giving people enough freedom so
> they felt like they could breathe. (Protégé, Dorothy
> Hunnicutt)

> Brenda believes in cooperative relationships, team kinds of
> decision-making. . . . I think she's comfortable with that ver-
> sus the talk-down kind of leadership. So the fact that I was
> that way and wanting to sort of share the decision-making
> and that type of thing, she felt comfortable with that.
> (Mentor Pam Egan).

The frequency of comments like these suggests that these are the
kinds of leadership approaches that will be reinforced and passed on
to the next generation of educational leaders.

Fundamentally, in this study, mentors as leaders were admired
for their ability to share freely knowledge and information that
would benefit protégés. In other words, this new discourse on leadership includes openness and outreach. Leadership is associated
firmly with the building of relationships. Contrary to beliefs found
in earlier studies, many women in this study were capable of promoting other women in an encouraging and noncompetitive environment. Although mentors had many and various motives for
choosing and training protégés, all were primarily focused on what
was good for the protégé herself. Evidence of unselfish caring surfaced in many of the relationships. Mentors cared that their protégés were successful professionally but also personally. In
response, protégés cared deeply about mentors and did not want to
let them down.

When translated into leadership practices, attitudes and beliefs such as these that have emerged through mentoring promise to re-shape the discourse of educational administration. As outlined ear-lier, success in administration, in the past, was often associated with exclusivity and privilege. In contrast, the potential of wider rela-tionships that can develop in an atmosphere of freely shared knowl-edge and information is exciting. In our study, both mentors and protégés reported benefiting from these relationships which empha-sized connectedness and caring. Moreover, protégés were engaged in other mentoring relationships with their own protégés. Several of these relationships emerged from the wish to give back to others what protégés had enjoyed in their mentoring pairs. For example:

> Mary Ann just took it upon herself to begin to lead me this way and it's one of the most valuable experiences I've had in my lifetime. . . . I've had some very strong women . . . that have supported me, that have led me down this path, which is why I try to give that back . . . as I said in my faculty meet-ings—I always say it and I tell the men on the faculty, I say, "I'm not trying to exclude you, but I have to say I'm very sup-portive of women. . . . it's not as easy for them black or white." (Protégé, Carol Pierce)

> [I mentor others] because it's the duty of every educator to give something back or to make their profession better. . . . I have said a hundred times if it weren't for Sarah I don't be-lieve I would be here today where I am [principal]. I said if I ever got a job or position where I could do for someone else what Sarah did for me—if nothing else, it would be my trib-ute to her, to say thank you. (Protégé, Bobbi Reeves)

THE VALUE OF INTERDEPENDENCE

In general, the capacity to enter into caring relationships with various others and to maintain them over time has not been tradi-tionally valued in educational leadership. The exceptions, of course, have been those relatively few mentoring relationships that have re-produced the status quo. On the contrary, administrators are often encouraged to keep their distance from others and to avoid the car-ing, connected relationships that we are advocating in this book.

This view of the administrator as distant professional is reflective of the traditional search for autonomy and independence that much of the adult growth and development literature supports. Johnsrud (1991) points out that it is essentially a male model of maturity. Drawing on R. Kegan (1982) and C. Gilligan (1993), L. K. Johnsrud (1991) argues: "Mentoring needs to be explored within a conceptual framework that moves beyond male-oriented models of adult development and encompasses values of affiliation, caring and interdependence" (p. 10). Her point is based on the idea that "mentoring has been viewed as a means to the goal of individuation; there has been no recognition of a maturity that moves beyond autonomy" (p. 9). She quotes Kegan (1982) who "describes growth as an evolving balance between two yearnings: the yearning to be independent and autonomous and the yearning to be included and connected" (p. 9).

The kind of mentoring that has been described in this book reveals that many mentors and protégés achieved interdependence. As outlined in chapter 4, many of the relationships evolved from the early stage of initiation and establishment to the maintenance stage. In order for this development to occur, protégés gained their independence from their mentors. They became educational administrators in their own right. Protégés who became assistant principal or central office administrator illustrated this. However, the final stage of interdependence that Johnsrud advocates eludes some participants in mentoring relationships. Not all relationships move into the maintenance stage.

Good mentoring as described in chapter 3 provides the environment within which protégés can move from being dependent to becoming independent. If the purposes of mentoring are fulfilled, the protégé emerges skilled and confident, ready to assume a different subject position in the discourse—for example, as assistant principal rather than teacher, or as superintendent who is comfortable with being a woman and being superintendent. It is through the mentoring process that the protégé negotiates a new subject position. If the mentoring has truly served the needs of the protégé, the protégé has not only moved up the ranks in administration, but she has also found a way to lead from her new rank that reflects her own philosophies and convictions. She has not been forced to disguise herself or fit into a gendered or racially acceptable notion of leader.

Beyond independence, then, is the possibility for interdependence, which comes from the evolved, collegial relationships that many participants reported. To value interdependence is to acknowledge the merit of being in relationship with others. It is to appreciate the synergy that flows from connecting with others. This stage allows individuals to move freely between mentor positions and protégé positions and ultimately to support each other in collegiality. This is the real promise of mentoring women into educational administration. If it is undertaken the way it is reported here, it cannot help but shape the kind of leader the protégé becomes. The study reveals that the kind of person who mentors women already demonstrates the power of being connected. The notion of giving back spins a web of relationships across districts. This suggests that the women administrators who emerge from the process will have a personal stake in remaining in relationship— not only with those who initiated the relationships, but also with others whom they can, in turn, benefit.

CHALLENGES

The question is how can women mentor collaboratively and yet still reap the benefits of positioning themselves more powerfully in the discourse. To avoid the dangers of reinforcing the status quo, mentoring needs to look more like wide pockets of support rather than narrow inner circles of preference. As the data inform us, traditionally, males mentored or sponsored like-minded males sometimes regardless of the quality of their leadership. Networks were in place that privileged those with the dominant attitudes and values. These same networks served to exclude those who thought and behaved differently. They regulated the gendered subject positions available to women who were mostly encouraged to remain in teaching. If women wished to pursue leadership, the networks demanded that women adopt the dominant beliefs but not male behaviors. Women were encouraged to lead enough like a man to gain approval within the networks. However, for many women this conflicted with who they were as women. Therefore the kind of mentoring we advocate in this book, has to focus on renegotiating what leadership looks like for women particularly, but also for men who wish to lead differently.

We argue that a shift in values towards doing what is best for all children, leading through others, demonstrating real attempts at collaboration with stakeholders not currently given a voice should be reinforced through mentoring practices. The practices themselves also need expanding. Theory guides our conception of how to bring about this change. Feminist poststructuralism helps us to understand the established meanings, values and power relations in the discourse of educational administration (Weedon 1997). This is important because it helps us to understand "where they come from, whose interests they support, how they maintain sovereignty and where they are susceptible to specific pressures for change" (p. 169). It is in the possibilities for mentoring that pressure for change can be applied. Mentors by virtue of their mode of subjectivity in the discourse, can influence who contributes to the development of educational administration. We approach this transformation, first, from the viewpoint of how to mentor and how to be a protégé, or how to attract mentoring.

How mentors can be transformers.   First, as transformers, mentors are charged with seeking leadership in individuals who might be different from themselves and to engage in mentoring that values and does not annihilate difference. For instance, white women and men have much to learn from mentoring women and men of color. It is important for mentors to recognize the potential for leadership in others who may not imagine themselves as future leaders. Leadership can be demonstrated variously and we encourage mentors to choose leaders whose potential might be expressed in forms other than the traditional ones. Mentors should care for their protégés inasmuch as they must primarily serve protégés' needs as the protégés define them.

Second, we also favor a more collaborative structure than the one-on-one which tends to be too limiting and exclusive. Recall protégé Diane Lynch's reaction when her mentor left the district: "I had a real sense of loss. My rock was gone." While it is helpful to have close one-on-one mentoring relationships, if this comes at the cost of exclusion from necessary broader collaborations and connections it can be counterproductive for women in the long run. Therefore, we want to see mentors as organizers of professional webs or support systems. We urge them to gather together several women to offer information and know-how that will provide women with access to the system. Lunch sessions, after hours get togethers and the like allow women to discuss informally work related structures that shape their development in the organization. Such work groups can be instrumental in providing women with inside knowledge and opportunities for career advancement. Instead of doing this for only one or two individuals in an organization, we envision a more widespread attempt to inform as many women as possible of the means by which they can reposition themselves in education.

Some examples are mentioned in the literature (see The Career Cooperative in Hall and Sandler 1983, 9). Geared toward higher education, R. Hall and B. Sandler also advocate various campus groups who provide junior faculty with information. Ideas include: workshops, growth contracts, designating faculty for career counseling responsibilities, small group sessions, and forming networks and alliances both within the organization and across region and state. Their focus also includes group mentoring to ensure that classified employees have access to the kinds of information about advancement that mentors often provide (p. 11). All of these ideas can be adapted for K-12 settings.

Third, we encourage educators whose leadership is founded on an ethic of care to mentor others actively. Caring in itself has the power to transform educational leadership. Some examples follow: (a) Mentors can be sensitive to and aware of a woman's potential and aspirations. By listening to her conflicts and struggles as she considers what the entry into a higher level position in educational leadership is going to mean for her both personally and professionally, mentors can do much to allay fears, provide encouragement and promote growth. (b) Together, mentors and protégés can purposively work out a plan for career development as well as personal growth. Career development goals might include the specific opportunities outlined in chapter 4. Whole person development might include professional advice and professional friendship. Chapters 5 and 8 clearly show how women's movement into educational leadership, particularly for women of color, is fraught with conflicts and challenges that can best be addressed by mentoring that is *for* women. Such mentoring might be characterized by the caring mentoring relationships and leadership shown in chapter 6 and 7. (c) Reciprocity is also key to caregiving relationships, not in the sense of quid pro quo, but rather in that the relationship is founded on mutual respect. Wisdom is being shared by both mentor and protégé. The protégé is teaching the mentor to see in new ways, even while she is benefiting from the mentor's counsel.

How protégés can be transformers.   Women protégés must actively seek mentors who demonstrate willingness and the necessary expertise to guide them effectively. They should identify several mentors who can offer different kinds of leadership and competence.

Having identified several mentors, protégés can cultivate mentoring efforts in their mentors through communication and showing a willingness to learn from their mentor. We recommend that protégés make themselves known to potential mentors. Mentors in this study spoke highly of those who were proactive in seeking advice and volunteering their leadership skills to work for the district. In addition, once a relationship of trust has developed, protégés with their own unique ways of leading can have a positive effect on mentors' own practices. Because it is a relationship of mutual respect, mentors often benefit from the new ideas and alternative approaches that protégés bring to situations.

Women protégés also need to let go of relationships that are not benefiting them. Instead of trying harder at the same difficult relationship in order to make that particular relationship work, women are encouraged to move on from unhelpful relationships that do not serve their needs. This does not mean that difficult situations and relationships are to be avoided. We often learn the most in situations of conflict and cognitive dissonance. It does mean that simply trying harder at a relationship that is unhelpful is not productive. It is better to move on, learn from the mistakes, and try to establish a better relationship with someone who is open to the protégé's leadership potential.

Protégés are also encouraged to become their own mentors in a sense. By this is meant that protégés can believe in themselves, and take some initiative to seek out difficult assignments and show their strengths and commitments. By personally mentoring oneself, at the same time as actively seeking mentors, a woman is better positioned to gain the advocacy of others. One's belief in oneself as a leader, and the aspiration to become a leader in one's own style, will become apparent to others. Mentors will come to see that the protégé is worthy of the investment of time and energy that mentoring requires. Of course this self-mentoring or care for oneself will only work as long as it is part of a way of leading that also includes relating to others and the wider web of interconnections that are at the heart of education.

Implications for Administrator Preparation Programs

For those of us involved in principal and superintendent preparation programs across the country, this study suggests that we include explicitly the mentoring of women and women of color in our classes. The nature of mentoring, its power and privilege need to be made clear. First of all, administrative aspirants in these courses, men and women, need to hear how mentoring is currently conducted, for what purposes it is practiced and what particular circumstances shape the experiences for white women and women of color. Our study clearly shows women of color have special mentoring needs, and this needs to be acknowledged. What must also be acknowledged, as we point out in chapter 8, is that just as the female gender does not reduce all women to sameness, nor does the experience of color suggest that any two individuals of color will have the same stories. The narratives in this book need to be told and, more important, the students in the classes must be encouraged to tell the stories of their own lives. Teachers and administrators all have experiences of mentoring, either professional or personal, that can help to define it as an activity and give it meaning.

Second, new ways of mentoring as suggested here, need to be explored. Many administrator preparation programs require formal internships that include some of the group mentoring processes that have been discussed. University professors mentor interns in many of the specific areas that our mentors covered in chapter 3 and 4 for instance. Educational administration students are encouraged to take on as many leadership opportunities as possible, chair committees, write memos, present to the school board, lead staff development workshops, and so on. Getting visibility will aid the prospective administrator in getting a job. As instructors, we need to reinforce all these kinds of mentoring, but at the same time we also need to advocate their continued use after the intern is successful in his or her first assistant principalship or assistant superintendency. Once those individuals become familiar with their new systems, or once they are comfortable as new administrators in their old systems, they need to mentor others in the same activities—particularly administrative aspirants who are women. Assistant superintendents are positioned very well for such group interaction. Lunch time sessions can be focused on providing information for "Moving into the Principalship in _____ County," for instance, or "Women's Ways of Leading" or "Alternative Approaches to the Superintendency." Above all, in our university classes, we need to teach mentoring as a virtue, mentoring that includes all potential aspirants in information giving that is free and open.

In advocating for mentoring networks and collaboratives, how can we ensure that the advantages of the one-on-one are included?

Women do benefit from the individualized attention that mentoring offers as the study has shown. Over and over again, we heard how encouraging mentors were of their protégés. A mentor's belief in the potential of a protégé, particularly when the protégé has not recognized these capacities in herself seems to have been especially powerful. Can the group processes advocated here and in other literature provide the same benefits?

Ultimately the most promising mentoring model seems to be a combination of one-on-one and general group mentoring opportunities. However, Johnsrud (1991) makes the point that in the academic setting at least, "to call for a collaborative, collegial relationship from the onset of the mentoring relationship is not realistic. Genuinely collaborative, interdependent work requires a level of maturity that may not be present in the early stages of the relationship" (p. 9). Coupled with that there are other reasons that might also make the notion of true collegial, collaborative relationships unrealistic. For instance, the supervisor / supervisee element that is present in most mentoring relationships at the beginning can hinder it. Indeed many bosses do not mentor and many administrative aspirants do not know how to avail themselves of potential opportunities. Therefore we must make an effort to teach men and women how to mentor women and we must teach women how to gain mentors.

Third, we have argued in this book that quality mentoring is leadership. The capacity to form meaningful relationships centered on the needs of others; the outreach and unselfish dissemination of information, and the willingness to care characterize good leaders. Stripped of its exclusivity, mentoring illustrates team building and participation. Mentors and protégés, who have experienced the full satisfaction of reaching the stage of interdependence, recognize the value of being connected with others. Interdependence promotes respectful collaboration.

The biggest task for those of us in preparation programs is to foster the appreciation of leadership ideas and approaches that challenge tradition. This is why we must work hard to include as many diverse others in educational administration as possible. Our traditional leadership practices and beliefs have not served all children well. What we propose here is a heightened awareness on the part of women and men who are in the field of educational administration in K-12 settings to the desirability of mentoring diverse others into the field. We also urge that those aspiring to educational administration recognize the value of mentoring, to be open to mentoring, and actively choose to be mentored by others. Our focus has been particularly on women, white and of color, although we are aware that diversity is expressed in many different ways.

In the end, quality mentoring focused on the needs of the individual offers the possibility for women to be administrators and leaders in their own right. They no longer have to be "women administrators" or "African-American administrators" or "Hispanic administrators" occupying a gendered and / or racially appropriate subject position that the discourse has reserved for them. Ultimately we hope to see educational leadership freed from its association with gender and color. That is to say that educational leaders will be judged on how good they are for all children, not on whether they are white or of color, or whether they are men or women.

Appendix A

Description of Mentoring Pairs

Washington Sample

1. *Mentor*   Dr. Jeff Stewart, Assistant Superintendent. White male
   Protégé   Dr. Susan Rembert, Assistant Principal, Middle
School. White female.

Mentor and protégé work in the same school district. The relation
ship is supervisory, but one step removed—Assistant Superintendent with Assistant Principal. Mentor initiated relationship. Protégé
established a close relationship with her mentor right from the start
when she was hired into the district as assistant principal. "He established that . . . I have access to a person that nobody seems to
have access to, not even the principal." He has been "very candid,
giving a behind closed doors discussion of all the staff and faculty at
my school." Mentor seems to trust protégé and values her perspective on the school, offering constant support, "much more real than
the faults mentorship or the kind that you talk when you're assigned
and you do what you feel like you have to. This is different. This is
very real." Dr. Rembert relies on her mentor for feedback on how
she's doing, and for guidance on those issues to which she should be
paying attention.

2. *Mentor*   Dr. Pat Sorensen, Principal, Elementary. White female.
   Protégé   Eileen Hales, Central Office Reading Specialist.
               White female.

Currently both mentor and protégé work in same school district, but fifteen years professional relationship in different settings. The relationship is non-supervisory, although Eileen Hales is doing an internship on the principalship, and she requested to work with Dr. Sorensen. Protégé initiated the relationship, although very mutual. The women first met as mothers: "We had children the same age and so I watched her then as an interested mother and PTA person. Then she had students in my classroom when she supervised student teachers at [name] University, so I knew her then as a student teaching supervisor. And when she was applying to be a principal, I was her greatest fan at Giles. However, the selection committee elected to have someone there who would make them more comfortable, because they could tell she was a mover / groover kind of person. So they picked a man that they thought would leave them alone to do things in the old way." Now that Dr. Sorensen is a principal, Eileen is trying to learn as much as possible from her mentor because she intends to move from central office into the elementary principalship, even though secondary teaching is her experience. A great deal of admiration and respect exists on both sides, over many years, but the caring of the mentoring relationship differs to that of intimate personal friendship: "We really only talk about, when we get together, well how are our children, that kind of thing first, but then she's very professional. I don't think it's ever been very personal, and when she says things I need to do, I always think that's professional, not personal."

3. *Mentor*   Dr. Les Johnson, Superintendent. Hispanic male.
   Protégé   Dr. Meredith Koval, Assistant Superintendent. White
               female.

Mentor and protégé currently work in different school districts, although the relationship was formerly supervisory in same school district. Protégé initiated this thirteen year relationship, but it has been mutually established. Protégé has two male mentors who have been mentoring her for the last 13–15 years. One mentor, (white male superintendent well-known in the state) has retired and is still mentoring her. He was the high school principal who valued instruction when the protégé was the trainer for the district; he hired her as a secondary assistant principal when it was unpopular to put women in these roles. She was thirty-nine years old when she first went into administration and her mentor was fifteen years older. Dr. Johnson, an Hispanic male, her primary mentor, is currently a superintendent in a different school district. He was formerly the assistant superintendent in Meredith's school district, and he had the responsibility for the professional development of principals. Relationships with both men are professional— of respect and admiration for their work and their administrative skills. "I don't mix personal and professional relationships," she says. However, the retired administrator, who is still a mentor, became a family friend when he retired. "My mentor and I became friends when he retired, and he moved, and then we made a point to drop by or they'd come by and see us when they were here and then my husband and he became kind of golfing friends. So then our friendship developed later. But I'm more comfortable keeping those things separate." Protégé Meredith Koval is also mentoring principals herself.

4. Mentor   Dr. Les Johnson, Superintendent. Hispanic male.
Protégé   Diane Lynch, Principal, Elementary School. White female.

Both mentor and protégé are presently in different school districts, with an eight year, non-supervisory relationship; formerly they were in same school district and in a supervisory relationship. Protégé initiated relationship, although mutually established. Protégé has had, and continues to have, a number of mentors, but Dr. Johnson is the most prominent and important one to her. Her first mentor was a white male who was her principal when she was a teacher. The next mentor was a white male professor who worked with her while she was working on her master's degree. Another important mentor in her view is her husband, "because any woman who goes into a position like a principalship or superintendency leadership role, needs a support network of some type and mine was my husband and continues to be." Also a helpful mentor was a white woman superintendent who supervised her for her principal internship and encouraged her to take an administrative role in a larger district: "You are very capable of being in a larger district; look at your background." And when Diane took her very first principalship her mentor became Dr. Johnson, an Hispanic male, "who as assistant superintendent was in charge of principals; he set very high expectations for his principals; met with me weekly, challenged me . . . he would say trust the process, you can do this." Protégé Diane Lynch is also mentoring two principals.

5. *Mentor*   Marcia Francis, Principal, Elementary School. White female.
    Protégé Rene Miles, Assistant Principal. Hispanic female.

Mentor and protégé work in same school district, but at different schools. They have had a five year relationship, non-supervisory, however it was established initially as a supervisory relationship when the protégé was mentor's assistant principal. Mentor initiated the relationship. Protégé was selected by mentor as her vice principal when mentor was principal of a largely Hispanic elementary school and, as she explained, she "needed an Hispanic vice principal who knew the community well and could speak the language fluently." Mentor is now principal of a different school, with a predominantly working-class, Hispanic population. Mentor sees herself becoming a superintendent—having been a principal for fifteen years. Her current mentor is her white male superintendent. Protégé admires mentor because of her professionalism and ability to separate the personal and the professional: "I have told her many times that I think that she is so good at what she does, because she leaves the personal piece out of the job. It is all professional and she is very careful about not putting in that personal piece. And I think what makes her so successful is that she goes by the book; if this is the discipline handbook, if this is what it says then this is what we go by and it is always like that. There is nothing different. You can always count on the same procedure happening."

6. *Mentor*   Gabriela Ramirez, Community College Professor. Hispanic Female.
    Protégé Leticia Martinez, Assistant Principal. Hispanic Female.

This is a non-supervisory relationship, spanning eight years. "We kind of identified with each other" (Mentor, Gabriela Ramirez). Both are Hispanic-American and first generation college, from working-class families. "We were actually on a bus trip to Westside College and so we had two-and-a-half hours of talk at that time. I was very much advocating that my daughter go into college and she was very much advocating her daughter to go to college. That's how we met initially, as mothers concerned for our children, particularly girls. She had a daughter, I had a daughter the same age, in the same classes, so as mothers we connected, and then we developed some friendship." Mentor met Leticia Martinez when she hadn't even finished high school, and she was just a "Mom." Mentor encouraged her to finish her GED which she did "in no time flat," and then went on to "go for her teaching credential," and the mentoring has continued from there. Relationship is both personal and professional.

7. *Mentor*   Joyce Stearns, President of Education Association. White female.

   Protégé   Lesley Kinnard, Union Leader / Teacher. White female.

Mentor initiated the relationship and it has continued for four years in the same school district in a non-supervisory capacity. "Philosophically we're always on the same page." Mentor cultivated relationship with protégé. The professional relationship "grew out of friendship. Friendship was always the main factor." Mentor has administrative credentials and feels she could be a principal or superintendent. She has chosen to be a union president instead, however, in order to have extra days off in summer and more time off each day (shorter hours) to spend more time with her children, and she feels that the role of teacher-leader can be a very powerful and influential one. "I got both administrators fired at K school the year I was there. They hadn't done their evaluations in a long time so it was pretty easy." Protégé and mentor are friends. It was also a conscious decision of the mentor to cultivate that friendship, because she wants her protégé to learn the skills of union leadership. "If you're a good leader you try to get a group of strong leaders under you that can then take over when you're gone and I have a group like that. There is one person in particular that I am mentoring who is my colleague and my age, but hasn't engaged in the politics I have; she hasn't been as active in some of the things I have. But I see that she has very high integrity and she is very bright and is willing to serve. She wants to learn."

8. *Mentor*   Othene Kirkland, Retired Principal. African-American female.

   Protégé   Doreen Ballard, Principal, Elementary School. African-American female.

The relationship was initiated in same school district, in a non-supervisory capacity. Mentor helped protégé get her first principalship. Twelve years of mentoring, although the women have known each other for over sixteen years. The mentoring relationship includes friendship, combined with professional intent and engagement. Both were African-American women principals in a school district with very few minorities. Mentor coached protégé through all the barriers. Protégé feels she is having an easier time than her predecessor, because she has gone to the administration—in particular the white female area director, and asked for support. So even though Dr. Clausen, the white female area director, is her supervisor, it is Mrs. Othene Kirkland, her longtime fellow principal (now retired) who is her "real mentor." Protégé also feels the support of her church, her husband and her "young kids who are always happy and busy." Therefore she feels she can't let professional challenges weigh her down—"can't dwell on them." Mentor is always encouraging and supportive, and was there through the crucial period of getting the principalship. She coached her through the process, and gave invaluable advice both in getting the job and keeping it. Protégé met mentor in the same church. "We were also in the same organization like a sorority together. We were in the same organizations and that's how I got to know her."

9. *Mentor*   Dr. Barbara Hansen, Former Director of Special Programs, now at law school. White female.
   Protégé   Maria Valdez, Director, Special Programs, Elementary. Hispanic female.

Mentor initiated the relationship which has lasted for twelve years. Non-supervisory relationship, mentor is no longer in school administration (went back to law school), but mentor initially hired her, and was her supervisor for a number of years. Protégé, an Hispanic woman, now has the former job of her mentor (Central Office Director). Protégé has been at the district administrator level for six years, and she came to the district without a degree. Maria Valdez had completed three years in college in California, and needed another two years. She began work as a bilingual aide, hired by her mentor. Her mentor was able to garner district financial support to support her through the teaching certificate, and always pushed her to the next step. Mentor would model and be "gracious" in her criticism, "pushing" her to the next level, and urging her to mentor and support others.

10. *Mentor*   Dr. Carlos Domingos, Dean of Community College. Hispanic male.
    Protégé   Ramona Gonzales, Director of Special Programs, Secondary. Hispanic female.

Protégé initiated the relationship, with mutual admiration described as the "glue" for this seven year relationship, which is non-supervisory. Protégé has had, and continues to have a number of mentors and considers: "It's hard for me to divide my mentors from personal and professional because I think I see them one and the same." Ramona's first mentor was a professor in college who was a former superintendent, an Hispanic male, who convinced her to go into educational administration. In her words, he said, "You need to go into administration. And I'll tell you one reason." He said, "I'm very selective who I want in the program, but when we're in class and you speak, you have that voice that tells people to listen to you." I'll always remember that, because I respected him so much; I never saw myself as a true leader until he said that." Another mentor is Dr. Barbara Hansen, a white woman, former director, [name] school district, who is now in law school and also is mentor to Maria Valdez. Her other mentor is her brother-in-law, an Hispanic male who is an administrator within her district. He was instrumental in getting her to move to the area from New Mexico. Her main mentor is the Dean of the Community College in her district, Dr. Carlos Domingos, an Hispanic male: "I use him a lot for mentoring in education as well as mentoring me in my community relations approach to the community, because I see that he has been successful in that and I admire that in him. So he's been really helpful. I'll just call him and run things by him, ask what do you think . . . and he'll call me as well to say what do you think of this? So it was a mentor / mentee role and now it's become more equalized, maybe. I would like to think so anyway." Mentor coaches and guides her through decisions, and assists her to make wise decisions. He knows everyone in the community and knows where the power is and who she should be including in decisions. She has always wanted an Hispanic woman mentor, but says she hasn't known any at a level where she believes they could mentor her.

11. Mentor   Dr. Sherrill Williams, Superintendent. White famale.
  Protégé   Peggy Hoffman, Central Office Specialist. White female.

Mentor initiated the relationship, which is supervisory in the same
school district. Protégé's goal is to be assistant superintendent for
curriculum and instruction in a large school district. "Mentorship I
feel is a responsibility to be really honest and evaluative," as op-
posed to personal friendship which does not have those responsibilities. Mentor, Dr. Williams, established a group of teacher leaders, of
which the protégé is one, who are given a lot of responsibility in the
district. Mentor saw the abilities of the protégé, and is nurturing her
aspirations, giving her opportunities and encouraging her to complete her doctorate (now in progress).

12. Mentor   Dr. Barbara Hansen, Former Director, now at law
            school. White female.
  Protégé   Emilia Head, Assistant Director, Special Programs,
            Elementary. White female.

Mentor initiated the relationship by hiring Emilia initially. Relationship has continued for seven years. Currently non-supervisory,
but was established as a supervisory relationship. "I believe mentoring
is more than being a boss, there's either a sense of I'm gonna help this
person find their strengths, refine their strengths and giving them the
resources and the encouragement to pursue that" (Protégé, Emilia
Head). Mutual admiration exists on both sides. Emilia says of her mentor, "The first words that come to mind is that she's very honest, has a
lot of integrity, is low key, and is dependable as far as how she tackles
problems, how she deals with you. Not to say she's nonemotional. It's
just that she's very steady, and that's one of the things I admire in her."

Virginia Sample

1. Mentor   Dr. Mary Ellen Remington, Superintendent. White
            female.
  Protégé   Dr. Julia Dawson, Associate Director of Instruction.
            White female.

Long relationship (twenty-six years) and a very close one—
professional / personal, but not as close since mentor became superintendent three years ago. Protégé feels in a way that mentor is now

less able to help her as it might be seen as favoritism. Always in same district together. Mentor has been protégé's direct supervisor at times over the years, but was not her supervisor for some years. Followed each other into administration from assistant principal to principal to central office. Both have been very successful in the district although protégé feels that she had fewer opportunities to advance than she would have liked. Some of this was due to major district restructuring several years ago. Type of mentorship: advice and encouragement both academic and job related. Mentor initiated—protégé would ultimately like an assistant superintendency. Protégé is not very willing to relocate. Not much difference in age / class and so forth.

2. *Mentor* Dr. Patty Burns, Superintendent. White female.
   Protégé Beverly Thompson, President of Education Association / Teacher. African-American female.

Relationship is about five years—very close—professional / personal. There is an interesting dimension since mentor is now superintendent and protégé is now president of teachers' association. Therefore there is potential for an adversarial relationship to develop, but it has not. They work in the same district. When the relationship began, mentor was assistant superintendent and protégé was a parent on a community multicultural committee on which they both served. Mentor hired protégé at first as a teacher aide. She supervises her, but at a distance. Type of mentorship: advice and encouragement both academic and job related. Protégé did not even have current teaching license at the beginning of relationship although she had the academic preparation. Protégé now completing master's degree and administrative endorsement. Mentor very active on her behalf and very supportive. Mentor initiated the relationship. Protégé would like to remain in teacher leadership although she is thinking about an assistant principalship once her endorsement is completed. Race difference and social class background difference.

3. *Mentor* Dr. Sarah Anderson, Superintendent. White female.
   Protégé Bobbi Reeves, Elementary School Principal. White female.

This relationship has been relatively long—about twelve years—close—more professional than personal but it is interesting that both see themselves as peers now. Each is able to write recommendations for the other. Same district in beginning, now different. At first, a very specifically tailored mentorship for a three year period while mentor was principal and protégé was a teacher in her building seeking an assistant principalship. Relationship was mentor initiated, but protégé was eager to become principal (had applied for the principalship that mentor got). Protégé had master's degree and administrative endorsement before the relationship began. Mentor has tried to recruit protégé to her new district. Protégé not willing to move but would love to work with mentor again. Type of mentorship: initially very job-centered and specific, developing later into advice and encouragement. Protégé achieved goal of principalship in about six years under mentor's advice. The relationship was mentor initiated. Protégé interested ultimately in central office position. Similar ages, same race.

4. Mentor	Dr. Pam Egan, Middle Sschool Principal. White female.
Protégé	Dr. Brenda Monroe, Director of Human Resources / staff development. African-American female.

Relationship ten-and-a-half years. Mentor sees it as professional / personal; protégé sees it as more professional than personal although there is a social dimension to it. They visited each other and spent time together out of the office. Same district initially, now different. Type of mentorship: very job specific and also career-oriented for four-and-a-half years—not academic since protégé had doctorate at the beginning of the relationship. Mentor initially supervised protégé in a central office position and mentor initiated the relationship for the good of the district and also for protégé's good. Mentor held powerful positions in the district (Assistant Superintendent then Acting Superintendent)—able to influence career development. Later mentor did not supervise protégé directly. The relationship was mentor initiated. At this point protégé feels she has reached her desired position, but superintendency not out of the question. Age and race difference. Protégé has had African-American mentors, although she believes that this mentor has been most influential in her career.

5. Mentor	Dr. Mary Ann Chase, Middle School Principal. White female.
Protégé	Carol Pierce, Principal of Alternative High School. African-American female.

Relationship was protégé initiated to some degree, but mentor recognized protégé's potential and actively arranged for protégé to do tasks specific to the principalship while protégé was a teacher in the building under the mentor who was the principal. Protégé describes herself as having been "hand picked by her mentor." Also she received advice and encouragement both academic and career related. Once mentor left the building, protégé continued to rely on mentor's experience within system to help her advance. Protégé has master's degree with endorsement and is working on her doctorate. Protégé aspiring to the superintendency relationship about ten years—professional. Same district initially, now different. Type of mentorship: initially very job specific to take mentor's place at the alternative school that mentor had founded. Mentor had very clear plan—chose two protégés and mentored them individually. Still calls mentor often although she now has other mentors. Mentor thinks protégé will be superintendent—sees protégé as someone she could work for in the future. Although race difference, mentor thinks that her being Jewish lessened this somewhat and protégé agrees. Relationship has developed into a friendship over the years, but not during period of direct mentoring while protégé was being supervised by mentor.

6. *Mentor*   Dr. Marsha Poole, Superintendent. White female.
   Protégé   Sara Murphy, Elementary School Principal. White female.

This relationship has been about eight years—very close—personal / professional. Same district initially, but now different. Type of mentorship: initially very job specific with the clear aim of preparing protégé for a principalship which she achieved within two years. Mentor initiated the relationship, but protégé was very interested in administration. Mentor issued a general invitation to women faculty at the school to be mentored into administration. Protégé responded the most enthusiastically of all. Mentor arranged for protégé to do specific tasks in the building and encouraged her to get coursework for necessary certification. Mentor trained protégé in the skills that would be tested at the county principal assessment center. Mentor had to convince district to allow protégé to be tested since protégé had not had the required leadership positions in the county—for example, assistant principalship. At that time, mentor was principal and protégé was teacher in her building. Since then, the relationship has continued on a personal level and mentor now brings protégé into her district to share skills. Relationship is described as friendship on a social level—both women know each other's husbands. Protégé happy with current position; she has some idea of university teaching down the road, however, Sara has no doctorate and not really wanting to pursue one. Some age difference but similar otherwise. Both traveled widely.

7. *Mentor*   Dr. George Street, Superintendent. White male.
   Protégé   Dr. Janet Cochran, Director Staff development and program evaluation. White female.

Very close and long seventeen year relationship—professional, but deep personal regard for each other. They have always worked in the same district. Interesting to note that the protégé does not use mentor's first name. Type of mentorship: very job specific and largely project based in the beginning while she was part-time—he wanted to teach her his work in the school financial office so that she could help him be successful and do the district good—possibly take over from him down the road. Mentor initiated the relationship, but protégé asked for specific mentoring to learn budget and finance. He held powerful positions (Assistant Superintendent for Finance then Superintendent) and could influence her career. He always supervised her, but after several years the relationship became more collegial than supervisory. He facilitated her move from a staff position to an administrative one, but she directed her own advancement. She made her own decisions about when to come on board full-time and what title to have. Protégé is happy with current position, which is a demotion from the assistant superintendency that she held for a year. She wanted to leave that position for personal reasons and feels that she has let him down badly. He said as much, but described it as "just kidding." He indicates that he is sorry she didn't remain assistant superintendent because he trusts her so much that it makes his work easier. He also says that the relationship is reciprocal and that he learns as much from her as she does from him. He understands and respects the personal reasons for her decision however. Some age difference in that he is older—she calls him a "surrogate parent"—similar otherwise.

8. *Mentor*   Joan Lewis, Retired Assistant Superintendent. White female.
   Protégé   Dorothy Hunnicut, Curriculum Coordinator. African-American female.

This relationship is about ten years—close professional / personal. Mentor is much older. Somewhat of a parent image. Same district although now mentor is retired. Mentor saw the relationship as more personal than protégé did. Since retirement, the relationship has changed however and protégé agrees that it has a personal dimension to it now. They are friends, but not in close contact any more. Type of mentorship: very job specific. Protégé had no real aspiration to become an administrator, but gained confidence with mentor's encouragement. Mentor chose protégé to work on a team of curriculum coordinators and took them all under her wing. She was responsible for hiring protégé into the central office and supervised her directly. Protégé has gone on to take a more senior position at the central office. Protégé has master's degree with administrative endorsement. Protégé is happy with her position—has no particular wish to ascend—though a promotion is possible since she is thought to be so good at her work. Age and race differences.

9. *Mentor*   Dr. Eve Farley, Superintendent. White female.
   Protégé   Vicky Fletcher, Director of Instruction. African-American female.

Relationship of fifteen years with ten years of active mentoring—quite close professional / personal. Mentor initiated the relationship. She describes herself as like a big sister to protégé. Same district during most of the relationship. Mentor recently took superintendency elsewhere and protégé moved into mentor's former position (although position was relabeled from assistant superintendent for instruction to director of instruction). Type of mentorship: advice and encouragement both academic and job specific. Mentorship largely career encouragement based on the friendly, trusting relationship that formed between them. Mentor feels that protégé was able to be particularly candid with her on matters of race and community issues; mentor very aware of how important and influential protégé is with African-American community and how good her input is for the district. Protégé does not use mentor's first name. Mentor suggests that is due to cultural differences. Protégé happy with position, no desire to relocate under any circumstances. Protégé went into administration for economic reasons rather than because she had always aspired to administration. Protégé gained master's degree and administrative endorsement. Protégé feels that this mentor is only one of many mentors who have helped her develop her career. Age and race differences—mentor about twelve years older.

Maryland Sample

   1. Mentor   Dr. Winoa Chambers, Principal, Elementary. White female.

      Protégé   Angela Patterson, Assistant Principal, Elementary. White female.

This long-term relationship of nine years began when Angela was a beginning teacher hired by Winoa as principal. It was primarily a professional relationship with Winoa as supervisor and Angela as subordinate. Protégé said, "We don't go shopping together or do so only when we are attending a conference together." Winoa provided opportunities for Angela to develop her leadership skills, gain visibility, debrief situations at school, gain more responsibility for the school as a whole. Both individuals were similiar in race, gender, philosophy, personality. There were no conflicts cited because according to the protégé, Winoa was not only open to suggestions, but also available as a supporter.

   2. Mentor   Clara Barnes, Associate Superintendent / staff development. African-American female.

      Protégé   Lauren Kente, Assistant Principal, Alternative Hgh School. African-American female.

This mentoring relationship first began through a mutual acquaintance in college. It was a long-term, professional relationship, not social or especially personal. It was mutually beneficial to both, in that mentor Clara could call upon Lauren for assistance on various committees, for example, BEST teacher support group for beginning teachers. Lauren benefited by gaining experience outside her school and demonstrating her leadership to a wider audience. Mentor Clara provided opportunities and encouragement to the protégé. There was a question about whether this was a mentoring relationship because Lauren said, "I would love to be mentored by Clara! I don't think our relationship is an official mentor / mentee relationship . . ." Both individuals were African-American females of about the same age. They also were similar in philosophy and sense of purpose "desiring to see things run better." Neither mentioned any difficulties.

3. *Mentor*   Clara Barnes, Associate Superintendent / Staff Development. African-American female.
   Protégé   Jennifer Davies, Director of School Improvement. White female.

Protégé met the mentor while they were involved in a school district sponsored writing project. They were first colleagues and when Clara was appointed as assistant superintendent, she asked Jenny to be director of school improvement under her leadership. Their relationship is professional and supervisory, with Jenny reporting directly to Clara. The type of mentoring is informal. Mentor was lauded as making time for protégé. For instance, Jenny cited an incident where Clara sat talking together with her in the parking lot after work for several hours. While both mentor and protégé share gender, they do not share race; Clara is African-American and Jenny is Caucasian. Jenny commented about their shared philosophies, that of win-win and collaboration. Jenny mentioned being religious and trusting what was happening. There were no difficulties mentioned, rather Jenny talked about how Clara helped her with a troubling situation with a colleague.

4. *Mentor*   Dr. Roberta Paulie, Superintendent. White female.
   Protégé   Elaine Bennett, Principal, Elementary School. White female.

This relationship began in 1984 when Elaine was a new teacher and Roberta was her principal. The two also lived in the same neighborhood but did not socialize together outside of work. According to Elaine, "It's not a friendship where I could call her up and go shopping . . .we never do that because she's my boss, she's my superintendent." They did respect their boss-subordinate relationship. Occasionally they would go to dinner with each other to check in and support each other. In terms of the type of mentoring activities, mentor Roberta as principal would frequently rely upon protégé Elaine for many projects. While the protégé felt some burnout as a result, the opportunities did give her a chance to advance into administration and later become a principal herself. Both mentor and protégé are white females of about the same age. The mentor did not mention any difficulties but the protégé spoke of burnout under the mentor who was her principal, and of fear of favoritism when she was selected to be an elementary school principal under Roberta as

superintendent. Elaine kept a distance from Roberta because of
that fear.

5. *Mentor*   Dr. Martha Ellison, Deputy Superintendent. African-
               American female.
   Protégé   Dr. Denise Oscar., Supervisor of Parent / Community
               Relations. African-American female.

These two individuals connected initially when they were in the
same university educational administration program. Coming
from the same district, they would ride to the university campus
together. Martha was ahead of Denise in her program and set an
example for her. However, their relationship is more of a peer-to-
peer in contrast with the protégé's relationship with Glenda, another assistant superintendent. Protégé Denise felt that she and
Martha were more complementary. She spoke about a reciprocal
mentoring relationship with Martha, encouraging her to seek the
superintendency some day. Likewise, Martha spoke about having
protégés who supported her by calling and going out to lunch periodically. Both women were African-American professionals in the
same school system. According to the protégé, she and her mentor
could speak the same language and that dialect communication enhanced their relationship. They also shared a similar philosophical
orientation toward children. There were no difficulties indicated
between them.

6. *Mentor*   Dr. Martha Ellison, Deputy Superintendent. African-
               American female.
   Protégé   Marion Bateson, Principal, Magnet School. African-
               American female.

The long-term mentoring relationship began when protégé Marion
was a middle school teacher and mentor Martha was at the district
office. Because Martha identified Marion's exceptional teaching
qualities, this mentor encouraged her to do committee work and to
instruct other teachers in effective teaching practices. Martha also
encouraged her to continue in a university program toward her master's degree. And even when Martha was in a different school system, she provided Marion constant feedback and support. Their
relationship was characterized by the protégé as both personal and
professional. Protégé Marion said that her mentor invited her into

her "inner circle." Similarly, Martha said that after her family, she considered her protégés her closest friends. Both women were African-American who shared a love of educating children and valued learning. Marion contrasted her relationship with another mentor Glenda, saying that Martha was someone who could come into her kitchen for a cup of tea or go shopping with. She and Glenda did not have that kind of friendship, relating in a more formal, professional way. In terms of difficulties, Marion was having difficulty in gaining acceptance to a leadership program and Martha encouraged her ("tough love") to continue to pursue it. They disagreed about how to proceed and fortunately, Marion was successful later.

7. *Mentor*   Dr. Glenda Alcott, Superintendent. White female.
   Protégé   Cassie McHenry, Principal, Alternative High School. White female.

In 1981, this pair met when they were both working in the same school system and involved in a writing project. Over time, the mentor selected this protégé to be her administrative assistant. The exposure and opportunity in this position gave the protégé much administrative experience. In talking about her mentor, protégé Cassie distinguished a boss from a mentor. She felt that while you could learn from both, not all bosses are mentors. Their mentoring relationship was "more intense than that of boss and subordinate with more time spent but in Cassie's words, "you're glad of it, you seek their company and enjoy being with them." At the same time, Cassie distinguished this relationship from a friendship, "we're not personal friends. . . .I mean that we're not social friends" (meaning someone to have dinner with and just chat). It was clearly professional and career related. Her mentor provided numerous opportunities for her. Conversely, she had Cassie act as her "eyes and ears" during meetings. The protégé spoke about learning a lot of Glenda's leadership style during these times. Both were similarly white females of about the same age. While they have not always agreed on everything, Glenda has always heard her out and has never disappointed her. Currently the mentor is a superintendent and the protégé is a high school principal in a magnet school.

8. *Mentor*   Dr. Glenda Alcott, Superintendent. White female.
   Protégé   Dr. Denise Oscar, Supervisor of Parent / Community Relations. African-American female.

This long-term relationship is over twenty years, beginning when Denise was a teacher who raised a concern about a racial situation in her school with the then Associate Superintendent, Dr. Alcott. In this relationship, the protégé spoke of the mentor as a dear friend as well as a highly esteemed superintendent. Throughout their years together, the mentor gave advice and provided counsel to the protégé on occasion, not in day-to-day matters. They are no longer in the same school system but remain in touch. Though they do not share racial-ethnic background, they do share a common philosophical orientation toward children. No difficulties were mentioned in their relationship.

9. *Mentor*   Dr. Glenda Alcott, Superintendent. White female.
   Protégé   Marion Bateson, Principal, Magnet school. African-American female.

As with mentor Dr. Ellison, this relationship began when the protégé Marion was a middle school teacher and mentor Dr. Alcott was the area superintendent. Mentor Glenda asked her to become an acting assistant principal, giving her an opportunity to advance into administration. Currently Marion is a magnet school principal. The two are still in contact and will see each other socially as well. Marion is African-American and Glenda is white but they are female leaders who are committed to "the business of children". There were no difficulties mentioned.

10. *Mentor*   Chuck Donnelly, Associate Superintendent. White male.
    Protégé   Dr. Sharon Perta, Principal, High School. White female.

This pair met in 1988 when Sharon was an assistant principal under Chuck as high school principal. She was one of three assistant principals but Chuck encouraged her, providing opportunities to develop her leadership styles to become a principal. A distinction was made of those who were interested in remaining Asssistant Principals and those like Sharon who sought to be principals. The relationship continued when Sharon left the position two years later to become a curriculum support person. It is both personal and professional. Both mentor and protégé mentioned the loss of Sharon's husband to cancer and their closeness during that difficult time. Both are white, from the same school system, and share similar philosophy ("we were on the same page"), and work styles (task-oriented). Sharon spoke of learning by watching Chuck at work, and what didn't work about his task-oriented style. With Chuck as associate superintendent and Sharon a high school principal, a current dilemma in their relationship was how to relate to each other when mentor is the "big boss" and Sharon reports to a middle manager between them.

11. Mentor   Dr. Sharon Perta, Principal, High School. White female.

    Protégé   Frances Dawton, Principal, Middle School. White female.

This mentoring relationship began when protégé Frances (Fran) was hired as Sharon's assistant principal. The appointment was made at the school level and Fran was a newly appointed assistant principal. In this relationship, the mentor provided opportunities for leadership, as well as encouraged her assistant principal to reflect on what was been done and why. Mentor believed that one of her roles was training assistant principals under her supervision. Currently both are principals at different schools. Protégé Fran contacts Sharon periodically now, acknowledging that her mentor was instrumental in her promotion to principalship at this middle school. Asked about difficulties, mentor Sharon identified a communication problem that made everything that Fran spoke about negative and described how Fran had transformed over time.

12. Mentor   Dr. Constance Lee, Superintendent. White female.

    Protégé   Grace Holly, Principal, Elementary School. White female.

The relationship between this mentor and protégé was not very long term, beginning when protégé Grace was hired to be principal in mentor Lee's school district. Dr. Lee was the overseer of all the principals in this small school district (two thousand students total). The mentor advised her protégé and encouraged her leadership development in a "coaching" style. The two frequently communicate via e-mail. The relationship is a mutual one, not one-sided. Mentor and protégé are similar in race and gender but not age; protégé Grace is the same age as mentor Constance's daughter. According to the protégé, one difficulty was that the mentor might think of her as a "daughter" and speak in a more familiar or personal tone than desired. Also, Grace was aware that Dr. Lee was her boss.

13. Mentor   Dr. Paula Jenkins, Retired Deputy Superintendent. White female.

  Protégé   Dr. Constance Lee, Superintendent. White female.

The two individuals went to a workshop together and later were asked to present what they had learned on instructional strategies to their county. That was the beginning of their relationship. They were personal as well as professional friends throughout many years of their careers in several school systems. Both spoke of encouraging each other in different positions. On trust, mentor Paula spoke about how this is a mutual thing. Mentor and protégé keep confidences because the two individuals share information about themselves. Any information shared must be used well and responsibly. Further, if trust and respect are present, then mutual disagreements are possible. There continues to be respect for other people's opinions. Paula felt that "there were no right answers" and that a mentor could be encouraging but should not decide for the protégé. For instance, she talked about a career move that Connie was considering that Paula discouraged. However, as they talked through the situation, Paula reconsidered and felt Connie was making a good decision. Interestingly, she also followed Connie to work at the state department. Now the mentor is retired and living in Virginia but the two remain close friends who vacation together. This could be thought of as a maturity of a mentoring relationship from boss to subordinate and later of peer-to-peer. The type of mentoring that occurred was advisement and coaching throughout. Both individuals were similar in race, gender, and age. Neither mentioned difficulties or conflicts between them.

14. Mentor   Dr. Nanette Morrison, Principal, Private School. African-American female.

  Protégé   Dr. Ellie Carlye, Assistant Superintendent C & I. African-American female.

This relationship began when the protégé Ellie Carlye was returning from a sabbatical leave and inquired about a position. While there was no formal position in the curriculum division, Ellie agreed to take an assignment as executive assistant to the then associate superintendent. As her boss, Dr. Morrison began to mentor Ellie, encouraging and advising her. Theirs was a formal mentoring, where the mentor was a role model and adviser for the protégé. Protégé Ellie commented that her mentor was able to keep to her values even in a politically charged school district. Both mentor and protégé are African-American female administrators who evoke warmth and strength. Protégé Ellie felt that it was natural to be mentored by African-American women, because there was an affinity and further that they needed to "look out for each other." Asked about conflicts and tensions, mentor Nanette said that while there were none, they did not always agree. She was willing to hear what Ellie thought and they would frequently talk together. In their separate positions now, Ellie regretted that they were not in closer communication as before.

15. *Mentor*   Dr. Monique Avery, Principal, High School. African-American female.

   Protégé   Dr. Ellie Carlye, Assistant Superintendent C & I. African-American female.

The pair met when the protégé came to the district office as a curriculum specialist and mentor was assistant superintendent of instruction (the position that protégé Ellie currently holds). Their mentoring relationships consisted of advising and providing opportunities for the protégé when her mentor was at the school district level. In Ellie's words, mentor Monique "took me under her wings." Both women are African-American administrators who in physical appearance are different. Monique is tall in stature and evokes a powerful presence; whereas Ellie, a petite woman, appears calm, gentle, kind yet strong. Both share a deeply religious conviction and that has been a source of strength, according to Monique. In terms of difficulties, during the interviewing for this mentoring study, Monique took a controversial stance in her position as high school principal, which resulted in upset parents and much media attention. Her protégé Ellie called to support her during this crisis.

Appendix B

You have been asked to provide information as part of a study on mentorship, which has been approved by the Washington State University Institutional Review Board. The information will be gathered through interviews, observations (formal and informal), and documents.

The interviews will range from forty minutes to an hour. They will be audiotaped and transcribed with your consent, and you are free to turn the tape recorder off at any time. Once the data has been analyzed, the tapes will be erased.

You will not be identified in any of the transcripts. Pseudonyms will be used, in order to provide for confidentiality.

Your participation is entirely voluntary. Even if you agree to participate in the study, you may discontinue at any time.

I am grateful for your time and participation in the study. Please feel free to contact me regarding the study (our addresses, telephone numbers and e-ail)

Thank you once again.

(Our names)

Name (Print) _____

Signature _____

Phone_____ Date _____

Appendix C

Interview Guide for Mentors

1. Please tell me about yourself, your position and work.
2. Tell me about the person you are mentoring. Describe your protégé.
3. What does mentorship mean to you?
4. How did your mentoring relationship begin? Over what period of time? How often do you meet together?
5. Who initiated it? Why did you assume the role of mentor to this person?
6. How would you describe your role as a mentor?
7. What mutual understandings resulted? How was rapport established?
8. How did the mentorship process work? What were the benefits on both sides? Were there costs as well?
9. What makes a good mentor?
10. How does a mentor encourage her protégé to be successful? Are there specific tasks that a mentor gives to a protégé to develop their capabilities in educational administration?
11. What are the most vital factors in creating a mentorship that works?

12. Please give me some specific examples of mentoring that you have done for your protégé.

13. Have there been conflicts, challenges, arguments, tensions in your mentoring relationship? Can you describe these? How do you deal with these differences?

14. How might you characterize your approach to mentoring? For example, tough love, caregiving, sink or swim, coaching?

15. How important is mentorship in career development of educational administrators?

16. What specific advice do you give to a person you are mentoring regarding job interviewing or networking?

17. Is there anything else you would like to comment on?

Interview Guide for Protégés

1. Please tell me about yourself, your position and work.

2. Tell me about the person who is mentoring you. Describe your mentor.

3. What does mentorship mean to you?

4. How did your mentoring relationship begin? Over what period of time? How often do you meet together?

5. Who initiated it? How did you come to be mentored by this person?

6. How would you describe your role in the mentorship relationship?

7. What mutual understandings have resulted? How was rapport established?

8. How does the mentorship work? Please describe specific things that your mentor has done that have been helpful to you.

9. What were the benefits on both sides? Were there costs as well?

10. What makes a good mentor?

11. How does your mentor encourage you to be successful?

12. Are there specific tasks that a mentor gives to a protégé to develop their capabilities in educational administration?

13. What are the most vital factors in creating a mentorship that works?

14. Have there been conflicts, challenges, arguments, tensions in your mentoring relationship? Can you describe these? How do you deal with these differences?

15. How might you characterize your mentor's approach to the mentorship relationship? for example, tough love, caregiving, sink or swim, coaching?

16. How important is mentorship in career development of educational administrators?

17. How active is your mentor on your behalf?

18. Is your mentor like you? Explain.

19. Do you think mentor and protégé are best matched when they share the same gender, ethnicity, philosophy, age, personality, interest? How about cross-gender or other differences in pairings?

20. Are there special needs that you are aware of that women or minorities have that needs to be addressed through mentorship?

21. Are there differences in your opinion between mentorship and friendship? If so, what might these be?

22. What about personal and professional relationships?

23. How would you describe your leadership style? Are you like your mentor in this respect? Do you see yourself developing the same style of leadership as your mentor?

24. What are the ways that educational leadership is changing and how are these changes reflected in mentorship?

25. Is there anything else you would like to comment on?

References

Acker, S. 1983. "Women, the Other Academics." *Women's Studies International Forum* 6 (2):191–201.

———. 1995. "The Head Teacher [Principal] as Career Broker: Stories from an English Primary School." In *Women Leading in Education*, Edited by Diane M. Dunlop and Patricia Schmuck, 49–70. Albany, NY: State University of New York.

Aisenberg, N., and M. Harrington. 1988. *Women of Academe: Outsiders in the Sacred Grove*. Amherst, MA: The University of Massachusetts Press.

Alasuutari, P. 1996. "Theorizing in Qualitative Research." *Qualitative Inquiry* 2 (4): 371–384.

Alston, J. 1999. "Climbing Hills and Mountains: Black Females Making it to the Superintendency." In *Sacred Dreams: Women and the Superintendency*. Edited by C. Brunner, 79–90. Albany, NY: State University of New York.

Babbie, E. 1994. *The Sociological Spirit*, 2nd ed. Belmont, CA: Wadsworth Publishing Co.

Bateson, M. C. 1990. *Composing a Life*. New York, NY: Plume.

Beck, L. 1992. "Meeting the Challenge of the Future: The Place of a Caring Ethic in Educational Administration. *American Journal of Education* 100: 454–496.

———. 1994. *Reclaiming educational administration as a caring profession*. New York, NY: Teachers College Press.

Beekley, C. 1999. "Dancing in Red Shoes: Why Women Leave the Superintendency." In *Sacred Dreams: Women and the Superintendency*.

Edited by C. Bruner, 161–176. Albany, NY: State University of New York.

Bell, C. 1995. "If I Weren't Involved with Schools, I Might Be Radical: Gender Consciousness in Context." In *Women Leading in Education.* Edited by D. Dunlap and P. Schmuck, 288–312. Albany, NY: State University of New York.

Benham Maenette, K. P. 1997. "Silences and Serenades: The Journeys of Three Ethnic Minority Women School Leaders." *Anthropology and Education Quarterly* 28 (2): 280–307.

Benton, S. Y. 1980. "Women Administrators for the 1980s: A New Breed." *Journal of the National Association of Women Deans, Administrators, and Counselors 43* (4): 18–23.

Beyer, L. 1996. "The Arts as Personal and Social Communication: Popular / Ethical Culture in Schools." *Discourse: Studies in the Cultural Politics of Education* 17 (2): 257–269.

Biklen, S., and C. Shakeshaft. 1985. "The New Scholarship on Women." In *Handbook for Achieving Sex Equity through Education.* Edited by S. Klein, 44–52. Baltimore, MD: The Johns Hopkins University Press.

Bizzari, J. 1995. "Women: Role Models, Mentors, and Careers. *Educational Horizons* (Spring): 145–152.

Blount, J. 1998. *Destined to Rule the Schools: Women and the Superintendency 1873–1995.* Albany, N.Y.: State University of New York.

Bolton, E. 1980. "A Conceptual Analysis of the Mentor Relationship in the Career Development of Women." *Adult Education* 30: 195–207.

Bova, B., and R. Phillips. 1982. "The Mentoring Relationships as an Educational Experience. ERIC Document Reproduction Service No. ED224944.

Brunner, C. 1999. "Power, Gender and Superintendent Selection." In *Sacred Dreams: Women and the Superintendency.* Edited by C. Brunner, 63–78. Albany, NY: State University of New York.

Burke, R., C. McKenna, and C. McKeen. 1991. "How Do Mentorships Differ From Typical Supervisory Relationships?" *Psychological Reports* 68: 459–466.

Card, C. 1995. "Gender and Moral Luck." In *Justice and Care.* Edited by V. Held, 79–100. New York, NY: Teachers College Press.

Capper, C. 1993. *Educational Administration in a Pluralistic Society.* Albany, NY: State University of New York.

Carter, H. 1982. *"Making It in Academia: Gurus Can Get You There?"* Paper presented at the annual meeting of the American Educational Research Association (AERA), New York, March 19–23.

Chase, S. 1995. *Ambiguous Empowerment.* Amherst, MA: University of Massachusetts Press.

Chronicle of Higher Education. 1998. 11 September, p. A15.

Cline, Z., and J. Necochea. 1997. "Mentoring for School Reform." *Journal for a Just and Caring Education 3* (2): 141–159.

Cole, M. 1996. *Cultural Psychology: A Once and Future Discipline.* Cambridge, MA: Belknap Press of Harvard University Press.

Covel, J. 1978. "Analysis of School Administrators' Careers in Riverside County from 1870–71–1974–75: A Study of Factors Which Affect Career Patterns for Men and Women in School Organizations. Dissertation Abstracts International, 38, 7044A–7045A. University Microfilms No. 7808275.

Daloz, L. 1986. *Effective Teaching and Mentoring.* San Francisco, CA: Jossey–Bass.

———. 1991. "Mentorship." In *Adult Learning Methods.* Edited by M. Galbraith, Malabar: Kreiger.

Daresh, J. C. 1987. "Mentoring: A Key Feature of the Danforth Program for the Preparation of Principals." Paper presented at the annual convention of the University Council for Educational Administration (UCEA). Charlottesville, VA.

Daresh, J. C., and M. Playko. 1992. *The Professional Development of School Administrators.* Boston, MA: Allyn and Bacon.

Davies, B. 1994. *Poststructuralist Theory and Classroom Practice.* Geelong, Vic.: Deakin University.

———. 1996. *Power, Knowledge, Desire: Changing School Organization and Management Practices.* Canberra: Commonwealth of Australia.

Davies, B., and R. Hunt. 1994. "Classroom Competencies and Marginal Positionings." *British Journal of Sociology of Education* 15 (3): 389–408.

Didion, C. 1995. "Mentoring Women in Science." *Educational Horizons* (Spring): 141–144.

Donmoyer, R., M. Imber, and J. J. Scheurich. 1995. *The Knowledge Base in Educational Administration: Multiple Perspectives.* Albany, NY: State University of New York.

Edson, S. 1988 *Pushing the Limits: The Female Administrative Aspirant.* Albany, NY: State University of New York Press.

———. 1995. "Ten Years Later: Too Little, Too Late?" In *Women Leading in Education*, Edited by Diane M. Dunlap and Patricia A. Schmuck, 36–48. Albany, NY: State University of New York.

Enomoto, E. 1995. "Gendered Construction of Educational Management." Paper presented at the annual meeting of the American Educational Research Association (AERA), San Francisco, April 4–8.

———. 1997. "Negotiating the Ethics of Care and Justice." *Educational Administration Quarterly 33* (3): 351–370.

Erikson, E. H. 1978. *Adulthood.* New York, NY: W. W. Norton.

Evetts, J. 1989. "The Internal Labor Market for Primary Teachers." In *Teachers, Gender and Careers.* Edited by S. Acker. Lewes: Falmer Press.

Fisher, B. 1982. "Professing Feminism: Feminist Academics and the Women's Movement." *Psychology of Women Quarterly* 7 (1): 55–69.

Foucault, M. 1980. "Two Lectures." In *Power/Knowledge: Selected Interviews and Other Writings 1972–1977.* Edited by C. Gordon, 78–108. New York, NY: Pantheon.

Freire, P. 1970. Pedagogy of the Oppressed. New York: Herder and Herder.

Fuss, D. 1989. Essentially Speaking. New York: Routledge.

Gardiner, M., M. Grogan, and E. Enomoto. 1999. "Women's Conflicts as They are Mentored into Educational Leadership in Public Schools." Paper presented at the annual meeting of the American Educational Research Association (AERA), Montreal, Canada, April 19–23.

Garland, S. B. 1991. "How to Keep Women Managers on the Corporate Ladder." Business Week, 2 September, p. 64.

Gehrke, N., and R. Kay. 1984. "The Socialization of Beginning Teachers Through Mentor-Protégé Relationships." Journal of Teacher Education 35: 21–24.

Gilligan, C. 1982. In a Different Voice: Psychological Theory and Women's Development. Cambridge, MA: Harvard University Press.

———. 1993. In a Different Voice: Psychological Theory and Women's Development. Revised. Cambridge, MA: Harvard University Press.

Ginn, L. W. 1989. "A Quick Look at the past, Present, and Future of Women in Public School Administation." Research in Education. (RIE Document Reproduction No. ED 310 498).

Glass, T. 1992. The Study of the American School Superintendency. Arlington, VA: AASA.

Grady, M., B. Krumm and K. Peery. 1998. "Pathways to Administrative Positions." In Women Leaders: Structuring Success. Edited by B. Irby and G. Brown, 88–98. Dubuque, IA: Kendall Hunt Publishing Company.

Grogan, M. 1996. Voices of Women Aspiring to the Superintendency. Albany, NY: State University of New York.

———. 1998. "Feminist Approaches to Educational Leadership: Relationships Based on Care. In Women Leaders Structuring Success. Edited by B. Irby, and G. Brown, 21–29. Huntsville, TX: Kendall Hunt Publishing Co.

Grogan, M., and M. Henry. 1995. "Women Candidates for the Superintendency: Board Perspectives." In Women as School Executives: Voices and Visions. Edited by B. Irby and G. Brown, 164–173. Huntsville, TX: Texas Council of Women School Executives.

Grogan, M. and F. Smith. 1998. "A Feminist Perspective of Women Superintendents' Approaches to Moral Dilemmas." Just and Caring Education 4 (2): 176–192.

Gupton, S. and G. Slick. 1994. "The Missing Pieces in Emerging female Leadership in the Profession: Support Systems, Mentoring, and Networking." Mississippi Educational Leadership 1 (1): 13–18.

———. 1996. Highly Successful Women Administrators: The Inside Stories of How They Got Here. Thousand Oaks, CA: Corwin Press.

Hall, R., and B. Sandler. 1983. Academic Mentoring for Women Students and Faculty: A New Look at an Old Way to Get Ahead. Washington, DC: Association of American Colleges.

Haraway, D. 1988. "Situated Knowledges: The Science Question in Feminism and the Privilege of Partial Perspective. *Feminist Studies* 14: 575–599.

Haring-Hidore, M. and L. Brooks. 1987. "Mentoring in Adademe: A Comparison of Protégés and Mentors Perceived Problems." Paper presented at the annual meeting of the American Educational Research Association (AERA), Washington, D.C., April-24.

Held, V. 1993. *Feminist Morality: Transforming Culture, Society, and Politics.* Chicago: University of Chicago Press.

———. (Ed.). 1995. *Justice and Care.* Boulder, CO.: Westview Press.

Hennecke, M. J. 1983. "Mentors and Protégés: How to Build Relationships That Work." *Training* 20: 36–41.

Henry, M. (now Gardiner, M., author). 1990. "Voices of Academic Women on Feminine Gender Scripts." *British Journal of Sociology of Education* 11 (2): 121–135.

———. 1996. *Parent-School Collaboration: Feminist Organizational Structures and School Leadership.* Albany, NY: State University of New York.

Hetherington, C., and R. Barcelo. 1985. Womentoring: A Cross-Cultural Perspective." *Journal of NAWDAC* (Fall): 12–15.

Hill, S., M. Hilton Bahniuk, J. Dobos, and D. Rouner, D. 1989. "Mentoring and Other Communication Support in the Academic Setting." *Groups and Organization Studies,* 14 (3): 355–368.

Jacobi, M. 1991. "Mentoring and Undergraduate Academic Success: A Literature Review. *Review of Educational Research* 61 (4): 505–532.

Jagger, A. 1991. "Feminist Ethics: Projects, Problems, Prospects." In *Feminist ethics.* Edited by C. Card, 78–104. Lawrence, KA. University Press of Kansas.

———. 1995. "Caring as a Feminist Practice of Moral Reason." In *Justice and Care.* Edited by V. Held, 179–202. New York, NY: Teachers College Press.

Jensen, R. 1998. "White People Need to Acknowledge Benefits of White Privilege." *Baltimore Sun.* Posted on the INTERNET, August 3.

Johnsrud, L. K. 1990. "Mentor Relationships: Those That Help and Those That Hinder." *New Directions for Higher Education* 72 (Winter): 57–66.

———. 1991. "Mentoring Between Academic Women: The Capacity For Interdependence." *Initiatives* 54 (3): 7–17.

Kanter, R. 1977. *Men and Women of the Corporation.* New York, NY: Basic Books.

Kegan, R. 1982. *The Evolving Self: Problem and Process in Human Development.* Cambridge, MA: Harvard University Press.

Klauss, R. 1981. "Formalized Mentor Relationships for Management and Executive Development Programs in the Federal Government." *Public Administration Review* 19: 489–496.

Klein, S. and P. Ortman. 1994. "Continuing the Journey Toward Gender Equity." *Educational Researcher* 23 (8): 13–21.

Kram, K. E. (1983). "Phases of the Mentor Relationship." *Academy of Management Journal* 26: 608–625.

Lakomski, G. 1998. "Training Administrators in the Wild: A Naturalistic Perspective." *UCEA Review* 39 (3): 1–11.

Lang, M., and C. A. Ford. Eds.. 1988. *Black Student Retention in Higher Education*. Springfield, IL: Charles C. Thomas Publishing.

LaPidus, J., and B. Mishkin. 1990. "Values and Ethics in the Graduate Education of Scientists." In *Ethics and Higher Education*. Edited by William W. May, 283–298. New York, NY: Macmillan Publishing Company.

Lather, P. 1992. "Critical Frames in Educational Research: Feminist and Post-structural Perspectives. *Theory into Practice* 31 (2), 87–99.

LeCompte, M. and J. Preissle. 1993. *Ethnography and Qualitative Design in Educational Research*. 2nd ed. San Diego, CA: Academic Press.

Lees, J. 1998. "Mentoring and Collegiality." Paper presented at the annual meeting of the American Educational Research Association, San Diego, April.

Levinson, D. J., C. N. Darrow, E. B. Klein, M. H. Levinson, and B. McKee 1978. *The Seasons of a Man's Life*. New York, NY: Knopf.

Lively, B., C. Barnett, B. Berger, M. Greer, and M. Holiday. 1992. "Mentoring of Faculty: Summary and Bibliographic Report." *American Journal of Pharmaceutical Education* 56: 82–83.

Lovelady-Dawson, F. 1980. "Women and Minorities in the Principalship: Career Opportunities and Problems." Paper presented at the American Association of School Administrators Third Annual Summer Instructional Leadership Conference, Chicago.

Lyons, W., D. Scroggins, and P. Bonham Rule. 1990. "The Mentor in Graduate Education." *Studies in Higher Education* 15 (3): 277–285.

Marshall, C. Ed.. 1994. *The New Politics of Race and Gender*. Washington, DC.: Falmer.

May, W. 1990. *Ethics and Higher Education*. New York: American Council on Education and Macmillan Publishing Company.

McIntosh, P. 1989. "White Privilege: Unpacking the Invisible Knapsack." *Peace and Freedom* (July/August): 10–12.

Merriam, S. 1983. "Mentors and Proteges: A Critical Review of the Literature." *Adult Education Quarterly* 33: 161–173.

Montenegro, X. 1993. *Women and Racial Minority Representation in School Administration*. Arlington, VA: AASA.

Moore, K. 1982. "The Role of Mentors in Developing Leaders for Academe." *Educational Record* (Winter): 23–28.

Moore, K. and A. Salimbene. 1981. "The Dynamics of the Mentor-Protégé Relationship in Developing Women as Academic Leaders." *Journal of Educational Equity and Leadership* 2: 51–64.

Nichols, I., H. Carter, and M. Golden. 1985. "The Patron System in Aca-
demica: Alternative Strategies for Empowering Academic Women."
Women's Studies International Forum 8: 383–390.

Nicholson, P. 1996. Gender, power and organization: A psychological perspective. London: Routledge.

Noddings, N. 1984. *Caring: A Feminine Approach to Ethics and Moral
Education*. Berkeley, CA.: University of California Press.

Noddings, N. 1990. "Feminist Critiques in the Professions." *Review of
Research in Education* 16: 393–424.

Noddings, N. 1992. *The Challenge to Care in Schools: An Alternative
Approach to Education*. New York, NY: Teachers College Press.

Office of the Superintendent for Public Instruction (OSPI). 1998. Personal
communication. Olympia, WA.

Pancrazio, S., and R. Gray. 1982. "Networking for Professional Women: A
Collegial Model." *Journal of NAWDAC* 45: 16–19.

Parkay, F. 1988. "Reflections of a Protégé." *Theory into Practice* 27 (3):
195–200.

Pavan, B. 1999. "The First Years: What Should a Female Superintendent
Know Beforehand?" In *Sacred Dreams: Women and the Superintendency*.
Edited by C. Brunner, 105–124. Albany, NY: State University of New York.

Pence, L. 1989. "Formal and Informal Mentorships for Aspiring and
Practicing Administrators." Ph.D. diss. Portland State University.

———. 1995. "Learning Leadership Through Mentorships." In *Women
Leading in Education*. Edited by Diane M. Dunlop and Patricia A.
Schmuck, 125–144. Albany, NY: State University of New York.

Poll, C. 1978. "No Room at the Top: A Study of the Social Processes that
Contribute to the Under-Representation of Women on the Administrative Levels of the New York City School System." *Dissertation
Abstracts International*, 39, 3165A. Ann Arbor, MI: University Microfilms No. 7821905.

Price, M. 1981. "Corporate Godfathers: By Appointment Only." *Industry
Week* 29 (June): 71–74.

Regan, H. B. 1990. "Not for Women Only: School Administration as a
Feminist Activity." *Teachers College Record*, 91 (4): 565–577.

Restine, L. 1993. *Women in Administration: Facilitators for Change*.
Newbury Park, CA: Corwin Press.

Roche, G. R. 1979a. "Probing Opinions." *Harvard Business Review*
(January–February): 14–28.

———. 1979. "Much Ado About Mentors." *Harvard Business Review* 57:
14–28.

Romero, M., and D. Storrs. 1995. "Is that sociology?" "The Accounts of
Women of Color Graduate Students in Ph.D. Programs. In *Women
Leading in Education*. Edited by D. Dunlop and P. Schmuck, 71–85.
Albany, NY: State University of New York.

Rothman, R. 1993. *Inequality and Stratification: Class, color, and Gender.* 2nd ed. Englewood Cliffs, NJ: Prentice-Hall.

Rowe, M. 1981. "Building Mentorship Frameworks as Part of an Effective Equal Opportunity Ecology." In *Sex Discrimination in Higher Education: Strategies for Equality.* Edited by J. Farley, 23–87. Ithaca, NY: Cornell University.

Saltzman, A. 1991. "Trouble at the Top." *U.S. News and World Report,* 17 June, 40–48.

Sandler, B., and R. Hall. 1983. *Academic Mentoring for Women Students and Faculty.* Washington, DC.: Project on the status of education of women.

Sandler, B. 1995. "Women as Mentors: Myths and Commandments." *Educational Horizons* (Spring): 105–107.

Sands, R., L. Parson, and J. Duane. (1991). "Faculty Mentoring Faculty." *Journal of Higher Education* 62 (2): 174–193.

Scherr, M. 1995. "The Glass Ceiling: Reconsidered Views From Below. In *Women Leading in Education.* Edited by Diane M. Dunlap and Patricia A. Schmuck, 313–323. Albany, NY: State University of New York.

Schmidt, J., and J. Wolfe. 1980. "The Mentor Partnership: Discovery of Professionalism." *NASPA Journal* 17 (3): 45–51.

Schmuck, P. 1995. "Advocacy Organizations for Women School Administrators." In *Women Leading in Education.* Edited by Diane M. Dunlap and Patricia A. Schmuck, 199–224. Albany, NY: State University of New York.

———. 1999. "Foreword." In *Sacred Dreams: Women and the Superintendency.* Edited by C. Cryss Brunner, ix–xiii. Albany, NY: State University of New York.

Scott, J. 1996. "Watching the Changes: Women in Law." In *Women and Minorities in American Professions.* Edited by Joyce Tang and Earl Smith, 19–42. Albany, NY: State University of New York.

Seelinger, K. 1998. "Fix-it Women: Rewriting Female Public School Leadership as Remedy." Roundtable presented at the annual meeting of the American Educational Studies Association, Philadelphia, November 4–8.

Sergiovanni, T. 1992. *Moral Leadership.* San Francisco, CA: Jossey-Bass.

Shakeshaft, C. 1987. *Women in Educational Administration.* Newbury Park, CA.: Sage.

———. 1989. *Women in Educational Administration.* 2nd ed. Newbury Park, CA: Sage.

———. 1993. "Gender Equity in Schools." In *Educational Administration in a Pluralistic Society.* Edited by Collen Capper, 86–109. Albany, NY: State University of New York.

———. 1995. Paper presented to the annual meeting of the American Educational Research Association.

———. 1999. "The Struggle to Create a More Gender-Inclusive Profession. In *Handbook of Research on Educational Administration.* 2nd ed.

Edited by J. Murphy and K. Seashore-Louis, 99–118. San Francisco, CA: Jossey-Bass.

Shapiro, E., F. Haseltine and M. Rowe. 1978. "Moving Up: Role Models, Mentors and the Patron System." *Sloan Management Review* 10 (3).

Stalker, J. 1994. "Athene in Academe: Women Mentoring Women in the Academy." *International Journal of Lifelong Education* 13 (5): 361–372.

Stanford University, 1988. "Graduate Student Academic Advising Guidelines for Departments." Office of Graduate Studies, Stanford University, Stanford, CA.

Starratt, R. 1994. *Building an Ethical School.* Washington, DC.: Falmer Press.

Stevens, N. 1995. "R and R for Mentors: Renewal and Reaffirmation for Mentors as Benefits From the Mentoring Experience." *Educational Horizons* (Spring): 130–137.

Stevenson, F. 1974. "Women Administrators in Big Ten Universities." Dissertation Abstracts International, 34, 5553A 5554A. Ann Arbor, MI: University Microfilms No. 74-6141.

Swoboda, M., and S. Millar. 1986. "Networking-Mentoring: Career Strategy of Women in Academic Administration." *Journal of NAWDAC* 49: 8–13.

Tallerico, M. 1999. "Women and the Superintendency: What Do We Really Know?" In *Sacred Dreams.* Edited by C. Brunner, 29–48. Albany, NY: State University of New York.

Tallerico, M., and J. Burstyn. 1993. *Gender and Politics at Work: Why Women Exit the Superintendency.* Fairfax, VA: The National Policy Board for Educational Administration.

———. 1995. "The Future of the Superintendency: Women Leaders Who Choose to Leave." *Educational Considerations* 22 (2) (Spring).

———. 1996. "Retaining Women in the Superintendency: The Location Matters." *Educational Administration Quarterly* 32 (December supplemental).

Tallerico, M., W. Poole, and J. Burstyn. 1994. "Exits From Urban Superintendencies: The Intersection of Politics, Race, and Gender." *Urban Education* 28 (4): 439–454.

Tetreault, M.K. 1976. "Feminist Phase Theory." *Journal of Higher Education* 56 (July/August): 363–384.

Tong, R. 1993. *Feminist Thought.* London, Eng.: Westview Press.

Tronto, J. 1993. *Moral Boundaries: A Political Argument for an Ethic of Care.* New York, NY: Routledge.

Turner, Mitchell, P., and Kegan, Paul. Ed.. 1993. *Cracking the Wall: Women in Higher Education Administration.* Washington, DC.: College and University Personnel Association. ISBN 1–878–240–21–8

Tyack, D., and E. Hansot. 1982. *Managers of Virtue: Public School Leadership in America, 1820–1980.* New York, NY: Basic Books.

USA Today. "Disparities Persist in Minority-Teacher Mix," 30 September 1997, p. 7d.

U.S. Department of Education. 1992. "Strengthening Support and Recruitment of Women and Minorities to Positions in Education Administration." Washington, DC: Superintendent of Documents.

Vertz, L. L. 1985. "Women, Occupational Advancement, and Mentoring: An Analysis of One Public Organization." *Public Management Forum* 45 (3): 415–423.

WASA. WASA Hotline. A Publication of the Washington Association of School Administrators. September 1997. Olympia, WA.

Weedon, C. 1997. *Feminist Practice and Poststructuralist Theory*. 2nd ed. New York, NY: Basil Blackwell.

Welch, O. M. 1993, May. *Mentoring in Educational Settings*. Newton, MA: Women's Educational Equity Act Publishing Center.

Woo, L. 1985. "Women Administrators: Profiles of Success." *Phi Delta Kappan* 67 (4): 285–288.

Zelditch, M. 1962. "Some Methodological Problems of Field Studies." *American Journal of Sociology* 67: 566–576.

Index